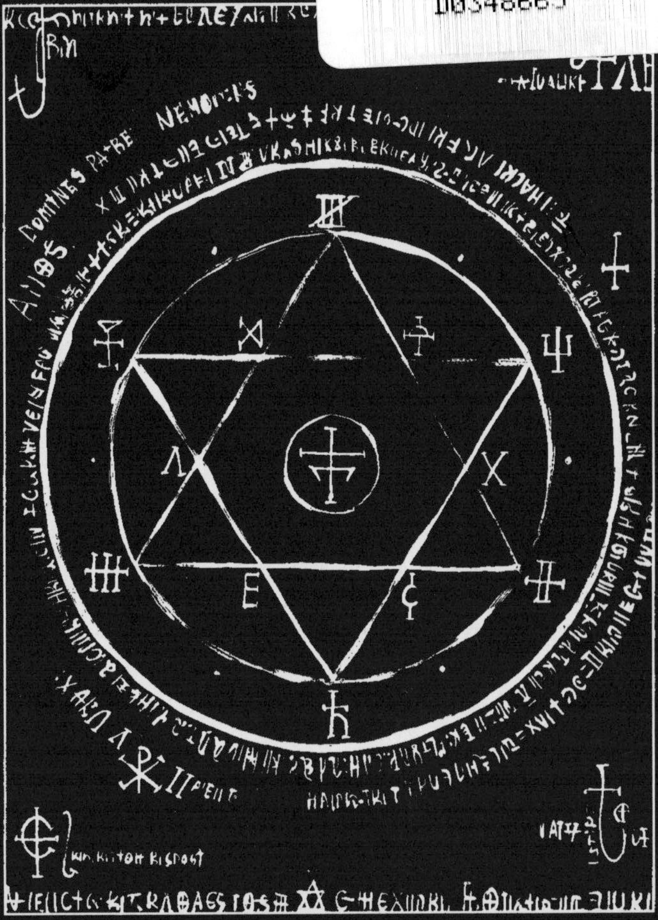

ALSO AVAILABLE FROM ⚙ TOKYOPOP®

MANGA

ANGELIC LAYER*
BABY BIRTH* (September 2003)
BATTLE ROYALE*
BRAIN POWERD* (June 2003)
BRIGADOON* (August 2003)
CARDCAPTOR SAKURA
CARDCAPTOR SAKURA: MASTER OF THE CLOW*
CLAMP SCHOOL DETECTIVES*
CHOBITS*
CHRONICLES OF THE CURSED SWORD (July 2003)
CLOVER
CONFIDENTIAL CONFESSIONS* (July 2003)
CORRECTOR YUI
COWBOY BEBOP*
COWBOY BEBOP: SHOOTING STAR* (June 2003)
DEMON DIARY (May 2003)
DIGIMON
DRAGON HUNTER (June 2003)
DRAGON KNIGHTS*
DUKLYON: CLAMP SCHOOL DEFENDERS* (September 2003)
ERICA SAKURAZAWA* (May 2003)
ESCAFLOWNE* (July 2003)
FAKE*(May 2003)
FLCL* (September 2003)
FORBIDDEN DANCE* (August 2003)
GATE KEEPERS*
G-GUNDAM* (June 2003)
GRAVITATION* (June 2003)
GTO*
GUNDAM WING
GUNDAM WING: ENDLESS WALTZ*
GUNDAM: THE LAST OUTPOST*
HAPPY MANIA*
HARLEM BEAT
INITIAL D*
I.N.V.U.
ISLAND
JING: KING OF BANDITS* (June 2003)
JULINE
KARE KANO*
KINDAICHI CASE FILES* (June 2003)
KING OF HELL (June 2003)

KODOCHA*
LOVE HINA*
LUPIN III*
MAGIC KNIGHT RAYEARTH* (August 2003)
MAGIC KNIGHT RAYEARTH II* (COMING SOON)
MAN OF MANY FACES* (May 2003)
MARMALADE BOY*
MARS*
MIRACLE GIRLS
MIYUKI-CHAN IN WONDERLAND* (October 2003)
MONSTERS, INC.
NIEA_7* (August 2003)
PARADISE KISS*
PARASYTE
PEACH GIRL
PEACH GIRL: CHANGE OF HEART*
PET SHOP OF HORRORS* (June 2003)
PLANET LADDER
PLANETS* (October 2003)
PRIEST
RAGNAROK
RAVE MASTER*
REAL BOUT HIGH SCHOOL*
REALITY CHECK
REBIRTH
REBOUND*
SABER MARIONETTE J* (July 2003)
SAILOR MOON
SAINT TAIL
SAMURAI DEEPER KYO* (June 2003)
SCRYED*
SHAOLIN SISTERS*
SHIRAHIME-SYO* (December 2003)
THE SKULL MAN*
SORCERER HUNTERS
TOKYO MEW MEW*
UNDER THE GLASS MOON (June 2003)
VAMPIRE GAME* (June 2003)
WILD ACT* (July 2003)
WISH*
X-DAY* (August 2003)
ZODIAC P.I.* (July 2003)

TOKYOPOP KIDS

STRAY SHEEP (September 2003)

ART BOOKS

CARDCAPTOR SAKURA*
MAGIC KNIGHT RAYEARTH*

ANIME GUIDES

GUNDAM TECHNICAL MANUALS
COWBOY BEBOP
SAILOR MOON SCOUT GUIDES

AKIRA*
CARDCAPTORS
JIMMY NEUTRON (COMING SOON)
KIM POSSIBLE
LIZZIE McGUIRE
SPONGEBOB SQUAREPANTS (COMING SOON)
SPY KIDS 2

SAILOR MOON
KARMA CLUB (COMING SOON)

VOLUME 6

BY
MIN-WOO HYUNG

LOS ANGELES ★ TOKYO

Translator - Jessica Kim
English Adaptation - Jake Forbes
Associate Editor - Bryce P. Coleman
Cover Artist - Raymond Swanland
Layout- Tomas Montalvo-Lagos
Retouch - Milissa Hackett
Production Coordinator - Tony DePietro

Editors - Jake Forbes & Mark Paniccia
Production Manager - Jennifer Miller
Art Director - Matt Alford
Editorial Director - Jeremy Ross
VP Production - Ron Klamert
President & C.O.O. - John Parker
Publisher & C.E.O. - Stuart Levy

email: editor@TOKYOPOP.com
Come visit us online at www.TOKYOPOP.com

A  MANGA

TOKYOPOP® is an imprint of Mixx Entertainment, Inc.
5900 Wilshire Blvd., Ste. 2000, Los Angeles, CA 90036

ISBN: 1-59182-202-5

First TOKYOPOP Printing: May 2003

10 9 8 7 6 5 4 3 2 1

Manufactured in the USA

INTRODUCTION

BY

MIKE CAREY

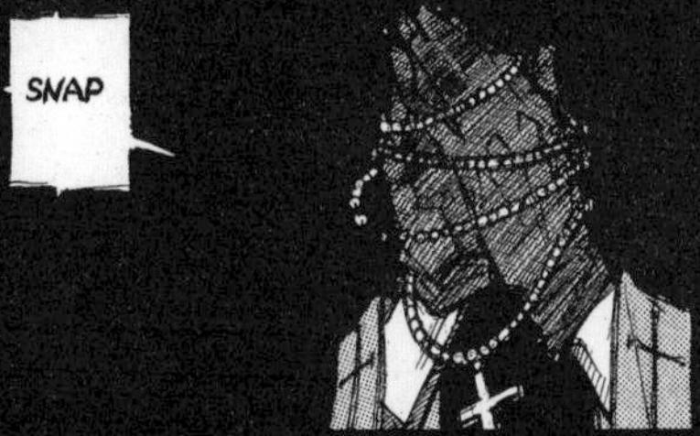
SNAP

You remember when Priest was just a gothic horror spaghetti Western with some spectacularly cinematic action sequences and a perversely engaging killer hero? It was lots of fun back then, wasn't it? But it went beyond being "lots of fun" a good while back now, and it's currently evolving into one of the most enthrallingly unpredictable stories in the entire medium.

"Evolving" seems like a good word to use, because the way Min-Woo Hyung's storyline is developing has the qualities that you tend to meet at the extreme edges of the Darwinian skirmish: like a giraffe or a duck-billed platypus, it leaves you gaping at first look and then, when you look again (as you have to), it seems inexplicably but wonderfully right.

From a start point that was already a melange of different genres, the story has expanded to cover three historical periods (the separate casts converging in some totally unexpected ways) and to include—alongside the visceral action that we've come to take for granted—a compelling mystery, a poignant romance and a meditation on faith and predestination. And it never telegraphs a single punch.

There's a moment in the fifth volume when the inquisitor, Betheal Gavarre, is winding his rosary around his fingers, contemplating the challenge posed to his faith and his methods by the heretic, De Guillon—and the rosary, wound too tightly, snaps, spilling the beads and the cross onto the floor. Gavarre stares down at them, vaguely puzzled, as though he's not quite sure how this happened. This is a trivial event in one way, but symbolically it's one of the central moments of the book, carrying the message that any faith that is adhered to too rigidly will sooner or later snap. We've now seen the moment of fracture in the case of De Guillon, when his wife and children are burned alive, and we're about to see it in the case of Ivan Isaacs seven centuries later in the American West. It remains to be seen how things are going to work out for the contemporary protagonist, Father Simon Talbot.

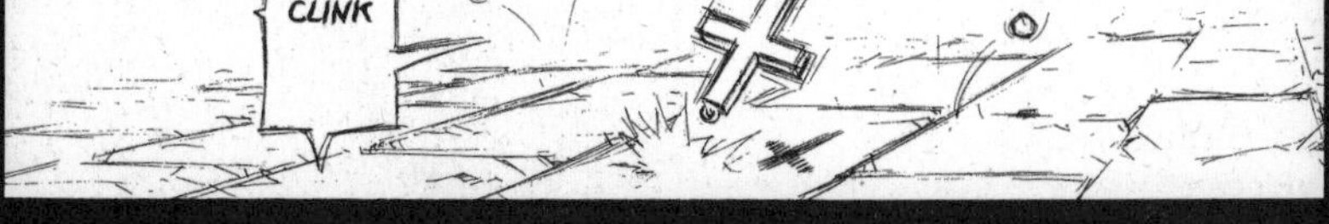
CLINK

And as I write this I'm thinking back to a moment in book two where Ivan deals with a pack of marauding zombies by throwing a stick of dynamite into their midst and then detonating it with a bullet from his revolver. Not many books have succeeded in fusing such unabashed and exhilarating action with such spiky intellectual matters. Let's face it, not many books have even tried.

So here we are, in the middle of at least three stories, with the great stone column of the domas poradas rising out of all of them "like a blasphemous finger, pointing at heaven" (as Mervyn Peake would say). And the background details are just beginning to be painted in, in a fourth story that deals with jealous angels and ancient cataclysms. Oh, and we've got a devil imprisoned in stone with the mortal man he tormented and destroyed along for company. A railroad line designed to draw a blasphemous sigil across the American deserts. An incestuous love that is entirely sympathetic and hopelessly doomed. The Vatican's secret strike force. A single man taking on the might of the inquisition so ruthlessly that you honestly don't know which evil is worse. Every chapter adds a new layer of queasy delight.

The very best comic books tend to give me exactly this combination of feelings: the feeling that I really can't make any predictions about how it's all going to come out, and the determination, wherever it goes, to be along right to the end of the ride. TOKYOPOP is doing a service to us all by making this incredible series available in English. But as I wait for the next volume I feel as if my own rosary beads are going to get wound up tighter, and tighter, and tighter…

Mike Carey
January 2003

THE STORY SO FAR...

In the beginning, God created man in his image and looked upon them and said, "THEY ARE GOOD." Unlike the angels who served him, mankind was not allowed to look upon God in life, and so was born the concept of Faith. While all men were sacred to God, not all men acknowledged his existence or honored his name, for they were granted a gift unique among all God's creations—Free Will. One of God's angels, his messenger Temozarela, became enraged that God would show more love for these flawed mortal beings than he did for his original creations, the seraphim. Having gathered 12 followers, Temozarela abandoned his post in heaven in order to turn mankind against God.

Many years later, a particularly righteous group of God's followers took it upon themselves to travel hundreds of miles to recapture the land of Jesus' birth. During these Crusades, the Knight Templar Vascar de Guillon came upon the ruins of an ancient cult that had built monuments to Temozarela and his minions. The spirit of Temozarela himself came to Sir Vascar and occupied the knight's body. For the next hundred years, Temozarela and his followers, in their human hosts, wandered the Holy Land, slaughtering all they encountered.

Eventually the unholy knights returned to Europe where Temozarela was put on trial for heresy. The heretic prosecutor Betheal Gavarre sentenced Sir Vascar/Temozarela to torture and execution. From his dungeon prison, Temozarela manipulated the mind of Betheal's ward, a young boy named Matthew, causing him to commit atrocities so horrific that Betheal cursed the name of God.

In the remote Stonetale Abbey, located somewhere in the frontier of the American West, Ivan Isaacs, a young religious scholar, reads about this forgotten history in his quest to unlock the secrets of the Domas Porada. We now return to his research...

PRIEST 프리스트 6

SYMPHONY OF BLOOD

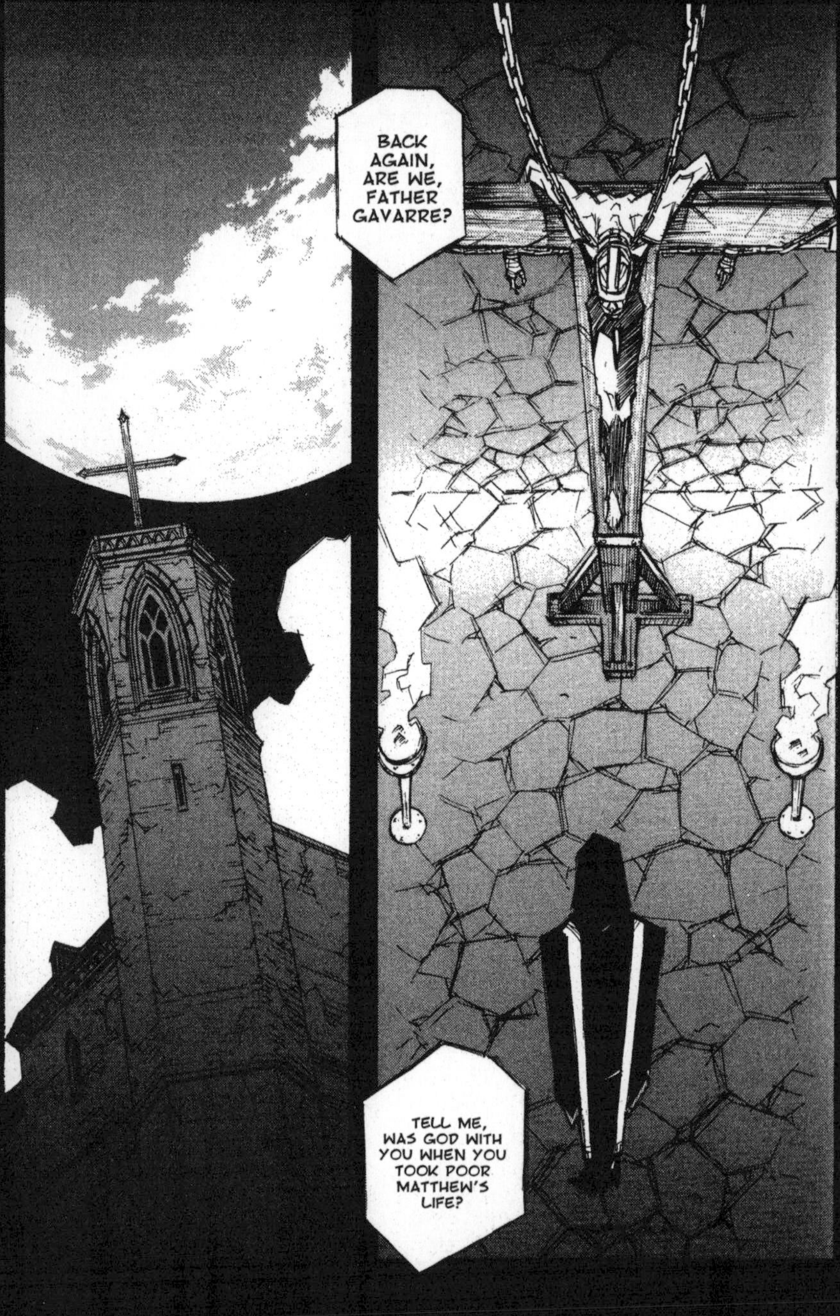
BACK AGAIN, ARE WE, FATHER GAVARRE?
TELL ME, WAS GOD WITH YOU WHEN YOU TOOK POOR MATTHEW'S LIFE?

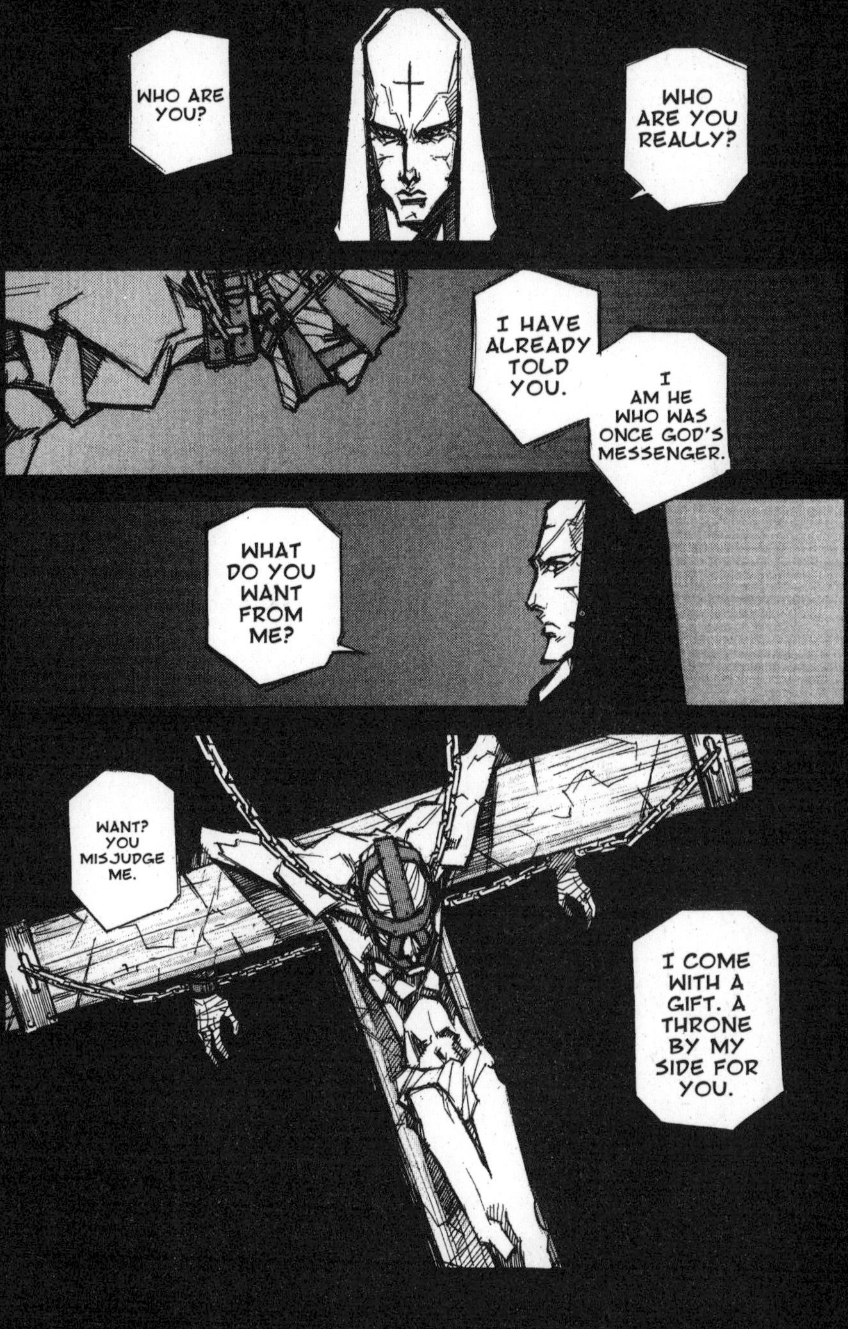
WHO ARE YOU?
WHO ARE YOU REALLY?
I HAVE ALREADY TOLD YOU.
I AM HE WHO WAS ONCE GOD'S MESSENGER.
WHAT DO YOU WANT FROM ME?
WANT? YOU MISJUDGE ME.
I COME WITH A GIFT. A THRONE BY MY SIDE FOR YOU.

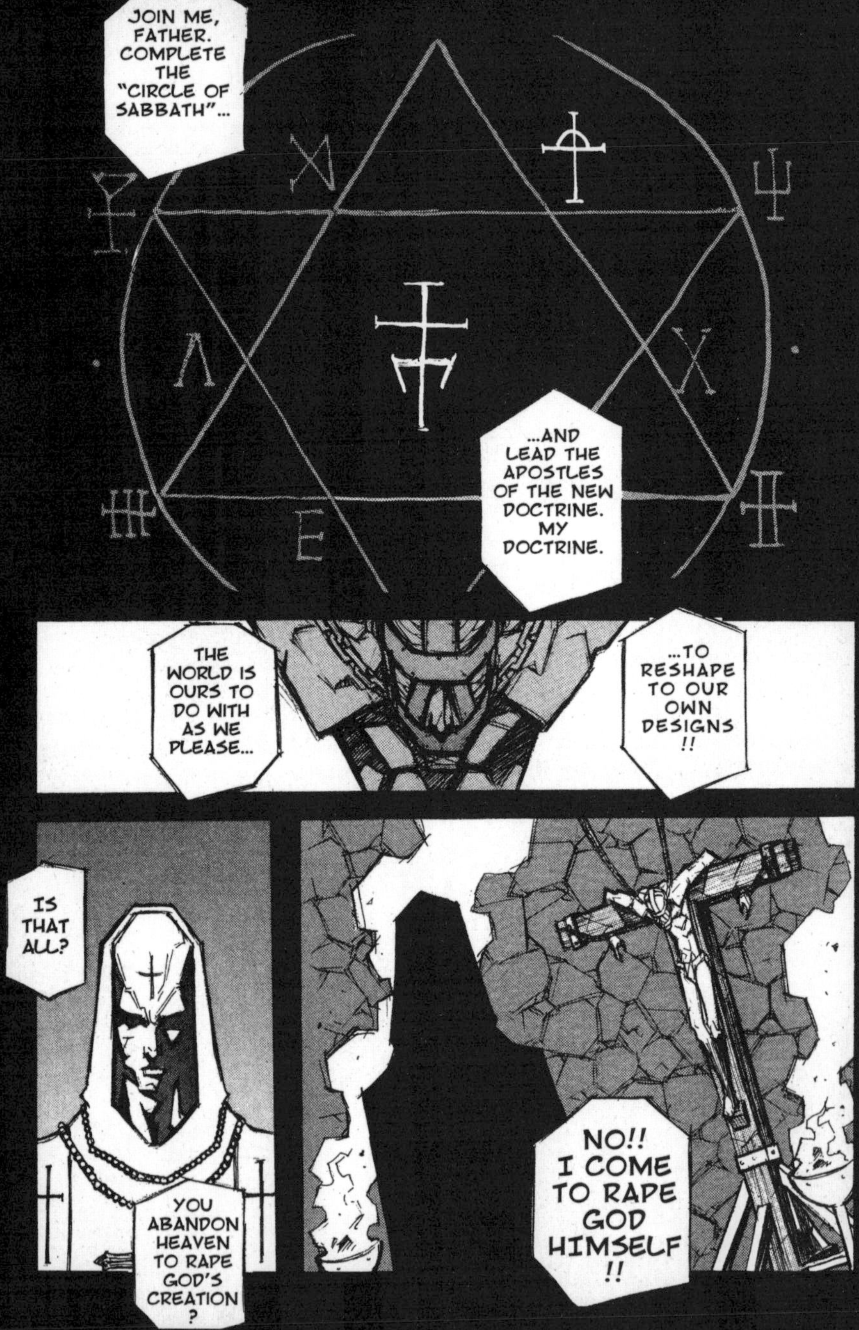
JOIN ME, FATHER. COMPLETE THE "CIRCLE OF SABBATH"...
...AND LEAD THE APOSTLES OF THE NEW DOCTRINE. MY DOCTRINE.
THE WORLD IS OURS TO DO WITH AS WE PLEASE...
...TO RESHAPE TO OUR OWN DESIGNS!!
IS THAT ALL?
YOU ABANDON HEAVEN TO RAPE GOD'S CREATION?
NO!! I COME TO RAPE GOD HIMSELF!!

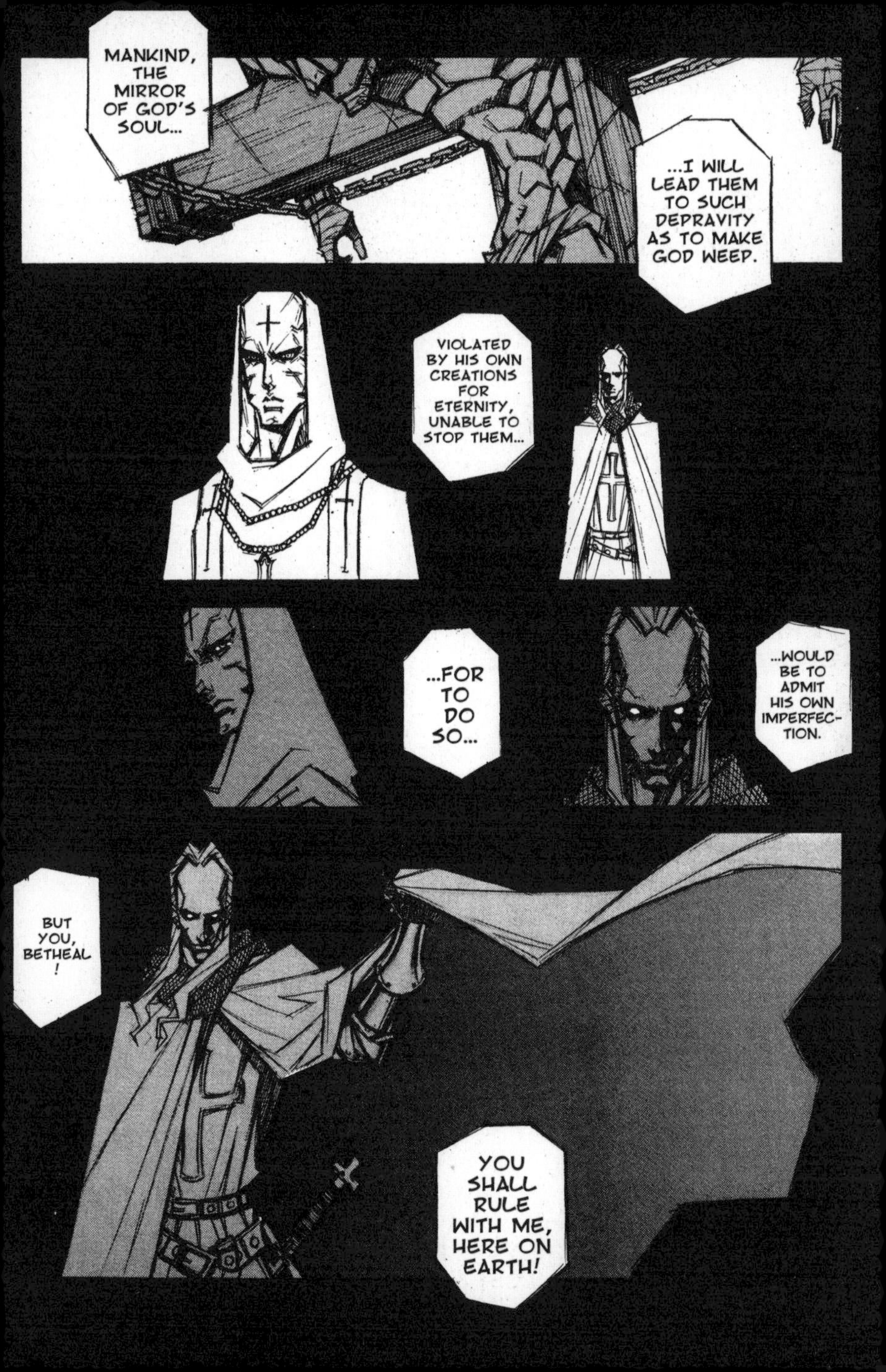
MANKIND, THE MIRROR OF GOD'S SOUL...
...I WILL LEAD THEM TO SUCH DEPRAVITY AS TO MAKE GOD WEEP.
VIOLATED BY HIS OWN CREATIONS FOR ETERNITY, UNABLE TO STOP THEM...
...FOR TO DO SO...
...WOULD BE TO ADMIT HIS OWN IMPERFEC-TION.
BUT YOU, BETHEAL!
YOU SHALL RULE WITH ME, HERE ON EARTH!

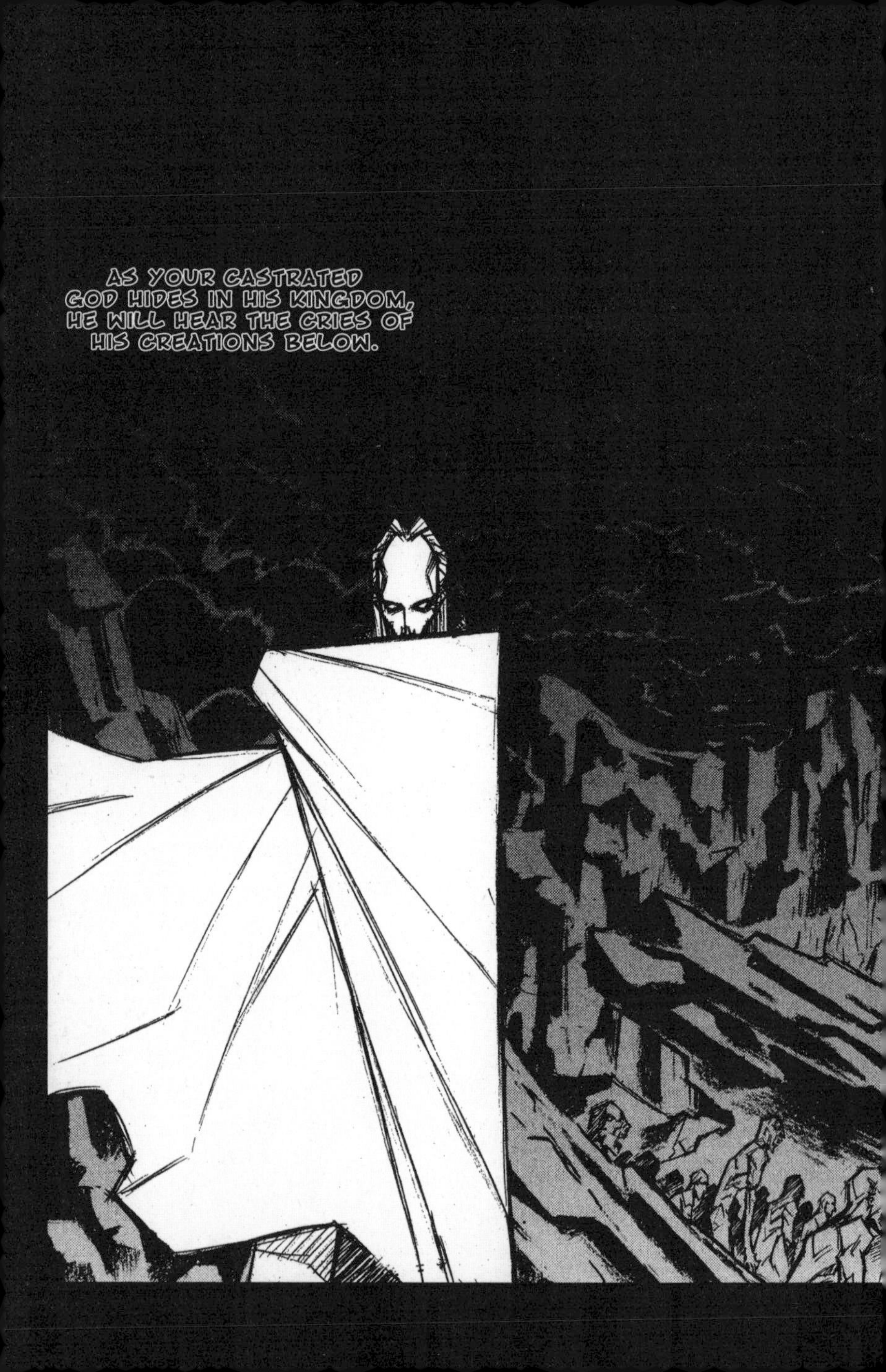
AS YOUR CASTRATED GOD HIDES IN HIS KINGDOM, HE WILL HEAR THE CRIES OF HIS CREATIONS BELOW.

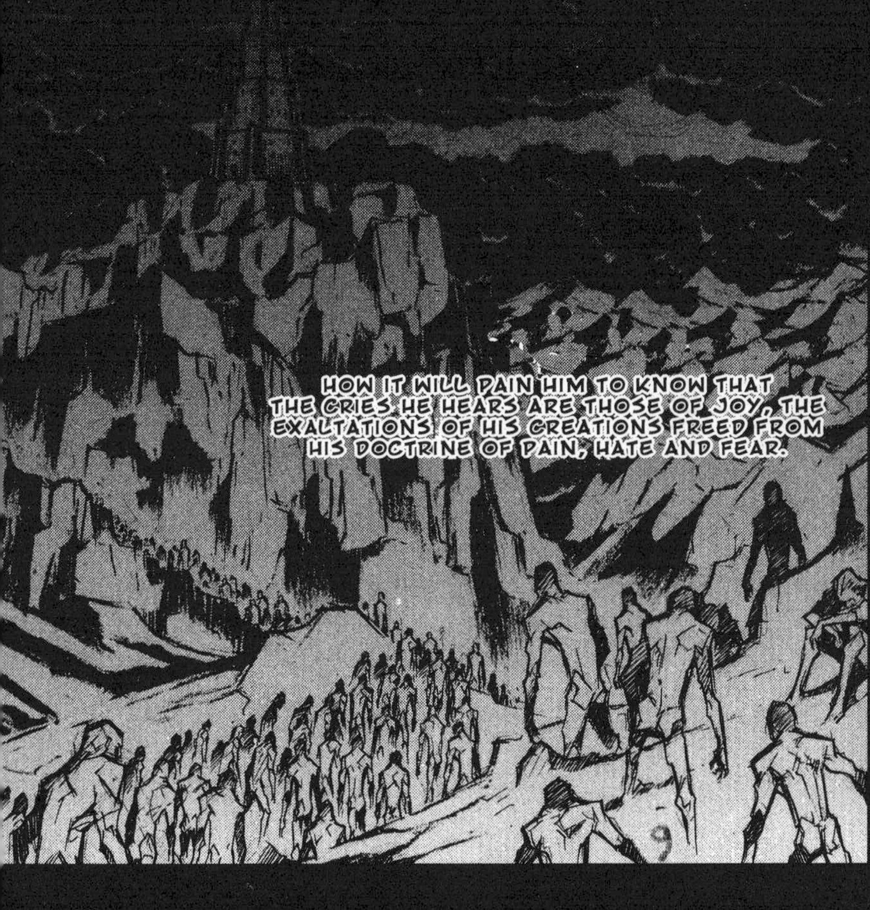
HOW IT WILL PAIN HIM TO KNOW THAT THE CRIES HE HEARS ARE THOSE OF JOY, THE EXALTATIONS OF HIS CREATIONS FREED FROM HIS DOCTRINE OF PAIN, HATE AND FEAR.

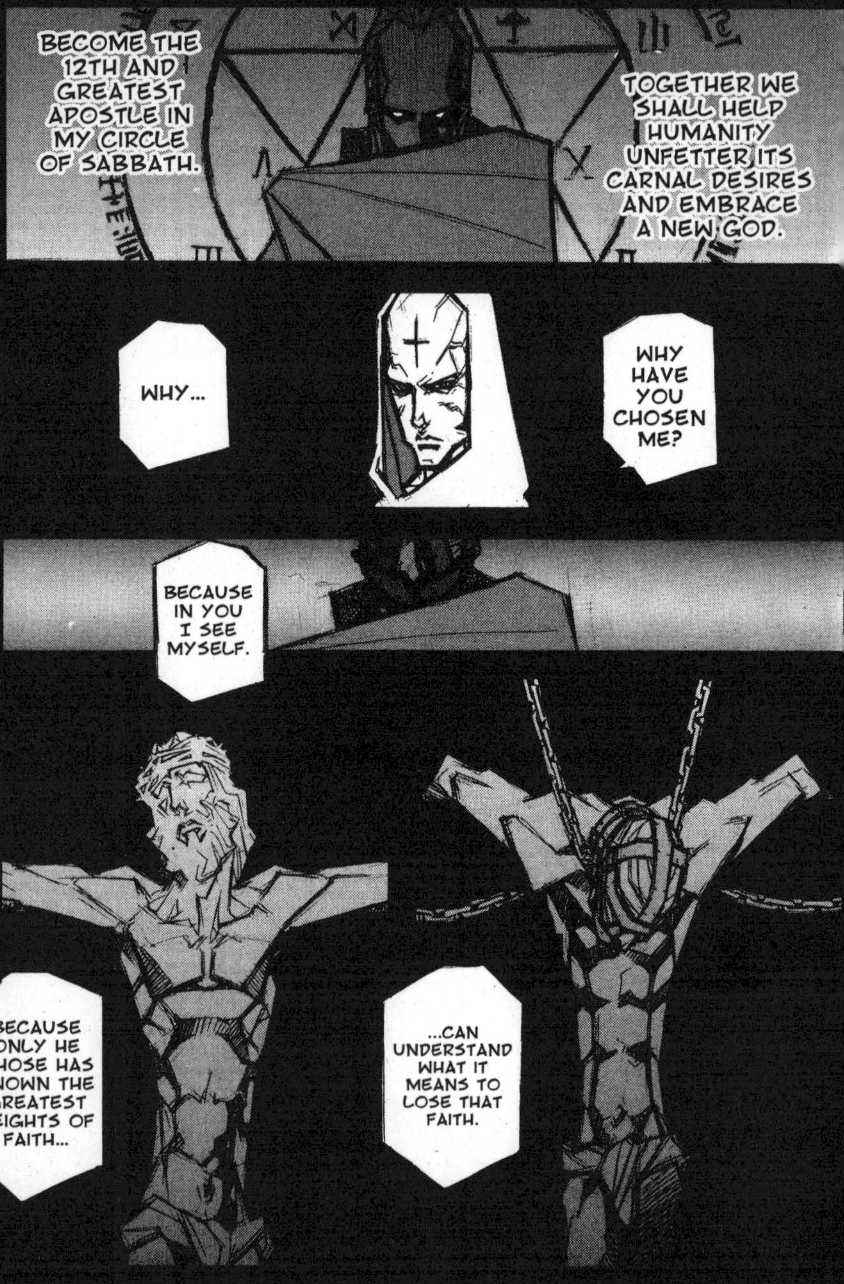
BECOME THE 12TH AND GREATEST APOSTLE IN MY CIRCLE OF SABBATH.
TOGETHER WE SHALL HELP HUMANITY UNFETTER ITS CARNAL DESIRES AND EMBRACE A NEW GOD.
WHY...
WHY HAVE YOU CHOSEN ME?
BECAUSE IN YOU I SEE MYSELF.
BECAUSE ONLY HE WHOSE HAS KNOWN THE GREATEST HEIGHTS OF FAITH...
...CAN UNDERSTAND WHAT IT MEANS TO LOSE THAT FAITH.

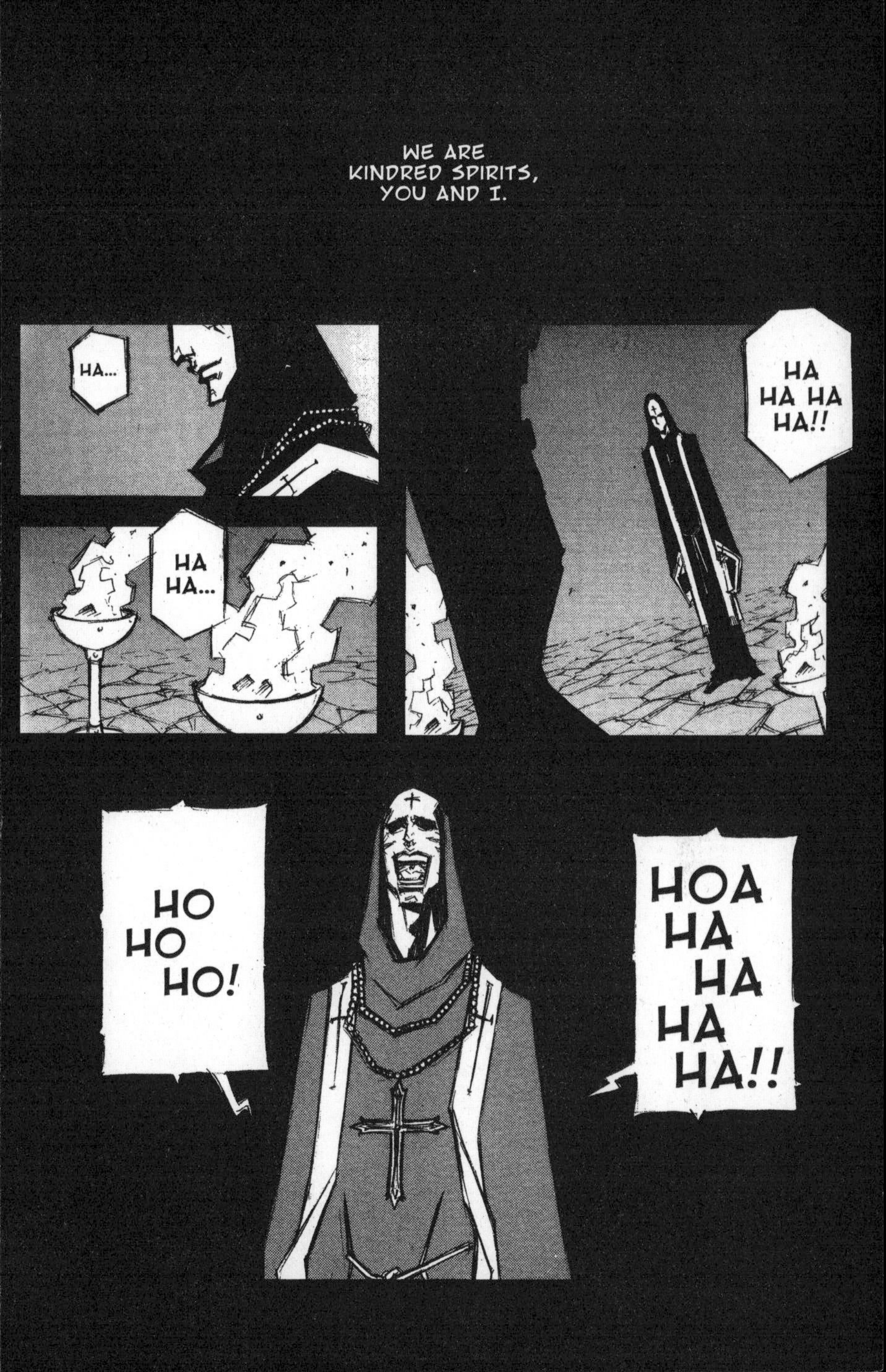
WE ARE KINDRED SPIRITS, YOU AND I.
HA...
HA HA...
HA HA HA HA!!
HO HO HO!
HOA HA HA HA HA!!

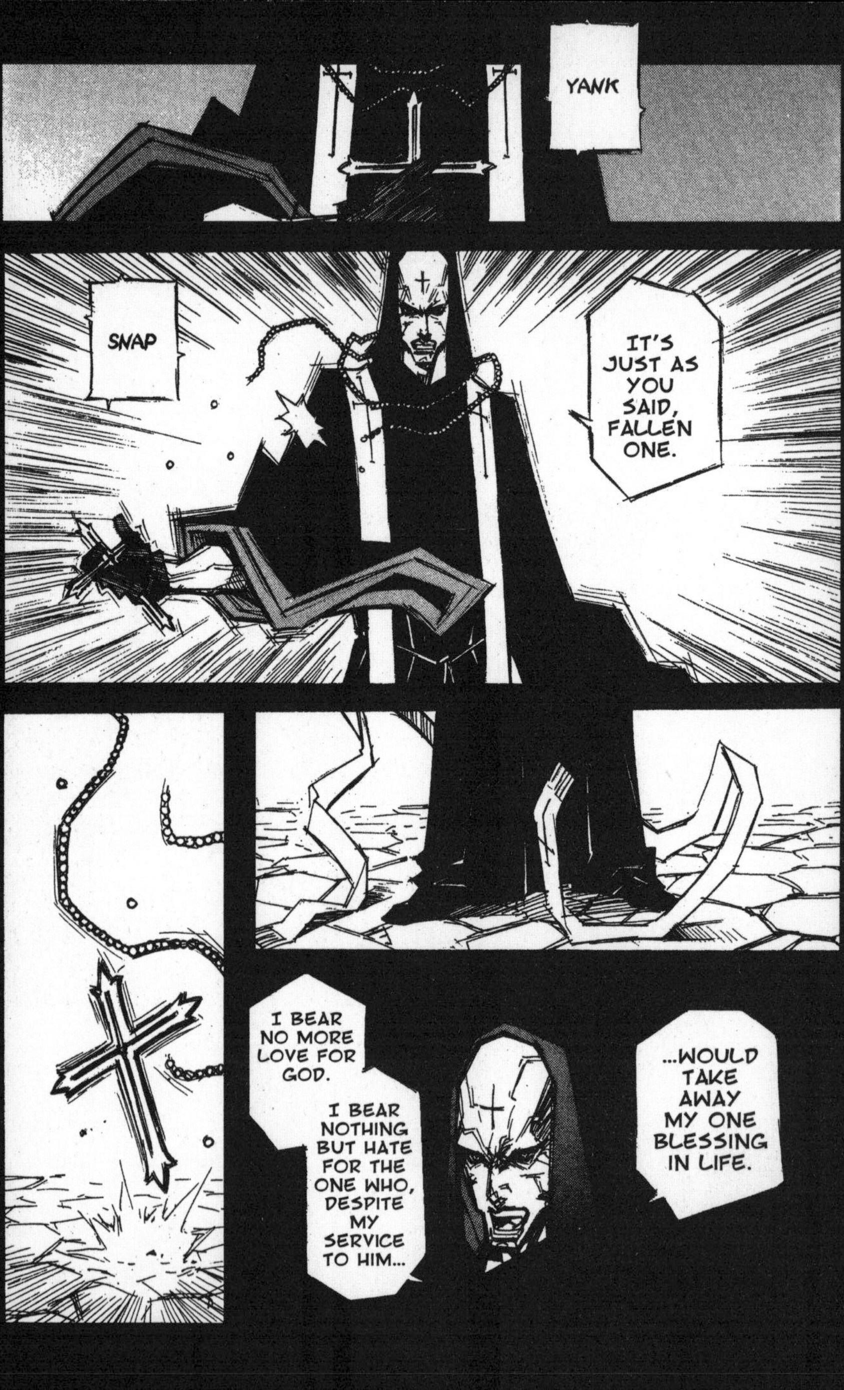
YANK
SNAP
IT'S JUST AS YOU SAID, FALLEN ONE.
I BEAR NO MORE LOVE FOR GOD.
I BEAR NOTHING BUT HATE FOR THE ONE WHO, DESPITE MY SERVICE TO HIM...
...WOULD TAKE AWAY MY ONE BLESSING IN LIFE.

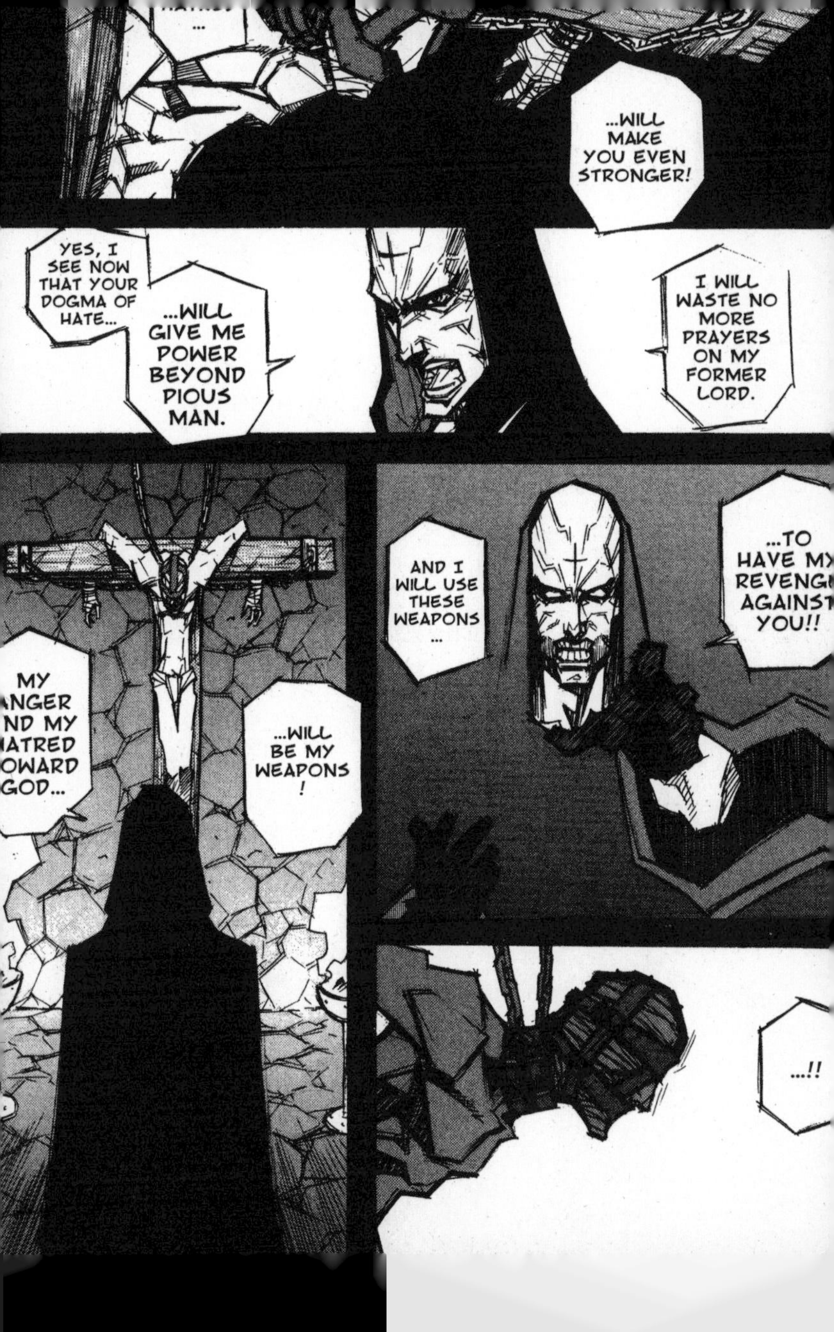
...WILL MAKE YOU EVEN STRONGER!
YES, I SEE NOW THAT YOUR DOGMA OF HATE...
...WILL GIVE ME POWER BEYOND PIOUS MAN.
I WILL WASTE NO MORE PRAYERS ON MY FORMER LORD.
MY ANGER AND MY HATRED TOWARD GOD...
...WILL BE MY WEAPONS!
AND I WILL USE THESE WEAPONS...
...TO HAVE MY REVENGE AGAINST YOU!!
...!!

THIS MAN...

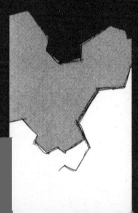

...I SEE...

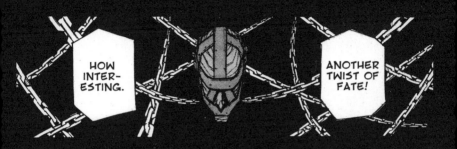

HOW INTERESTING.

ANOTHER TWIST OF FATE!

YOU ARE THE ONE DESTINED TO COMPLETE THE CIRCLE...

...AND BRING ABOUT MY RESURRECTION.

YOU CANNOT ESCAPE YOUR DESTINY AS MY APOSTLE, BETHEAL.

IF THAT DESTINY GRANTS ME POWER...

...I WILL GLADLY ACCEPT IT SO THAT I MIGHT USE IT AGAINST YOU!

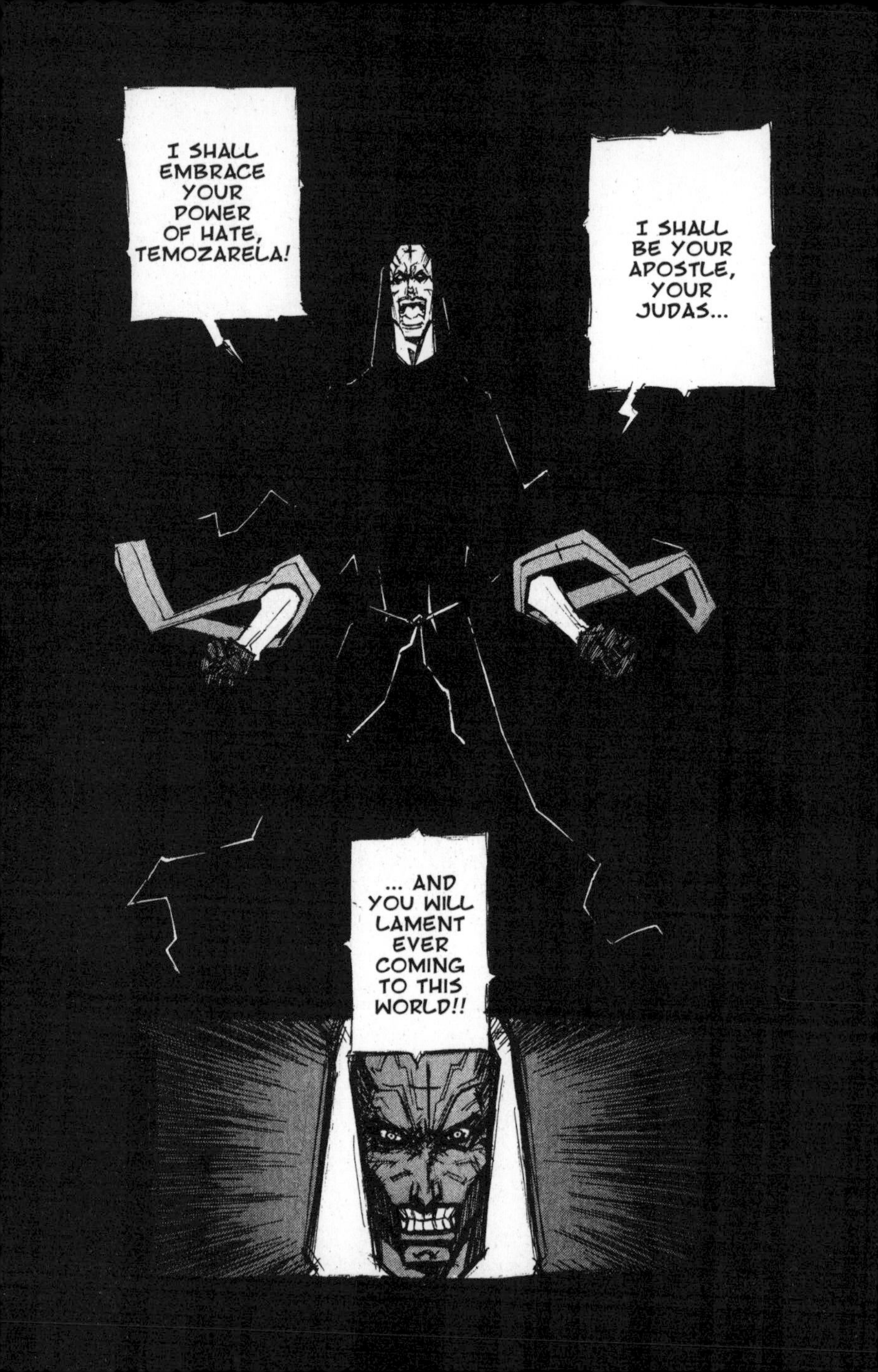
I SHALL EMBRACE YOUR POWER OF HATE, TEMOZARELA!
I SHALL BE YOUR APOSTLE, YOUR JUDAS...
... AND YOU WILL LAMENT EVER COMING TO THIS WORLD!!

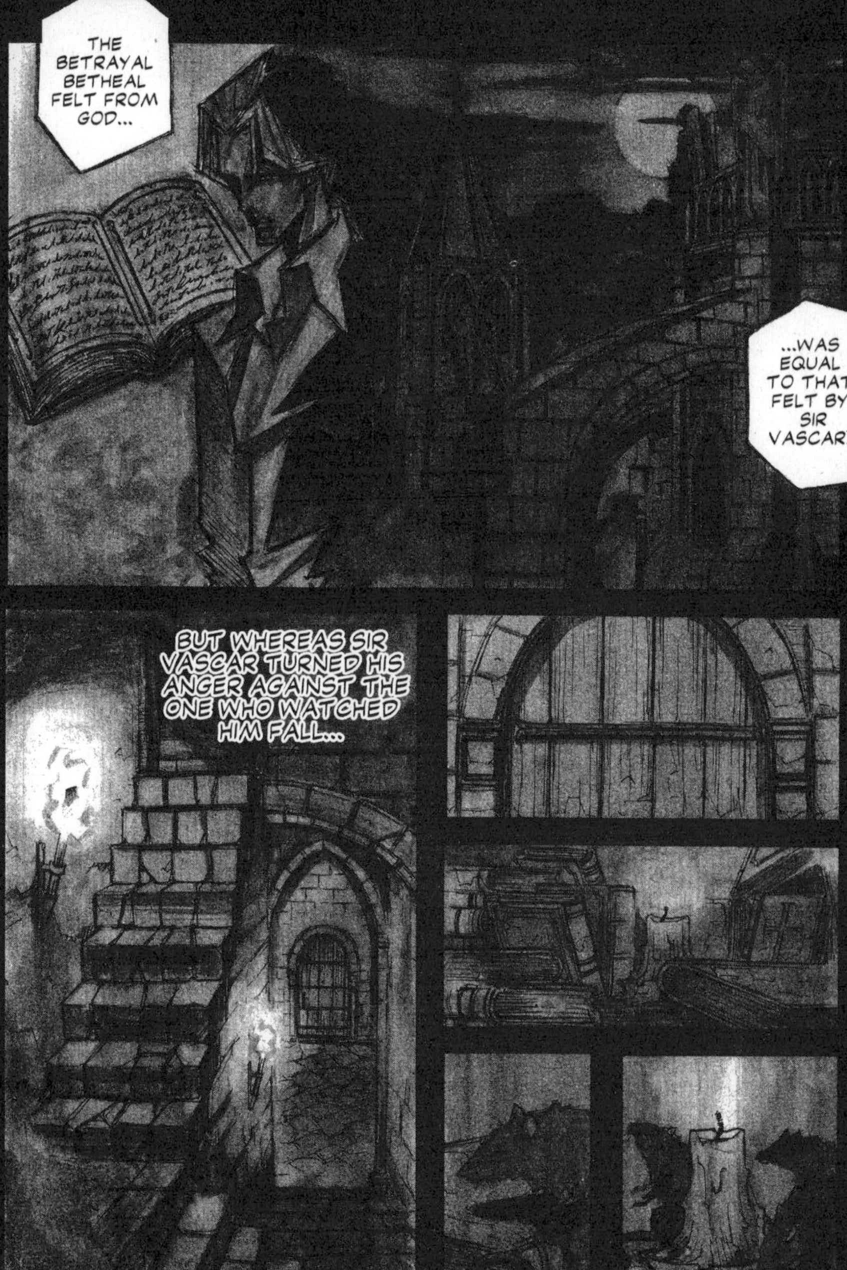
THE BETRAYAL BETHEAL FELT FROM GOD...
...WAS EQUAL TO THAT FELT BY SIR VASCAR.
BUT WHEREAS SIR VASCAR TURNED HIS ANGER AGAINST THE ONE WHO WATCHED HIM FALL...

...BETHEAL TURNED HIS RACE TOWARDS THE ONE WHO LED HIM TO FALL—TEMOZARELA.

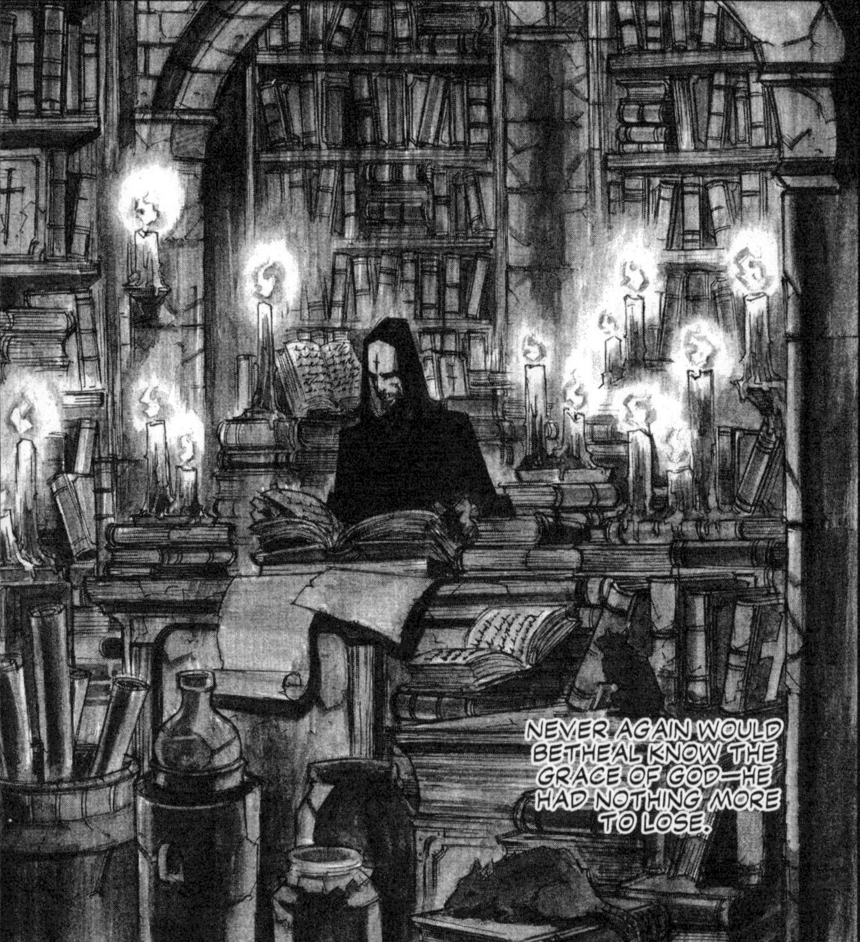
NEVER AGAIN WOULD BETHEAL KNOW THE GRACE OF GOD—HE HAD NOTHING MORE TO LOSE.

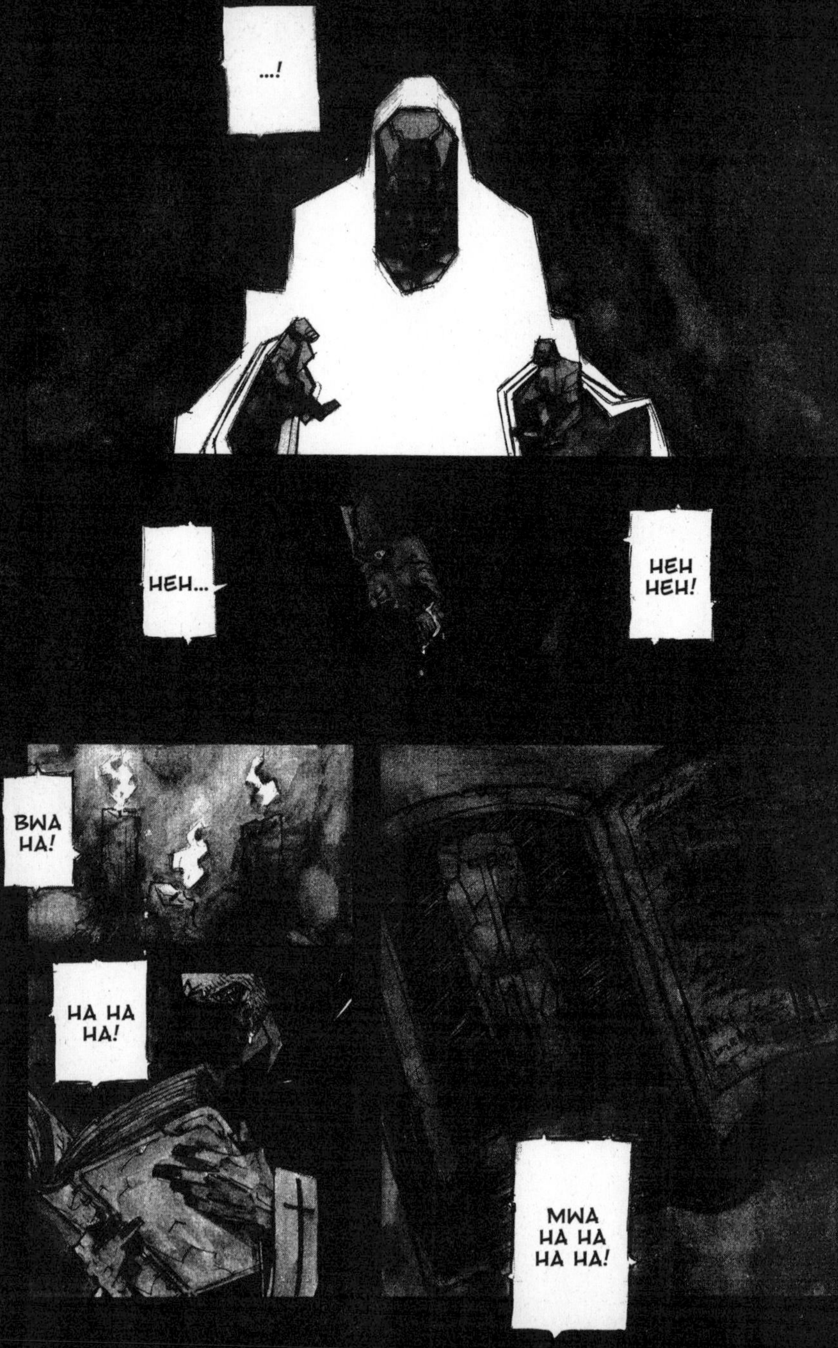
...!
HEH...
HEH HEH!
BWA HA!
HA HA HA!
MWA HA HA HA HA!

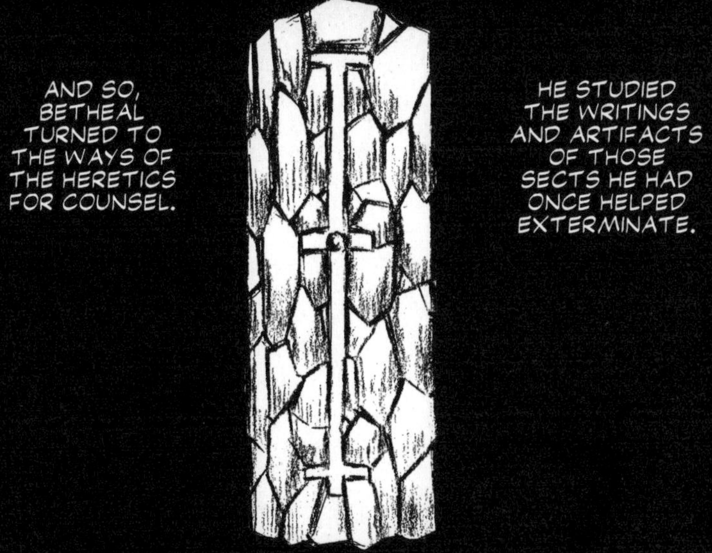
AND SO, BETHEAL TURNED TO THE WAYS OF THE HERETICS FOR COUNSEL.
HE STUDIED THE WRITINGS AND ARTIFACTS OF THOSE SECTS HE HAD ONCE HELPED EXTERMINATE.

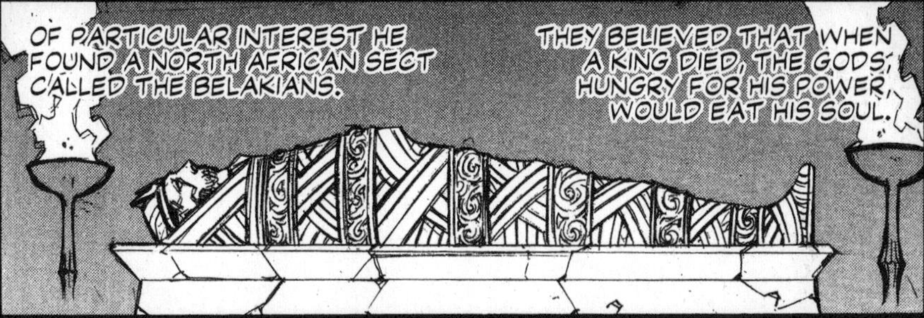
OF PARTICULAR INTEREST HE FOUND A NORTH AFRICAN SECT CALLED THE BELAKIANS.
THEY BELIEVED THAT WHEN A KING DIED, THE GODS, HUNGRY FOR HIS POWER, WOULD EAT HIS SOUL.

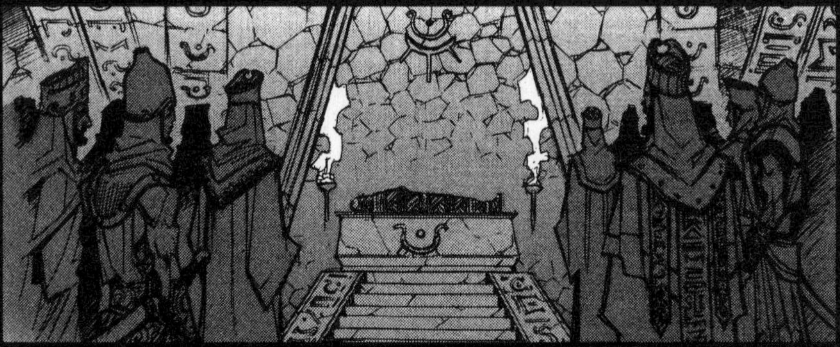

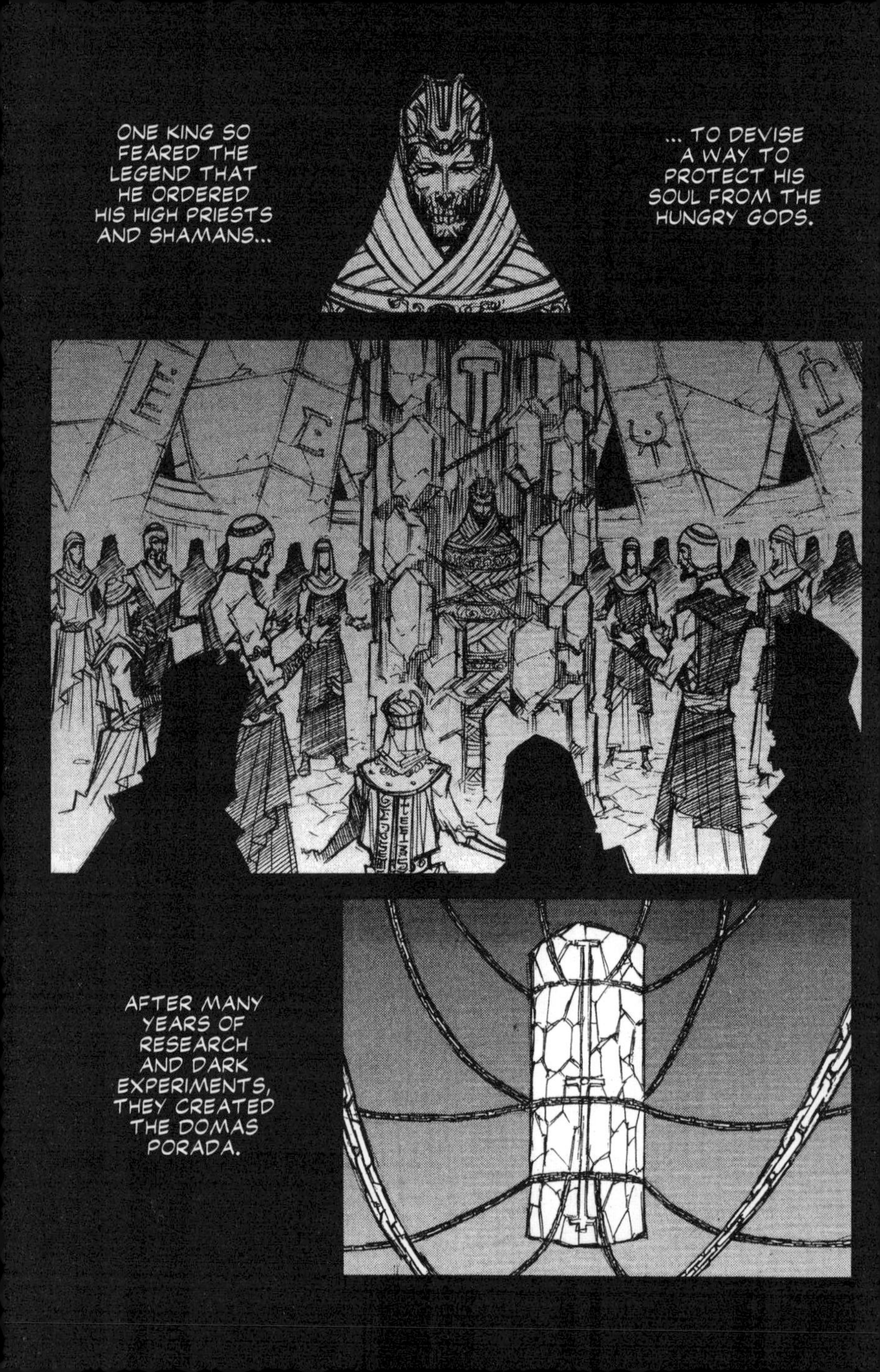
ONE KING SO FEARED THE LEGEND THAT HE ORDERED HIS HIGH PRIESTS AND SHAMANS...
... TO DEVISE A WAY TO PROTECT HIS SOUL FROM THE HUNGRY GODS.
AFTER MANY YEARS OF RESEARCH AND DARK EXPERIMENTS, THEY CREATED THE DOMAS PORADA.

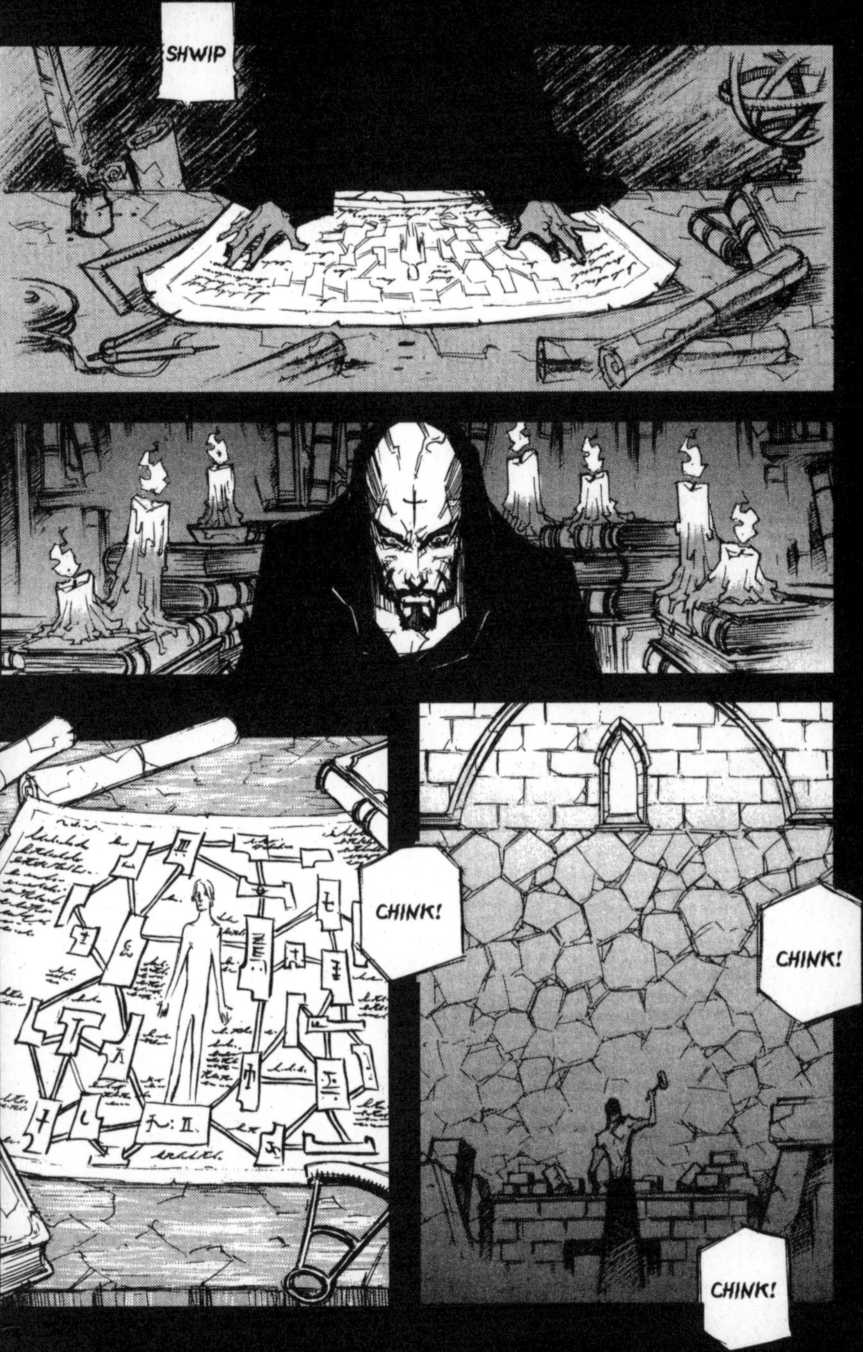
SHWIP
CHINK!
CHINK!
CHINK!

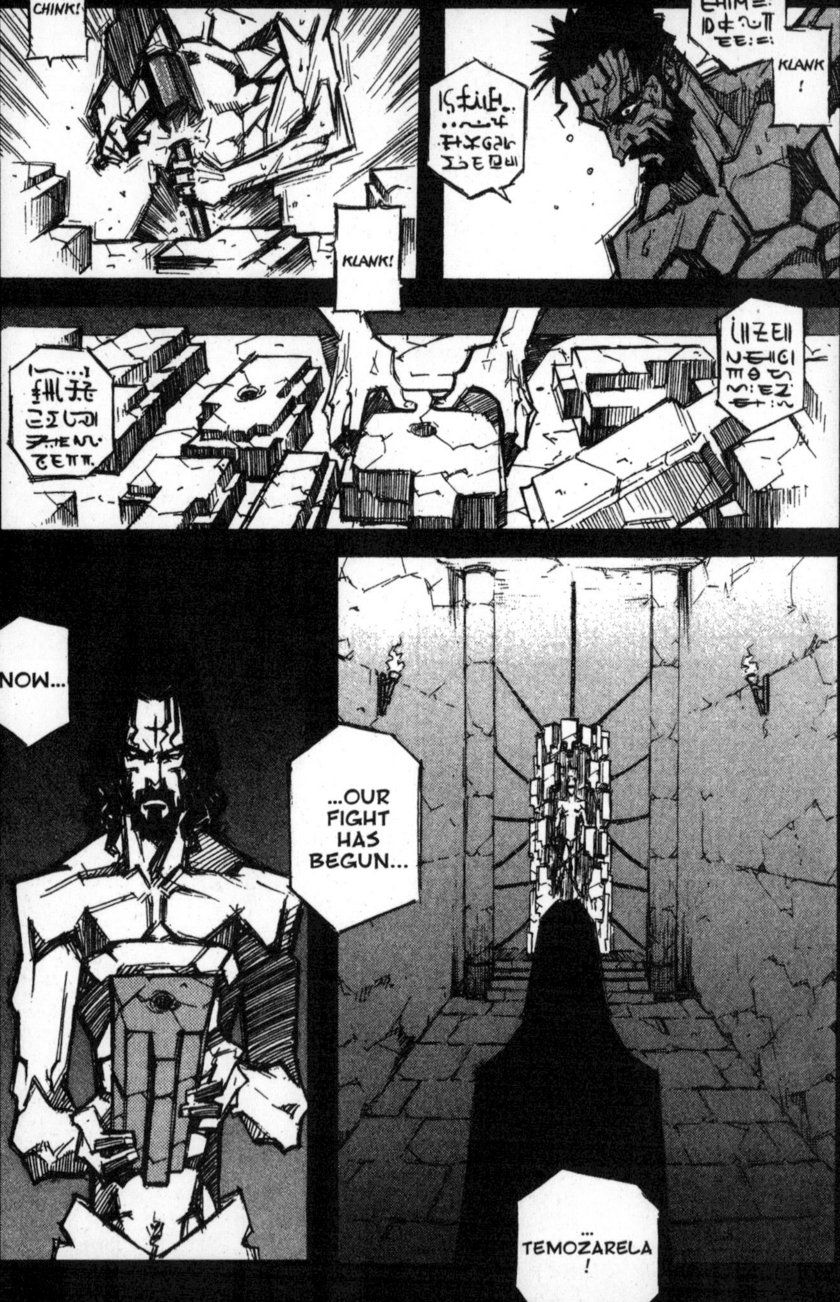
CHINK!
KLANK!
KLANK !
NOW...
...OUR FIGHT HAS BEGUN...
... TEMOZARELA !

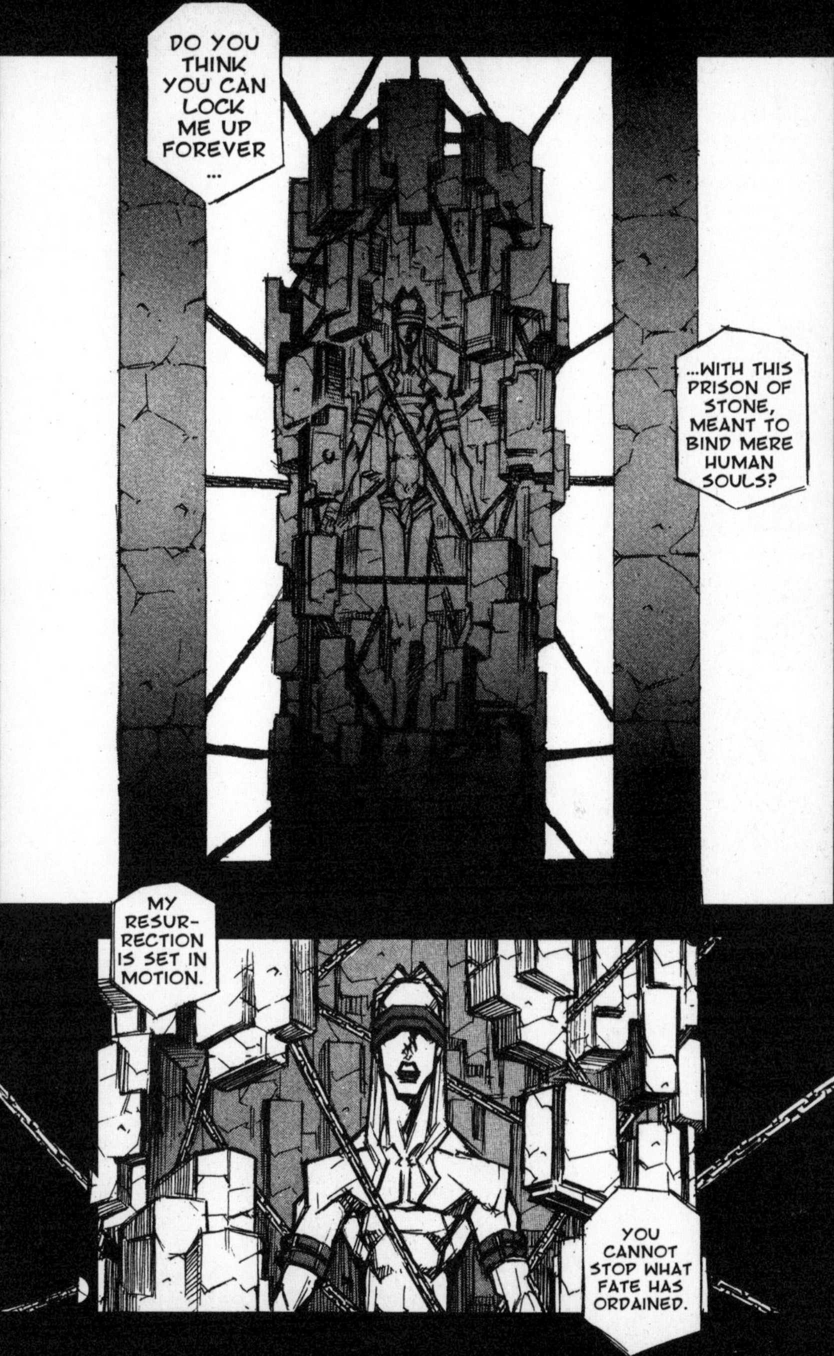
DO YOU THINK YOU CAN LOCK ME UP FOREVER ...
...WITH THIS PRISON OF STONE, MEANT TO BIND MERE HUMAN SOULS?
MY RESUR-RECTION IS SET IN MOTION.
YOU CANNOT STOP WHAT FATE HAS ORDAINED.

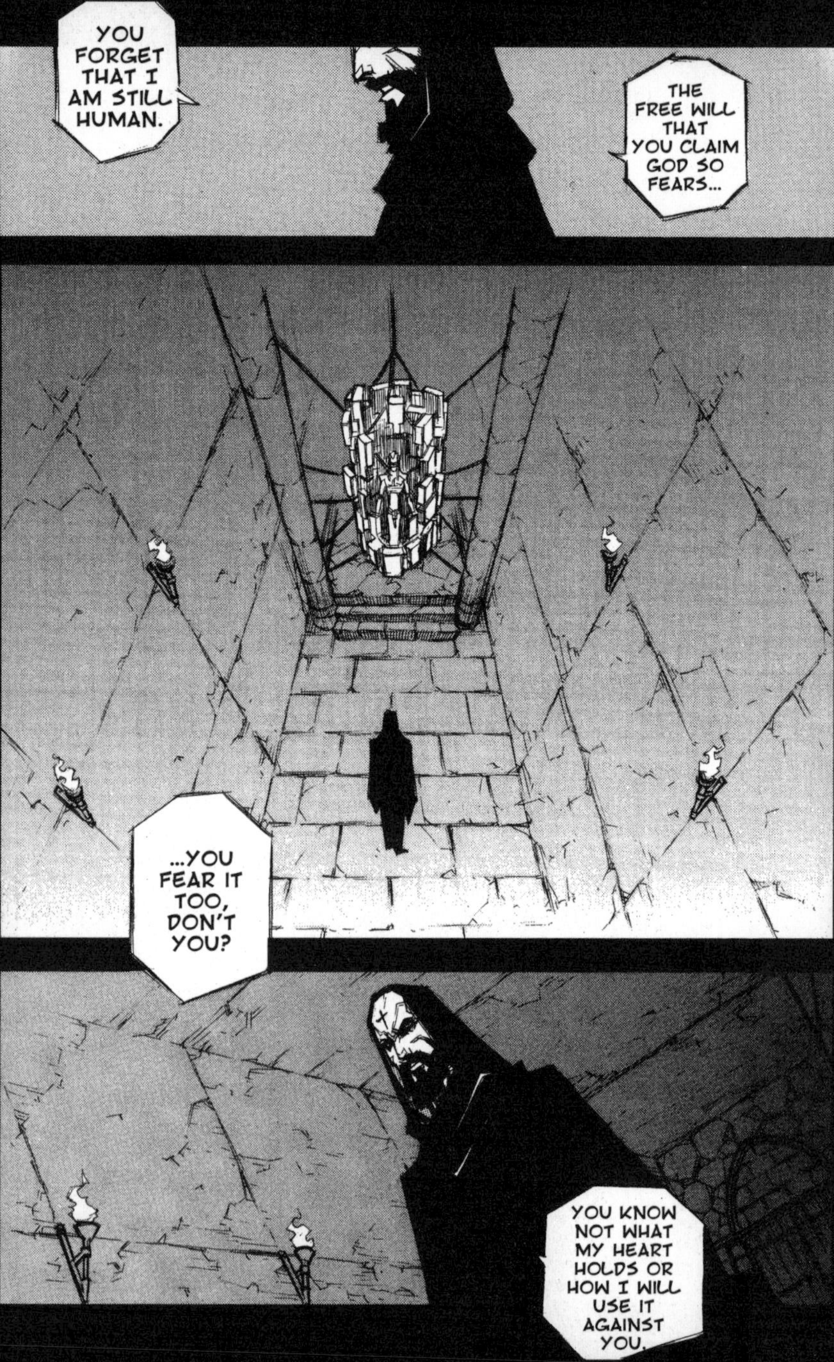
YOU FORGET THAT I AM STILL HUMAN.
THE FREE WILL THAT YOU CLAIM GOD SO FEARS...
...YOU FEAR IT TOO, DON'T YOU?
YOU KNOW NOT WHAT MY HEART HOLDS OR HOW I WILL USE IT AGAINST YOU.

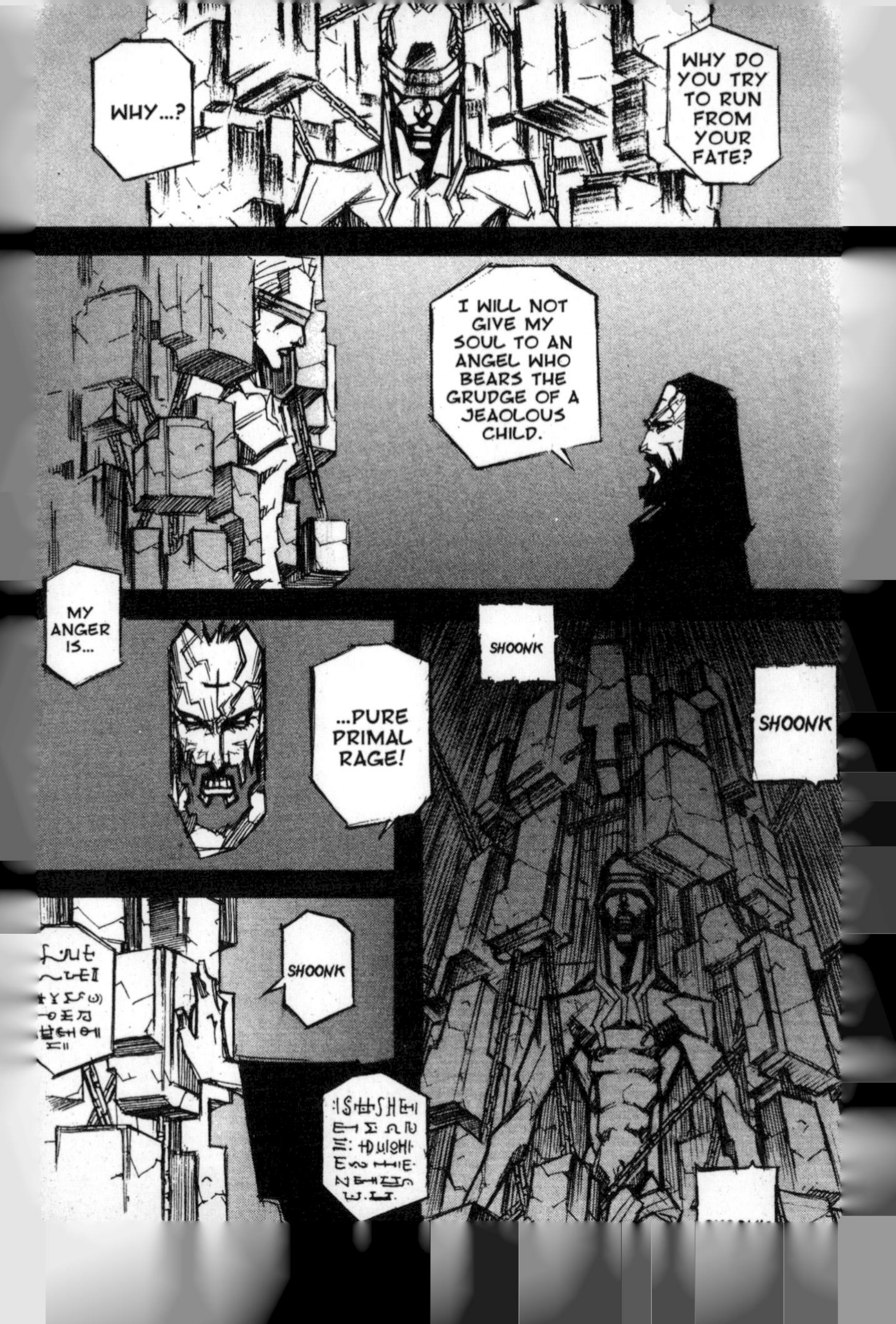
WHY...?
WHY DO YOU TRY TO RUN FROM YOUR FATE?
I WILL NOT GIVE MY SOUL TO AN ANGEL WHO BEARS THE GRUDGE OF A JEAOLOUS CHILD.
MY ANGER IS...
...PURE PRIMAL RAGE!
SHOONK
SHOONK
SHOONK

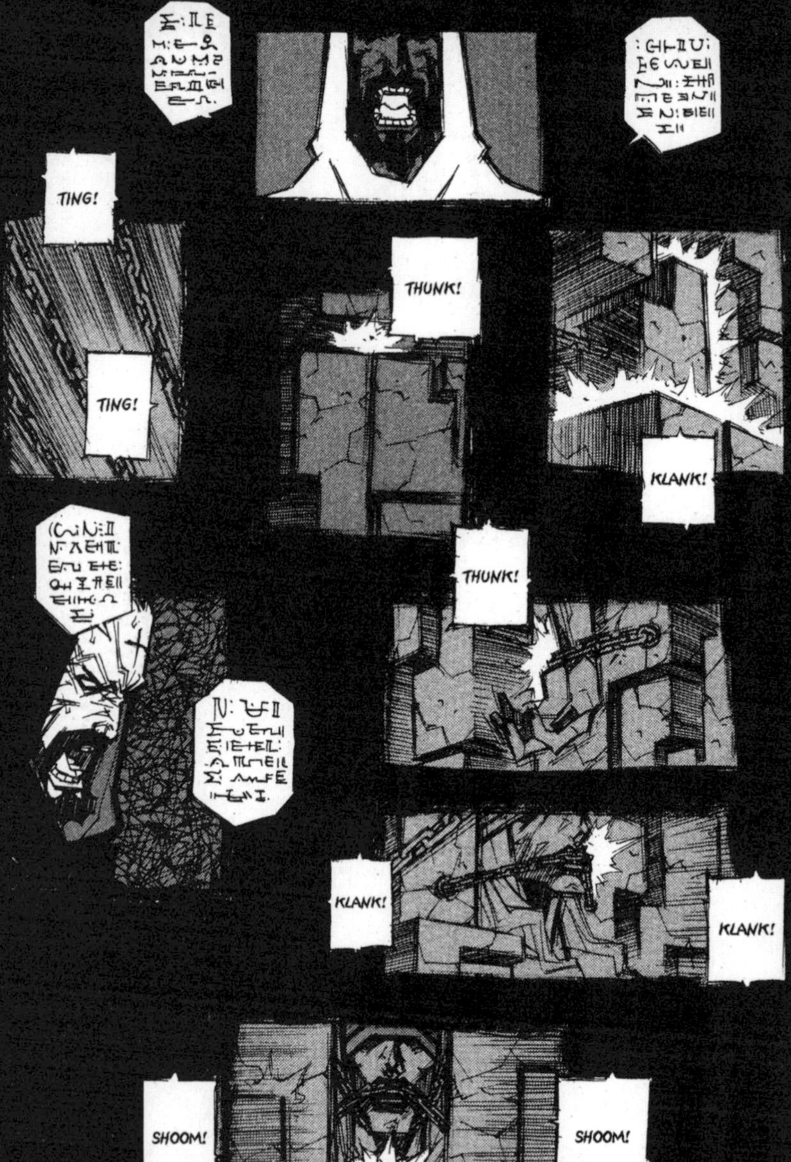
TING!
TING!
THUNK!
KLANK!
THUNK!
KLANK!
KLANK!
SHOOM!
SHOOM!

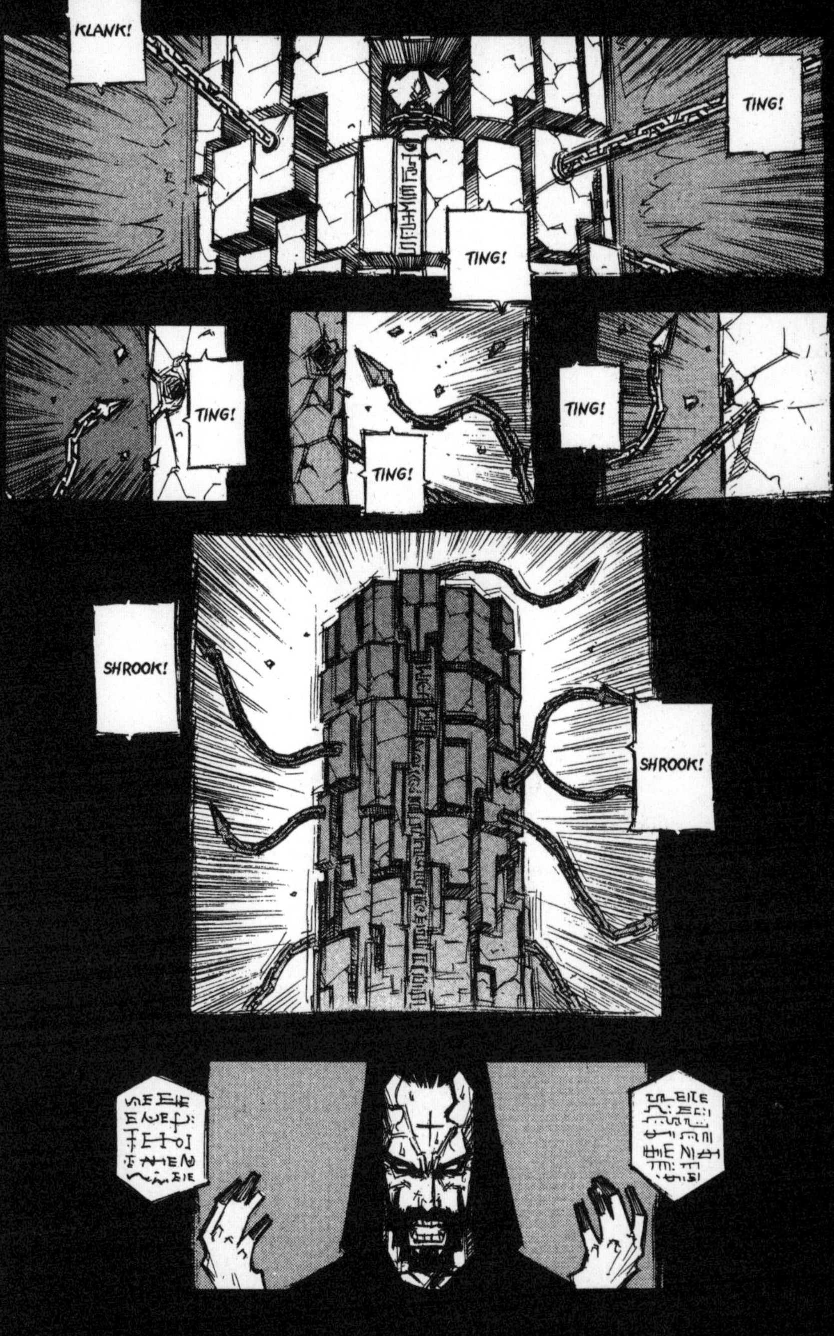
KLANK!
TING!
TING!
TING!
TING!
TING!
SHROOK!
SHROOK!

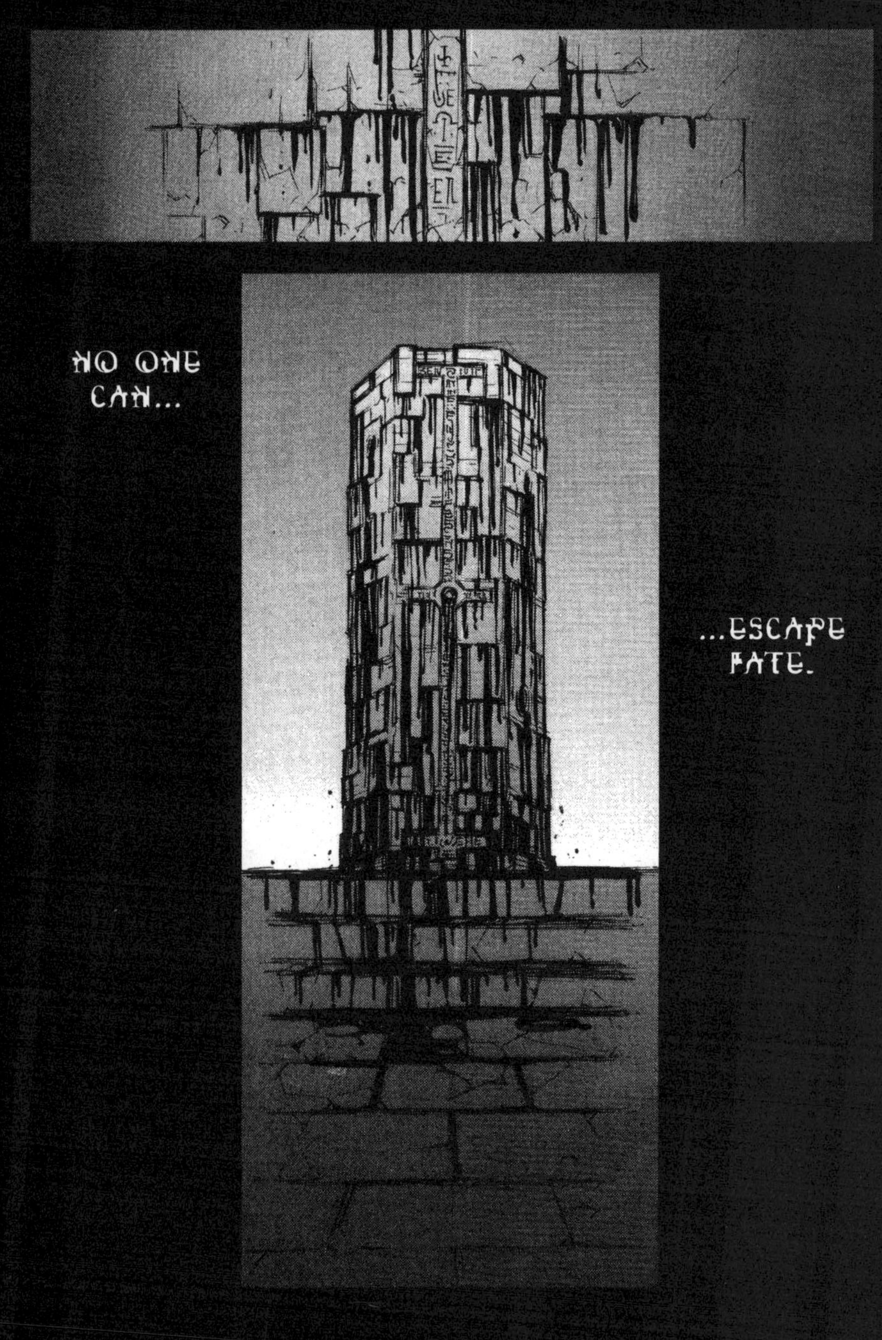
NO ONE CAN...
...ESCAPE FATE.

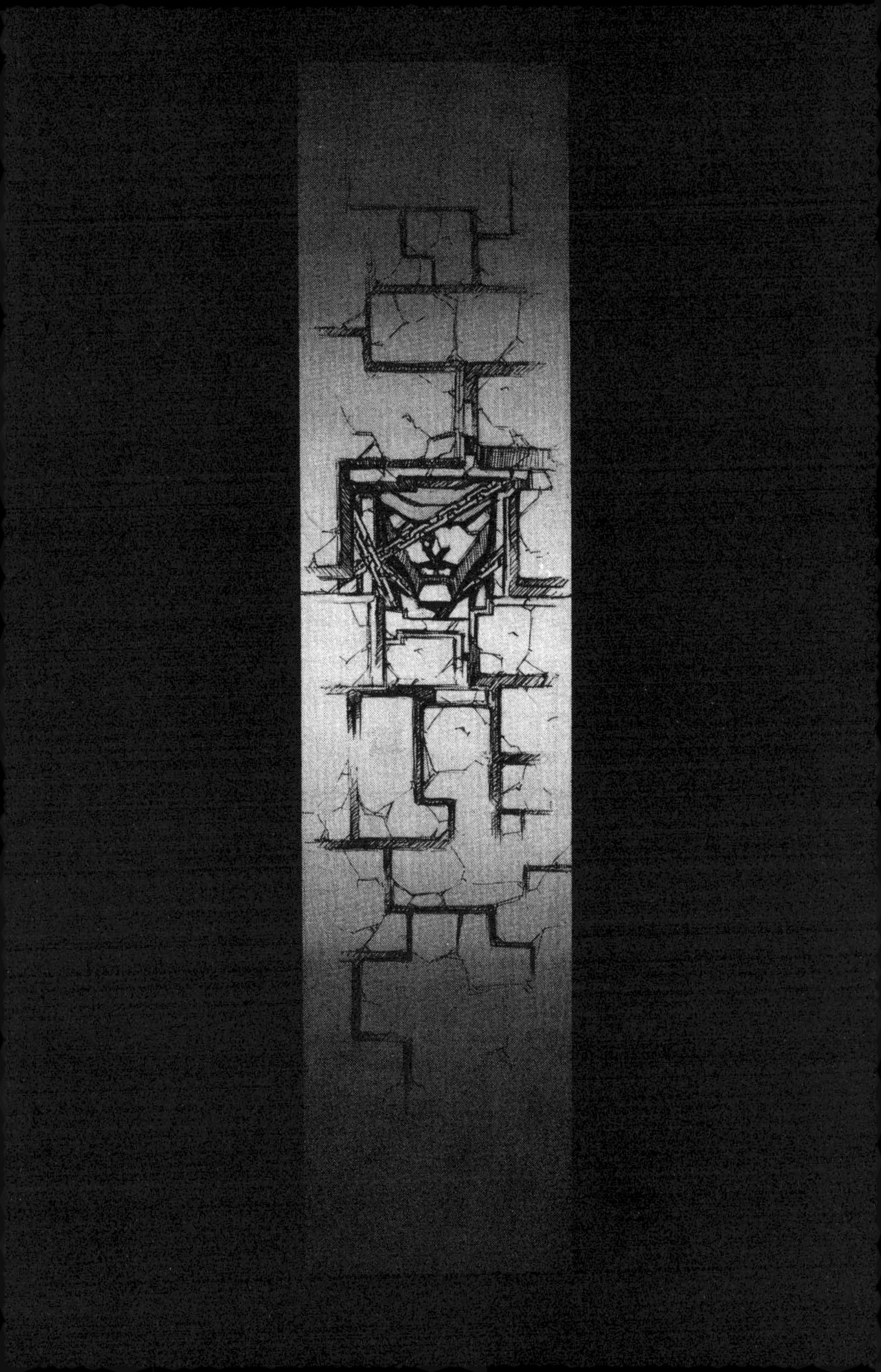

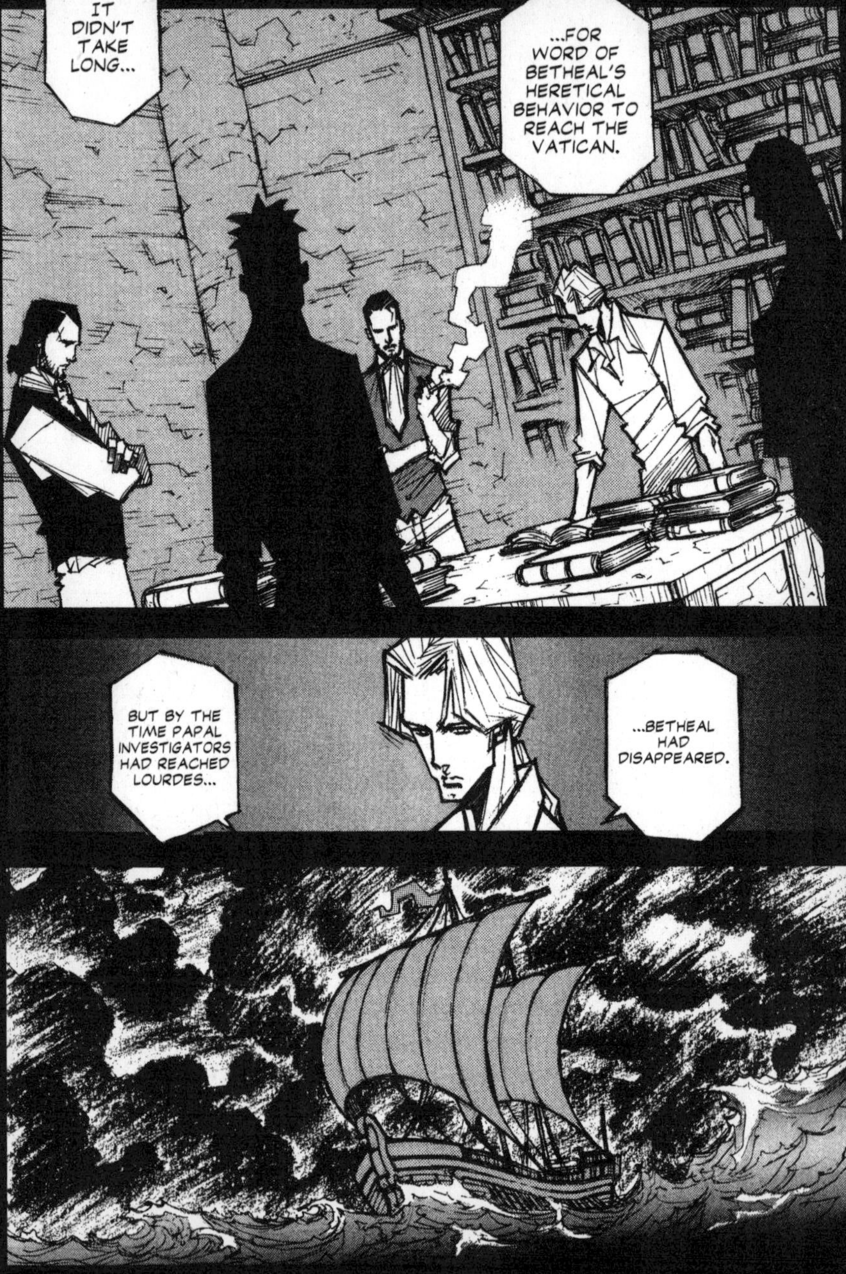
IT DIDN'T TAKE LONG...
...FOR WORD OF BETHEAL'S HERETICAL BEHAVIOR TO REACH THE VATICAN.
BUT BY THE TIME PAPAL INVESTIGATORS HAD REACHED LOURDES...
...BETHEAL HAD DISAPPEARED.

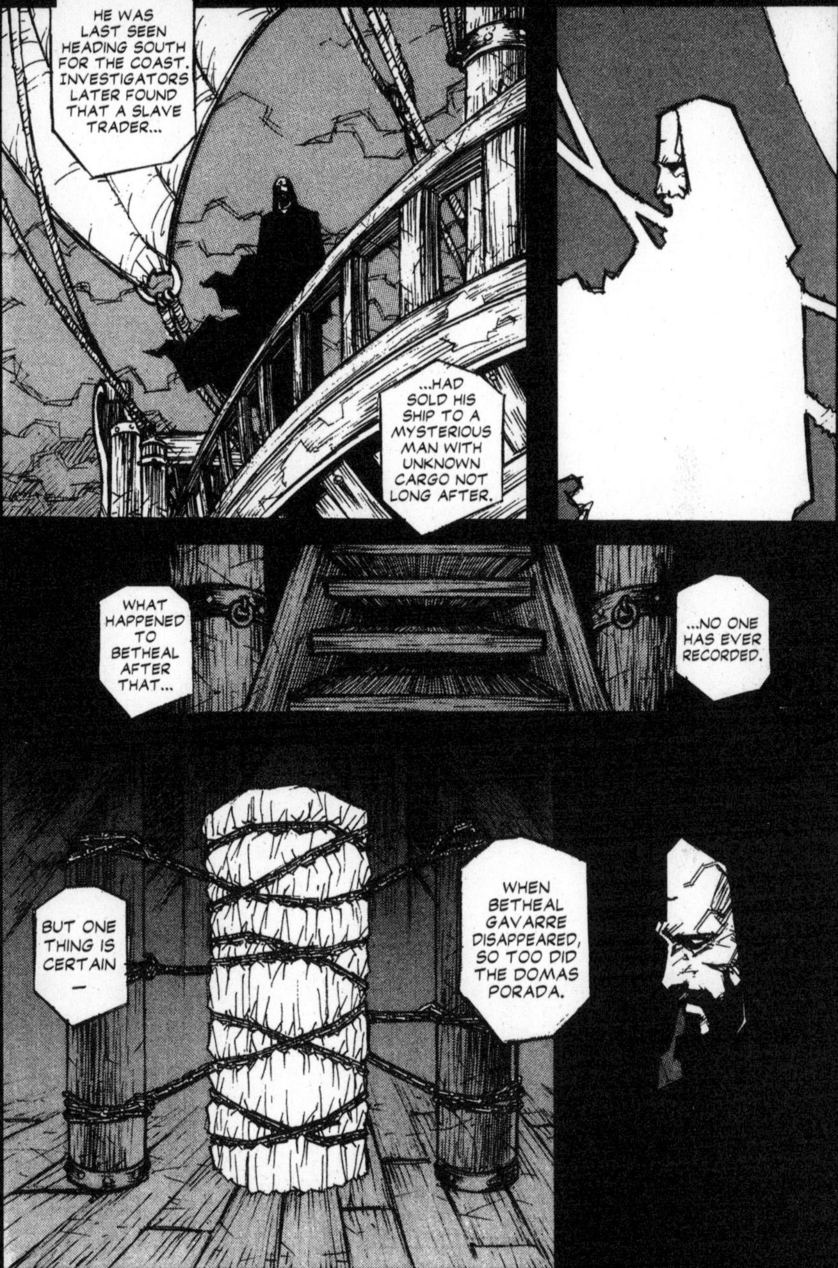
HE WAS LAST SEEN HEADING SOUTH FOR THE COAST. INVESTIGATORS LATER FOUND THAT A SLAVE TRADER...
...HAD SOLD HIS SHIP TO A MYSTERIOUS MAN WITH UNKNOWN CARGO NOT LONG AFTER.
WHAT HAPPENED TO BETHEAL AFTER THAT...
...NO ONE HAS EVER RECORDED.
BUT ONE THING IS CERTAIN —
WHEN BETHEAL GAVARRE DISAPPEARED, SO TOO DID THE DOMAS PORADA.

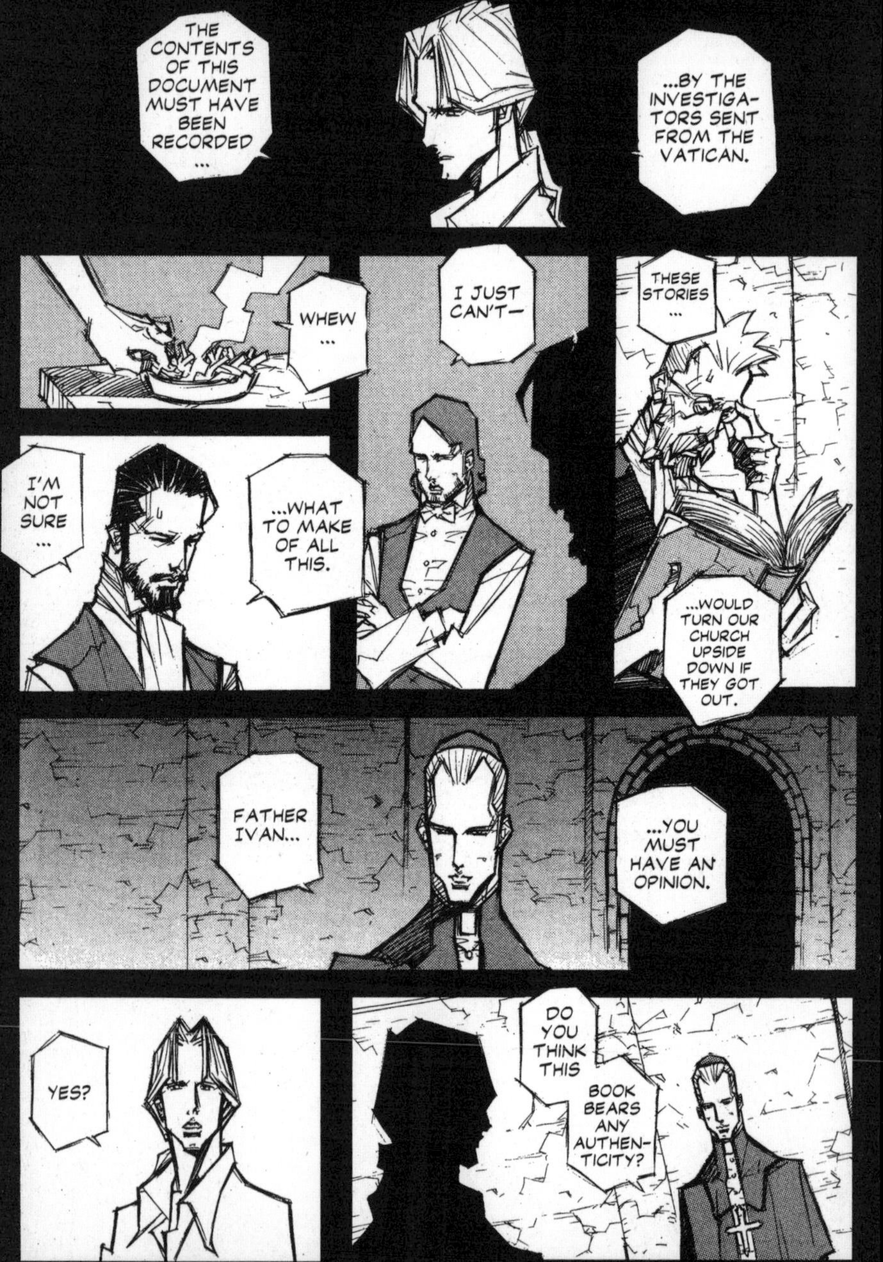
THE CONTENTS OF THIS DOCUMENT MUST HAVE BEEN RECORDED ...
...BY THE INVESTIGA-TORS SENT FROM THE VATICAN.
WHEW ...
I JUST CAN'T—
THESE STORIES ...
I'M NOT SURE ...
...WHAT TO MAKE OF ALL THIS.
...WOULD TURN OUR CHURCH UPSIDE DOWN IF THEY GOT OUT.
FATHER IVAN...
...YOU MUST HAVE AN OPINION.
YES?
DO YOU THINK THIS
BOOK BEARS ANY AUTHEN-TICITY?

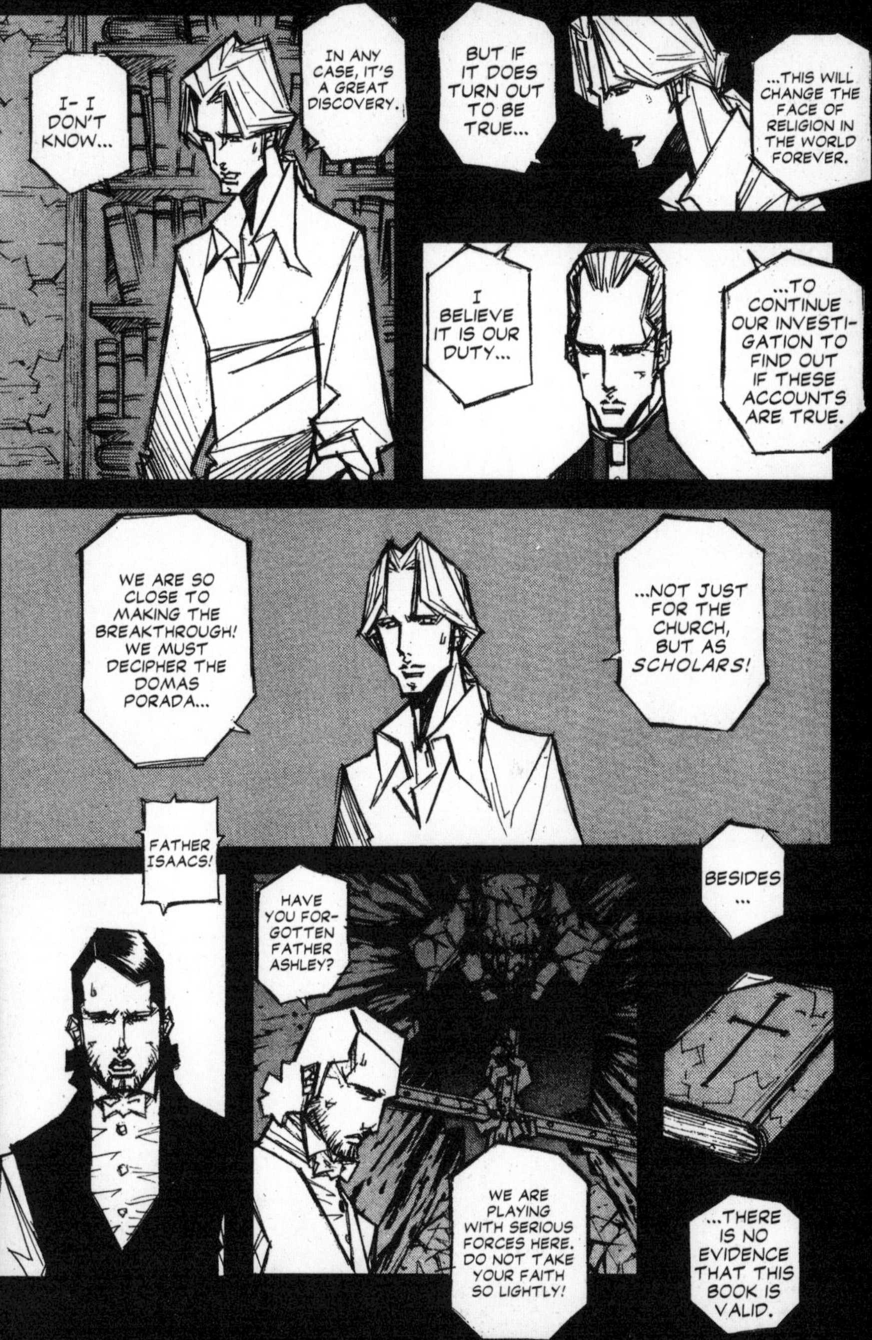
I- I DON'T KNOW...
IN ANY CASE, IT'S A GREAT DISCOVERY.
BUT IF IT DOES TURN OUT TO BE TRUE...
...THIS WILL CHANGE THE FACE OF RELIGION IN THE WORLD FOREVER.
I BELIEVE IT IS OUR DUTY...
...TO CONTINUE OUR INVESTIGATION TO FIND OUT IF THESE ACCOUNTS ARE TRUE.
WE ARE SO CLOSE TO MAKING THE BREAKTHROUGH! WE MUST DECIPHER THE DOMAS PORADA...
...NOT JUST FOR THE CHURCH, BUT AS *SCHOLARS!*
FATHER ISAACS!
HAVE YOU FORGOTTEN FATHER ASHLEY?
WE ARE PLAYING WITH SERIOUS FORCES HERE. DO NOT TAKE YOUR FAITH SO LIGHTLY!
BESIDES...
...THERE IS NO EVIDENCE THAT THIS BOOK IS VALID.

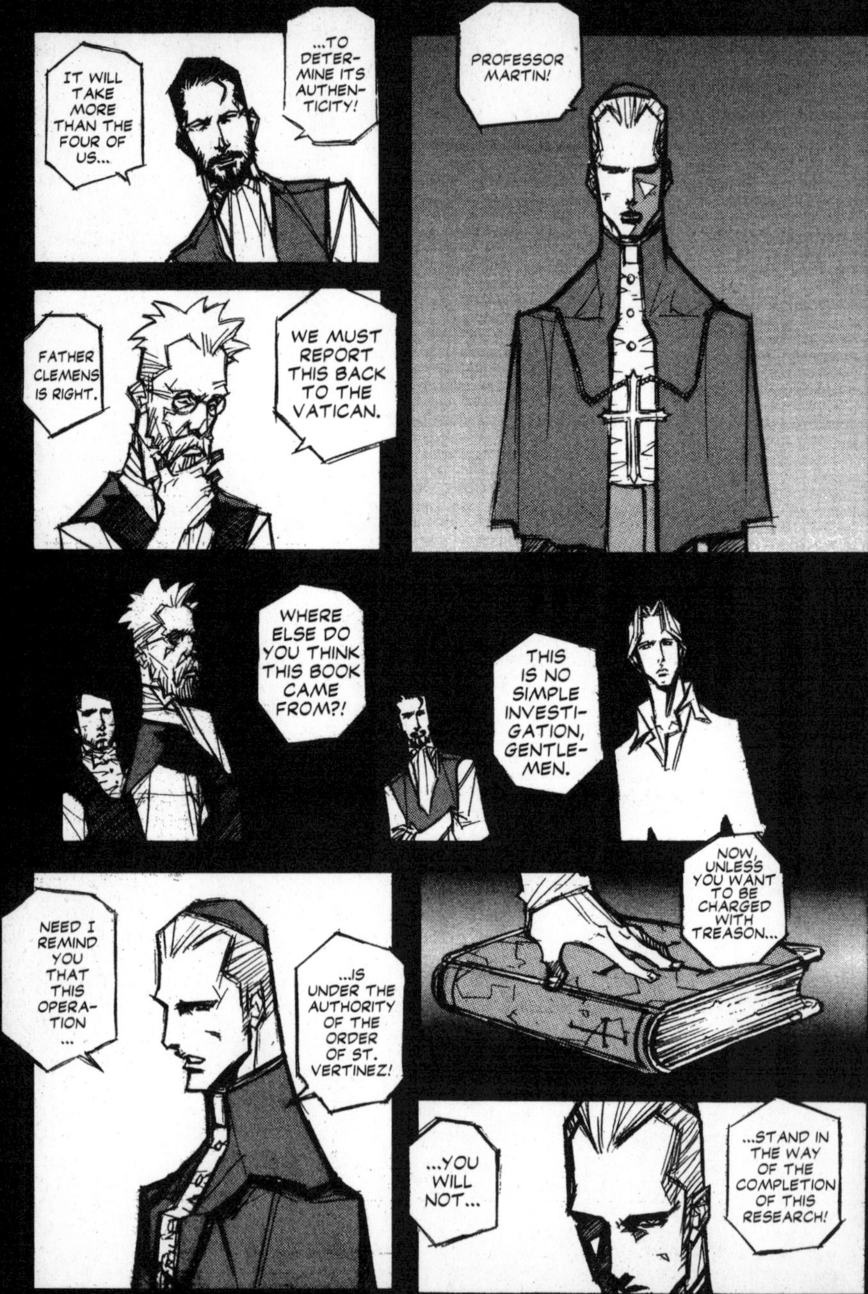
IT WILL TAKE MORE THAN THE FOUR OF US...
...TO DETERMINE ITS AUTHENTICITY!
FATHER CLEMENS IS RIGHT.
WE MUST REPORT THIS BACK TO THE VATICAN.
PROFESSOR MARTIN!
WHERE ELSE DO YOU THINK THIS BOOK CAME FROM?!
THIS IS NO SIMPLE INVESTIGATION, GENTLEMEN.
NEED I REMIND YOU THAT THIS OPERATION...
...IS UNDER THE AUTHORITY OF THE ORDER OF ST. VERTINEZ!
NOW, UNLESS YOU WANT TO BE CHARGED WITH TREASON...
...YOU WILL NOT...
...STAND IN THE WAY OF THE COMPLETION OF THIS RESEARCH!

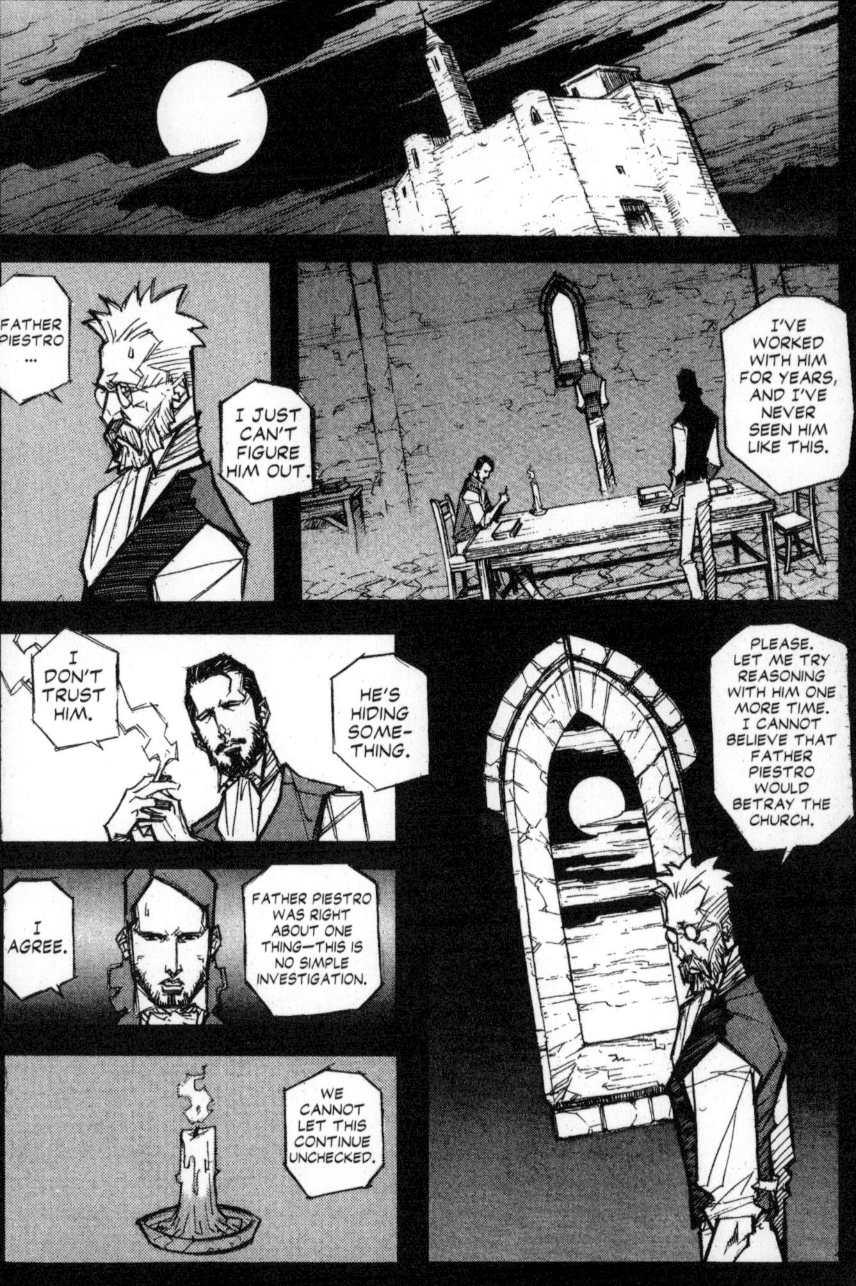
FATHER PIESTRO ...
I JUST CAN'T FIGURE HIM OUT.
I'VE WORKED WITH HIM FOR YEARS, AND I'VE NEVER SEEN HIM LIKE THIS.
I DON'T TRUST HIM.
HE'S HIDING SOME-THING.
I AGREE.
FATHER PIESTRO WAS RIGHT ABOUT ONE THING—THIS IS NO SIMPLE INVESTIGATION.
WE CANNOT LET THIS CONTINUE UNCHECKED.
PLEASE. LET ME TRY REASONING WITH HIM ONE MORE TIME. I CANNOT BELIEVE THAT FATHER PIESTRO WOULD BETRAY THE CHURCH.

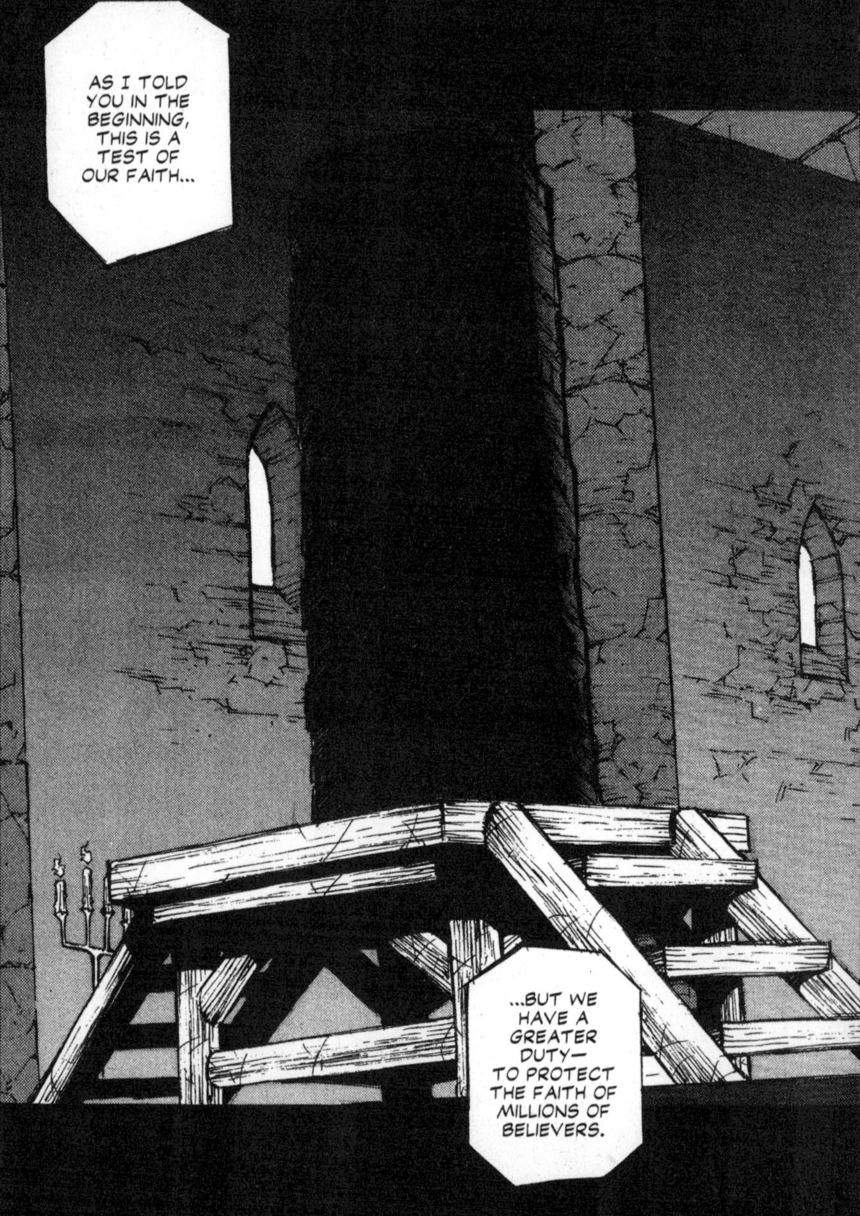
AS I TOLD YOU IN THE BEGINNING, THIS IS A TEST OF OUR FAITH...
...BUT WE HAVE A GREATER DUTY— TO PROTECT THE FAITH OF MILLIONS OF BELIEVERS.

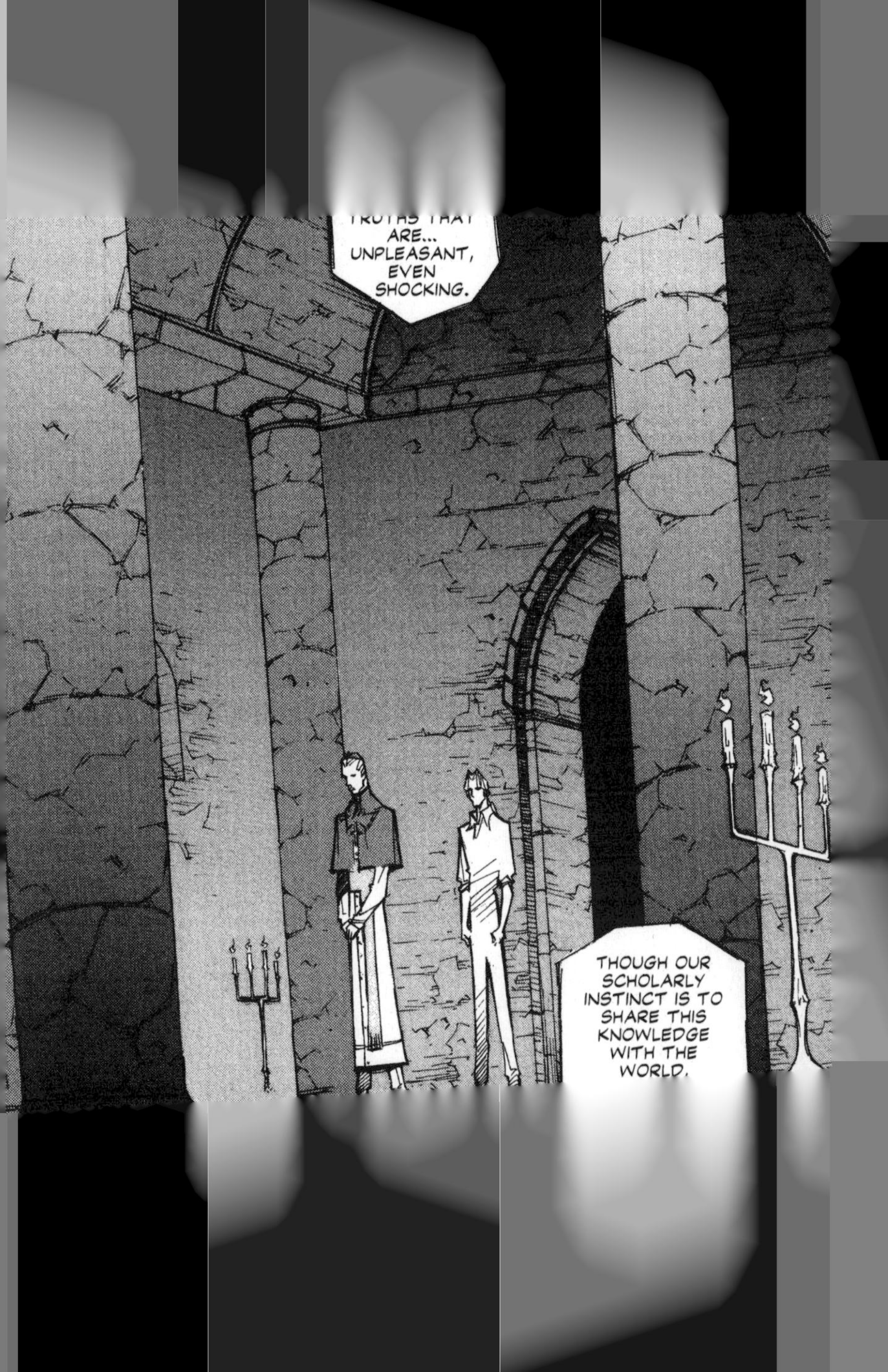
ARE... UNPLEASANT, EVEN SHOCKING.
THOUGH OUR SCHOLARLY INSTINCT IS TO SHARE THIS KNOWLEDGE WITH THE WORLD,

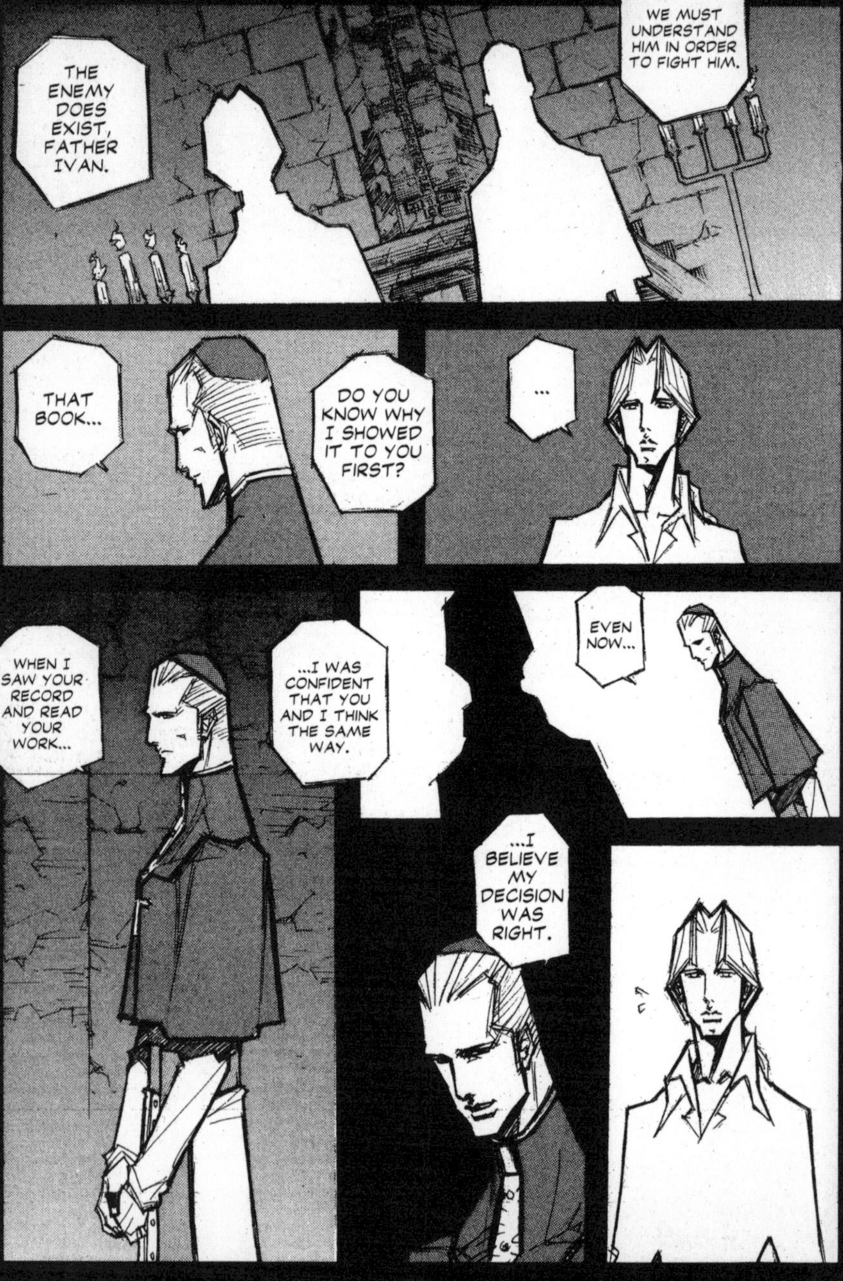
THE ENEMY DOES EXIST, FATHER IVAN.
WE MUST UNDERSTAND HIM IN ORDER TO FIGHT HIM.
THAT BOOK...
DO YOU KNOW WHY I SHOWED IT TO YOU FIRST?
...
WHEN I SAW YOUR RECORD AND READ YOUR WORK...
...I WAS CONFIDENT THAT YOU AND I THINK THE SAME WAY.
EVEN NOW...
...I BELIEVE MY DECISION WAS RIGHT.

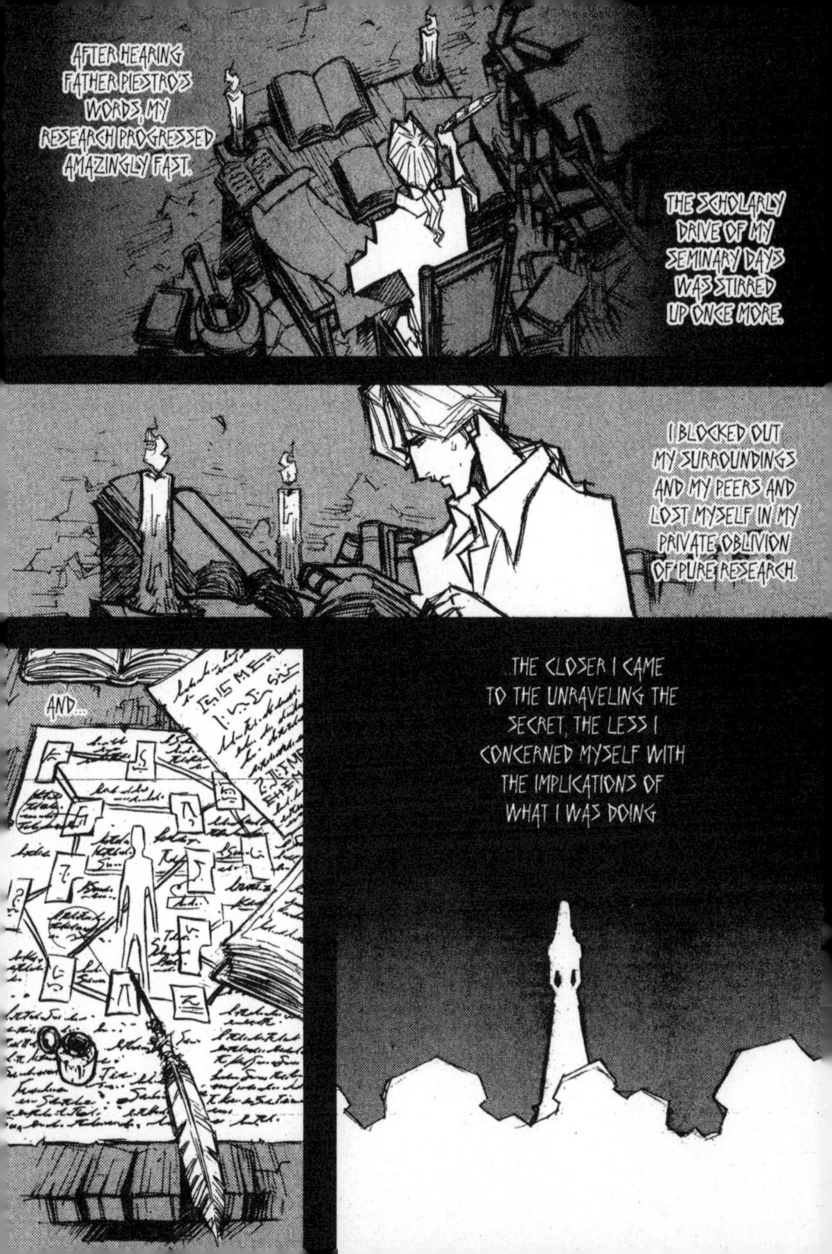
AFTER HEARING FATHER PIESTRO'S WORDS, MY RESEARCH PROGRESSED AMAZINGLY FAST.
THE SCHOLARLY DRIVE OF MY SEMINARY DAYS WAS STIRRED UP ONCE MORE.
I BLOCKED OUT MY SURROUNDINGS AND MY PEERS AND LOST MYSELF IN MY PRIVATE OBLIVION OF PURE RESEARCH.
AND...
...THE CLOSER I CAME TO THE UNRAVELING THE SECRET, THE LESS I CONCERNED MYSELF WITH THE IMPLICATIONS OF WHAT I WAS DOING.

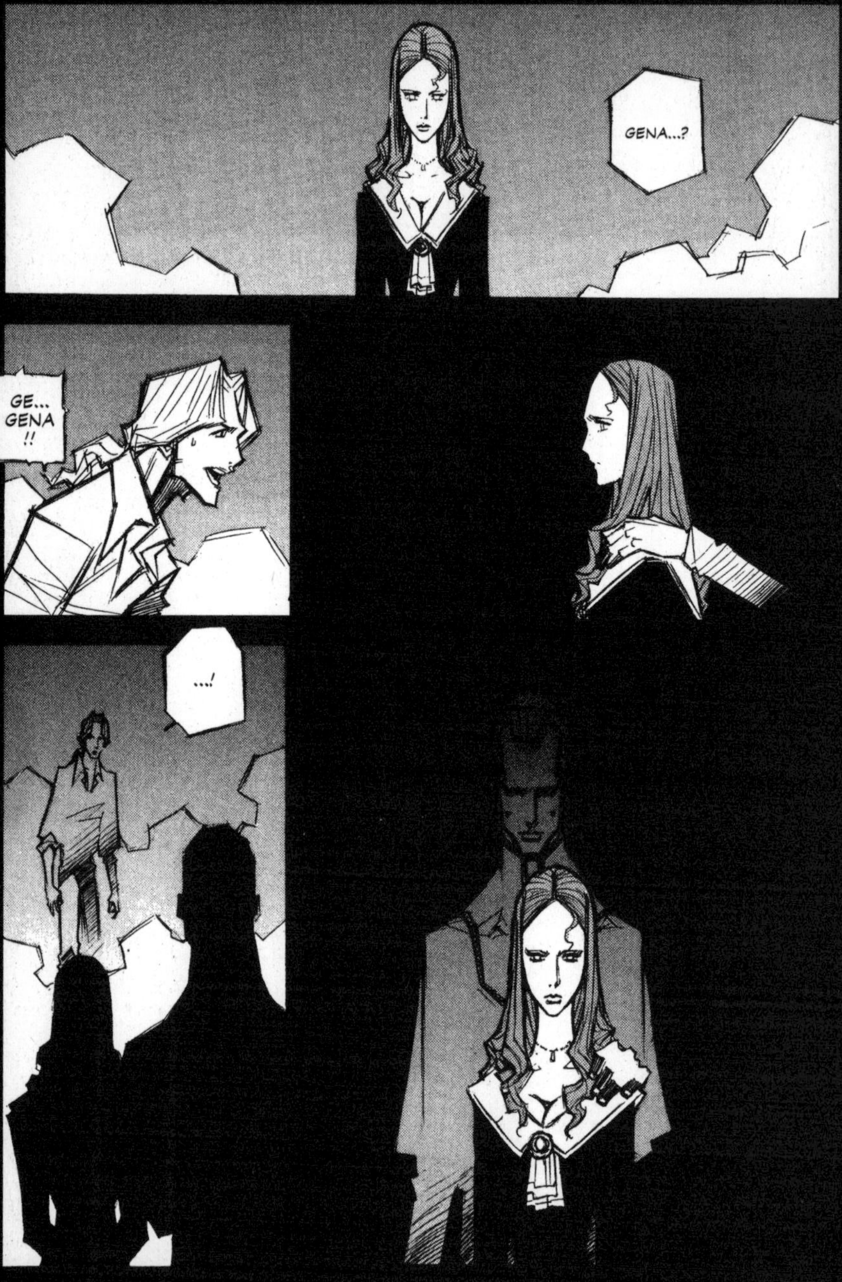
GENA...?
GE... GENA !!
...!

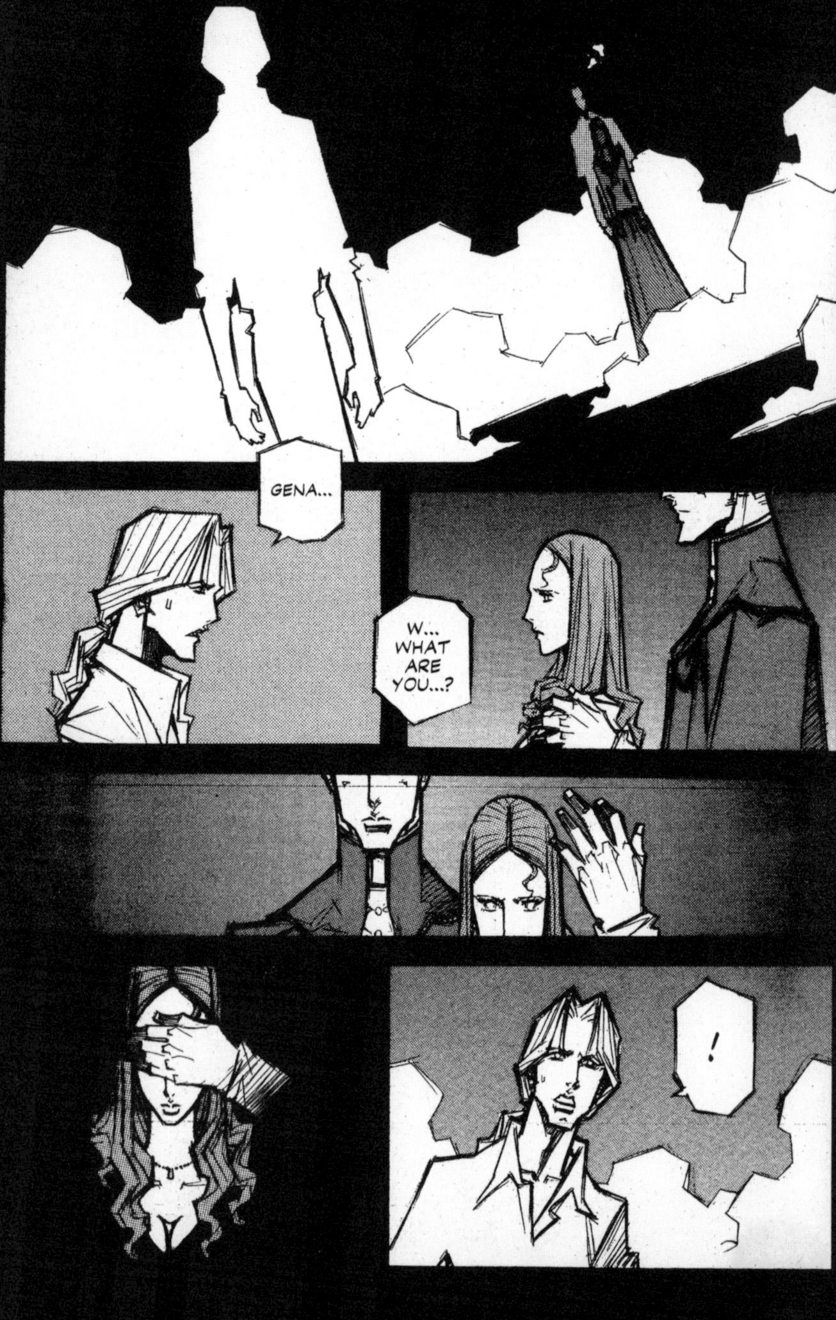
GENA...
W... WHAT ARE YOU...?
!

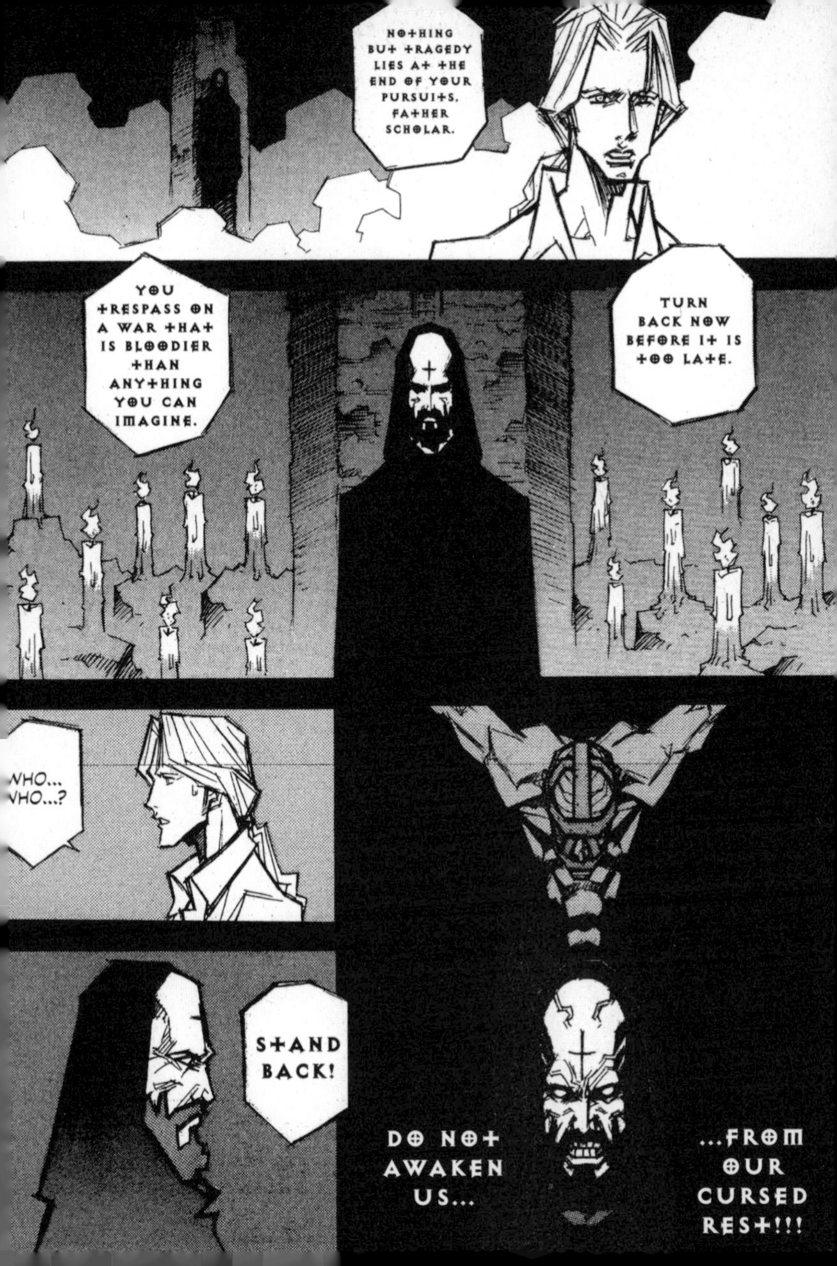
NOTHING BUT TRAGEDY LIES AT THE END OF YOUR PURSUITS, FATHER SCHOLAR.
YOU TRESPASS ON A WAR THAT IS BLOODIER THAN ANYTHING YOU CAN IMAGINE.
TURN BACK NOW BEFORE IT IS TOO LATE.
WHO... WHO...?
STAND BACK!
DO NOT AWAKEN US...
...FROM OUR CURSED REST!!!

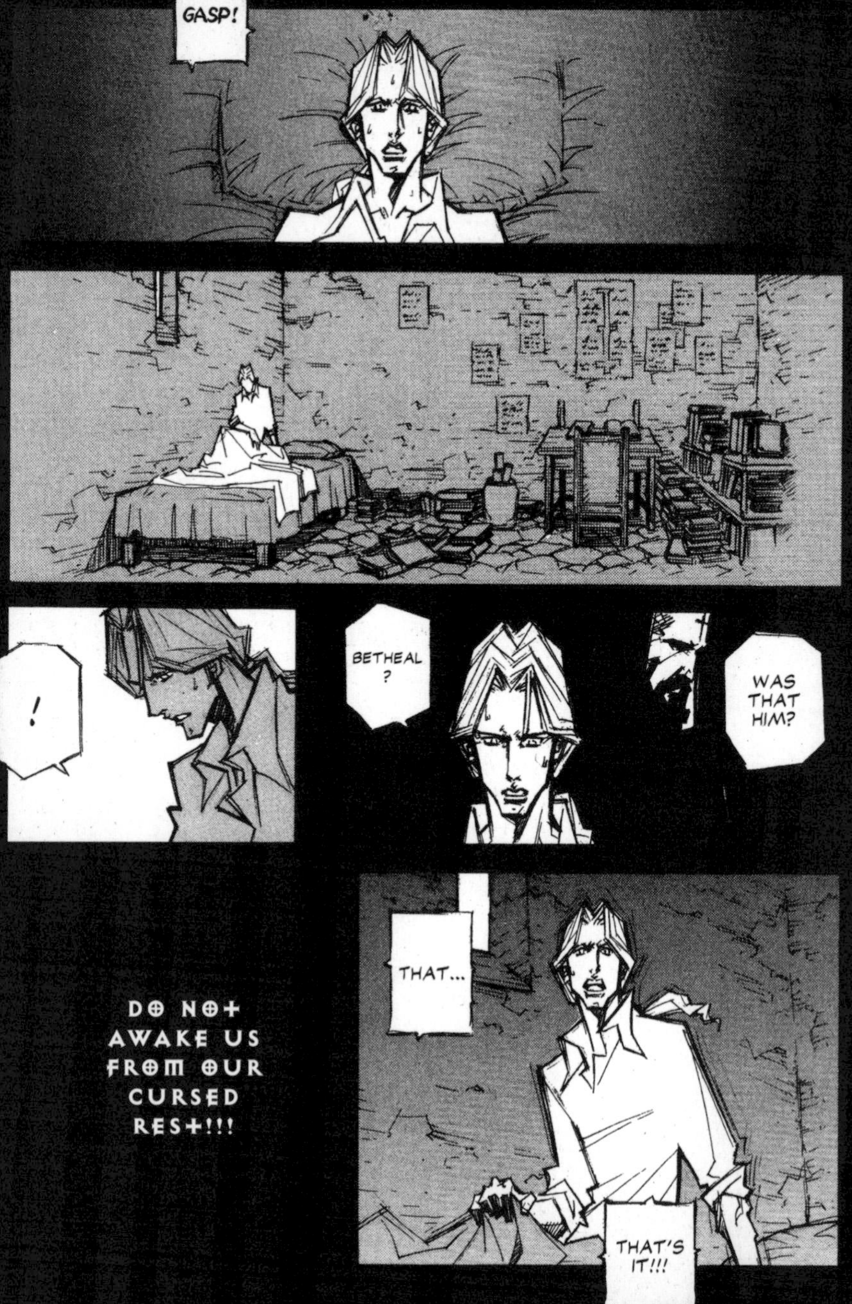
GASP!
!
BETHEAL
?
WAS
THAT
HIM?
DO NOT
AWAKE US
FROM OUR
CURSED
REST!!!
THAT...
THAT'S
IT!!!

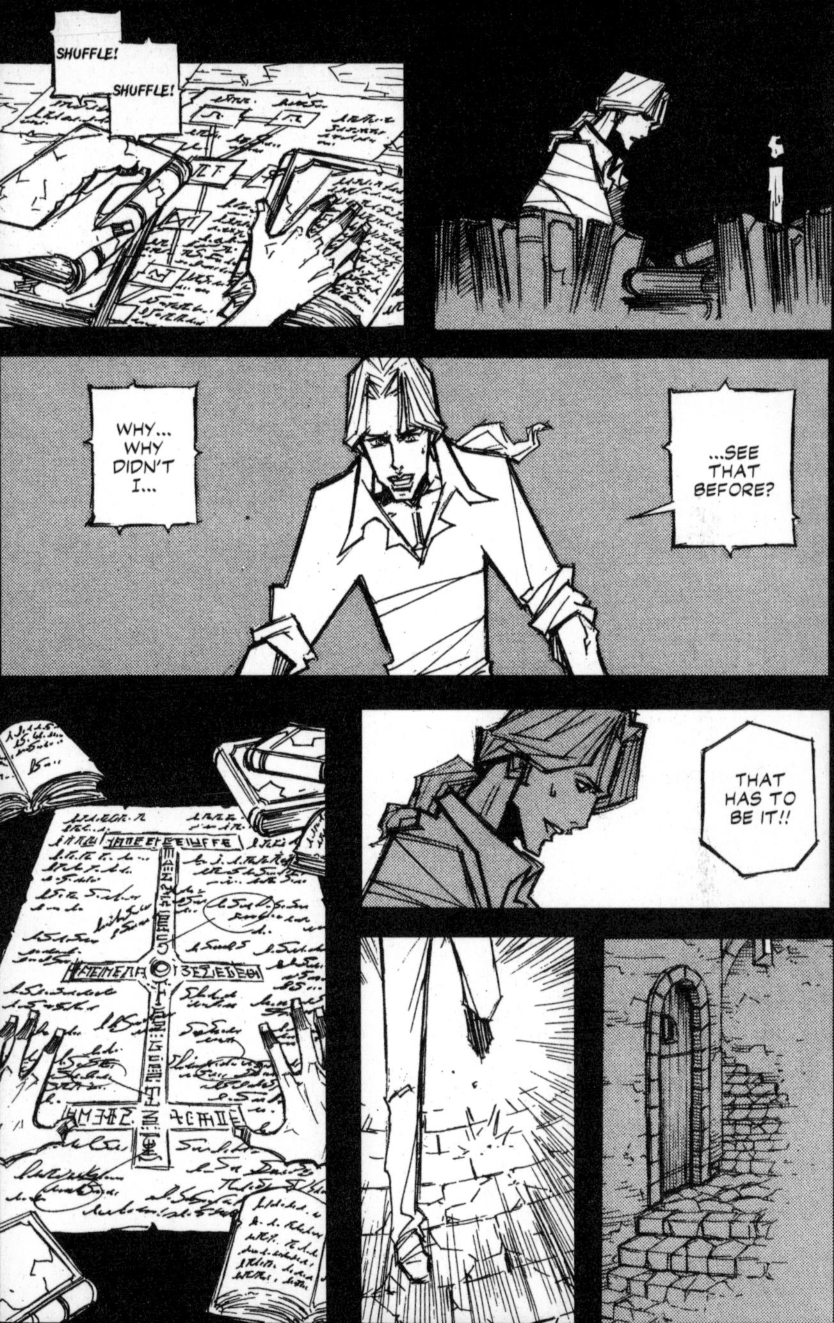
SHUFFLE!
SHUFFLE!
WHY... WHY DIDN'T I...
...SEE THAT BEFORE?
THAT HAS TO BE IT!!

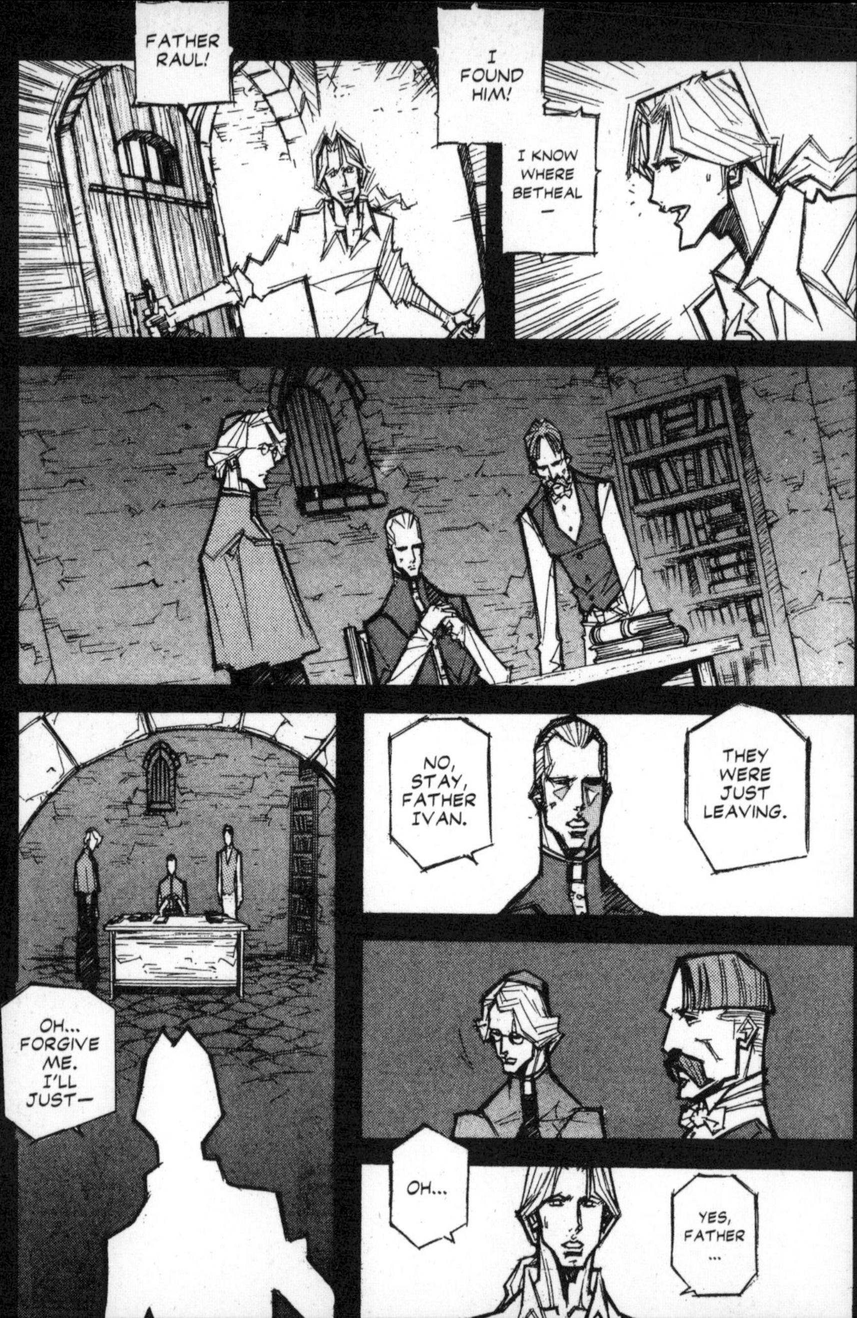
FATHER RAUL!
I FOUND HIM!
I KNOW WHERE BETHEAL —
OH... FORGIVE ME. I'LL JUST—
NO, STAY, FATHER IVAN.
THEY WERE JUST LEAVING.
OH...
YES, FATHER ...

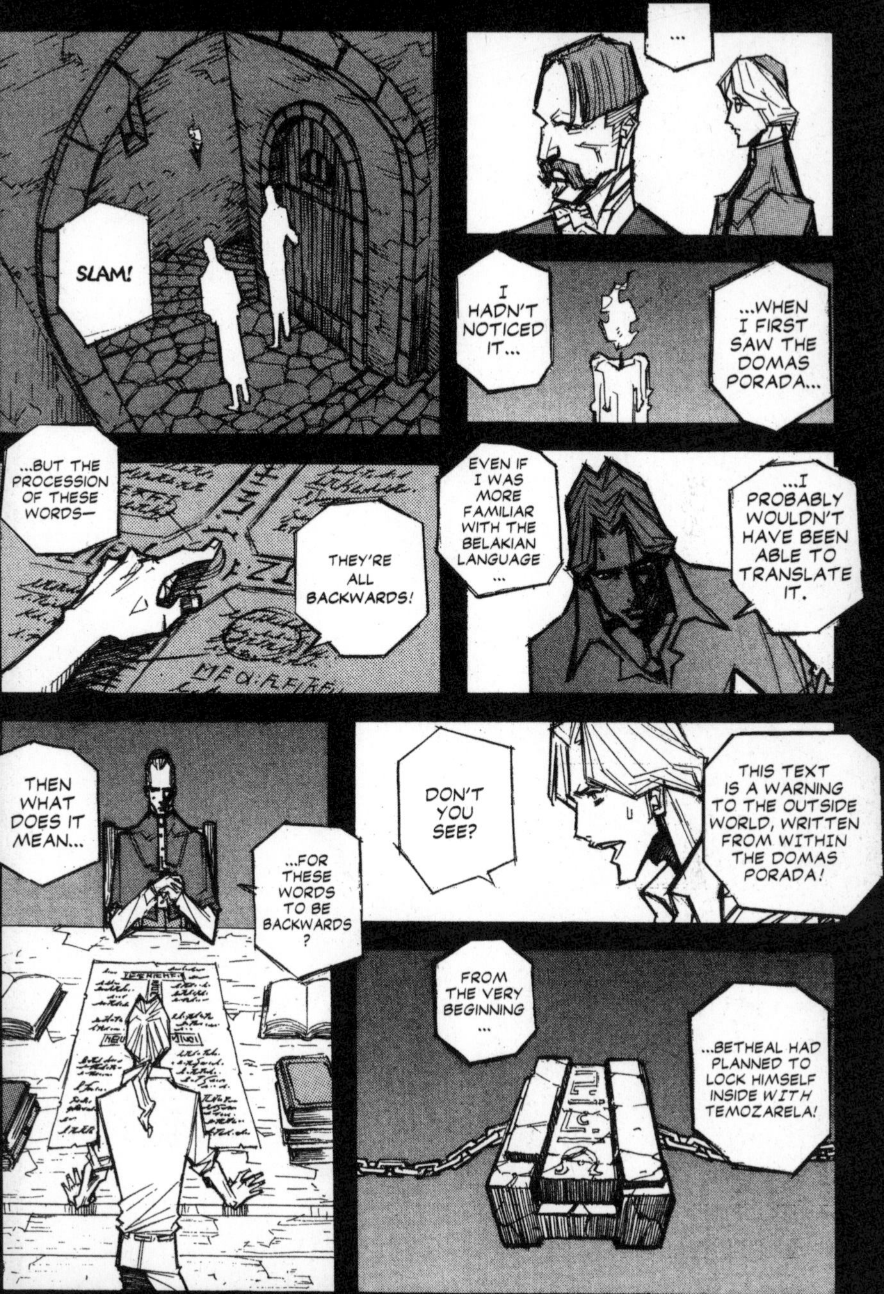
SLAM!
...
I HADN'T NOTICED IT...
...WHEN I FIRST SAW THE DOMAS PORADA...
...BUT THE PROCESSION OF THESE WORDS—
THEY'RE ALL BACKWARDS!
EVEN IF I WAS MORE FAMILIAR WITH THE BELAKIAN LANGUAGE ...
...I PROBABLY WOULDN'T HAVE BEEN ABLE TO TRANSLATE IT.
THEN WHAT DOES IT MEAN...
...FOR THESE WORDS TO BE BACKWARDS ?
DON'T YOU SEE?
THIS TEXT IS A WARNING TO THE OUTSIDE WORLD, WRITTEN FROM WITHIN THE DOMAS PORADA!
FROM THE VERY BEGINNING ...
...BETHEAL HAD PLANNED TO LOCK HIMSELF INSIDE *WITH* TEMOZARELA!

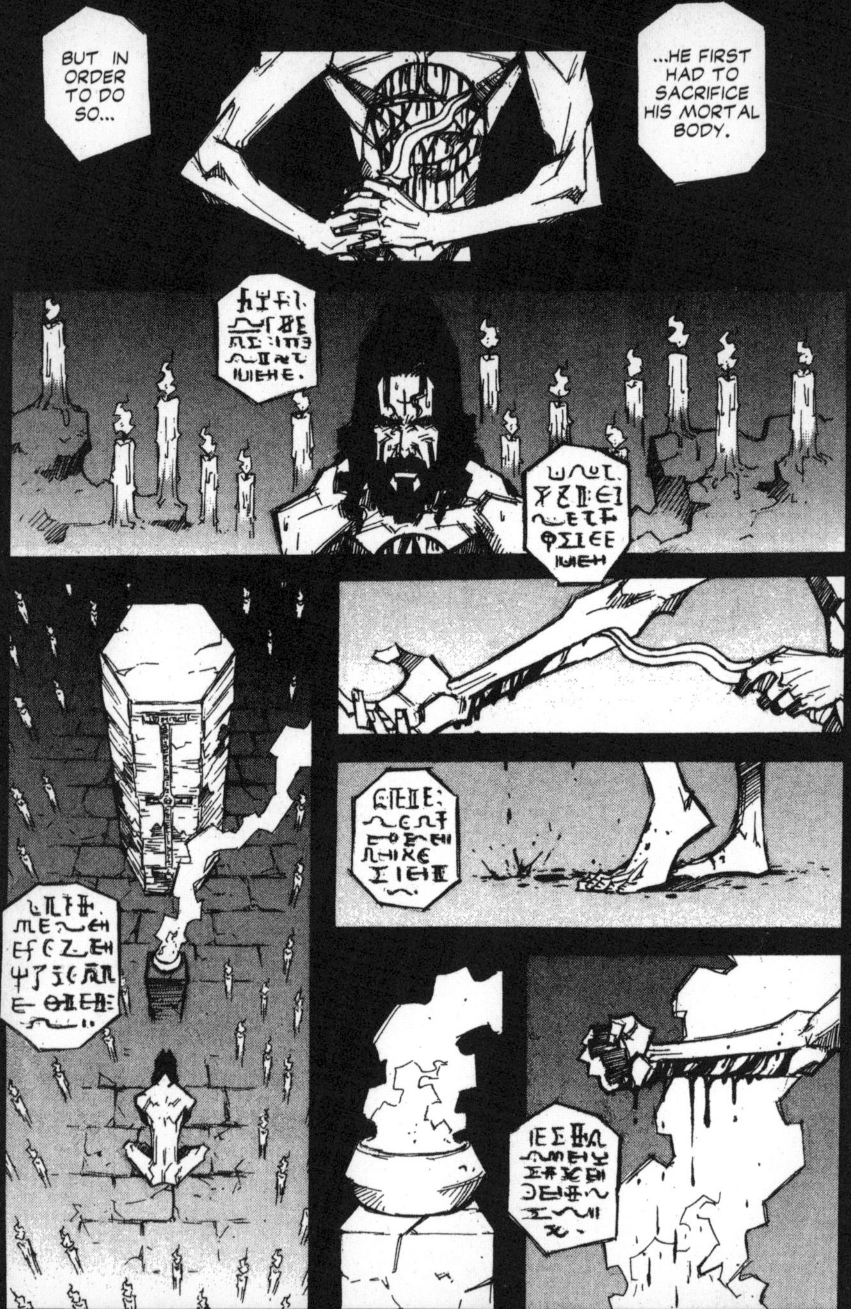
BUT IN ORDER TO DO SO...
...HE FIRST HAD TO SACRIFICE HIS MORTAL BODY.

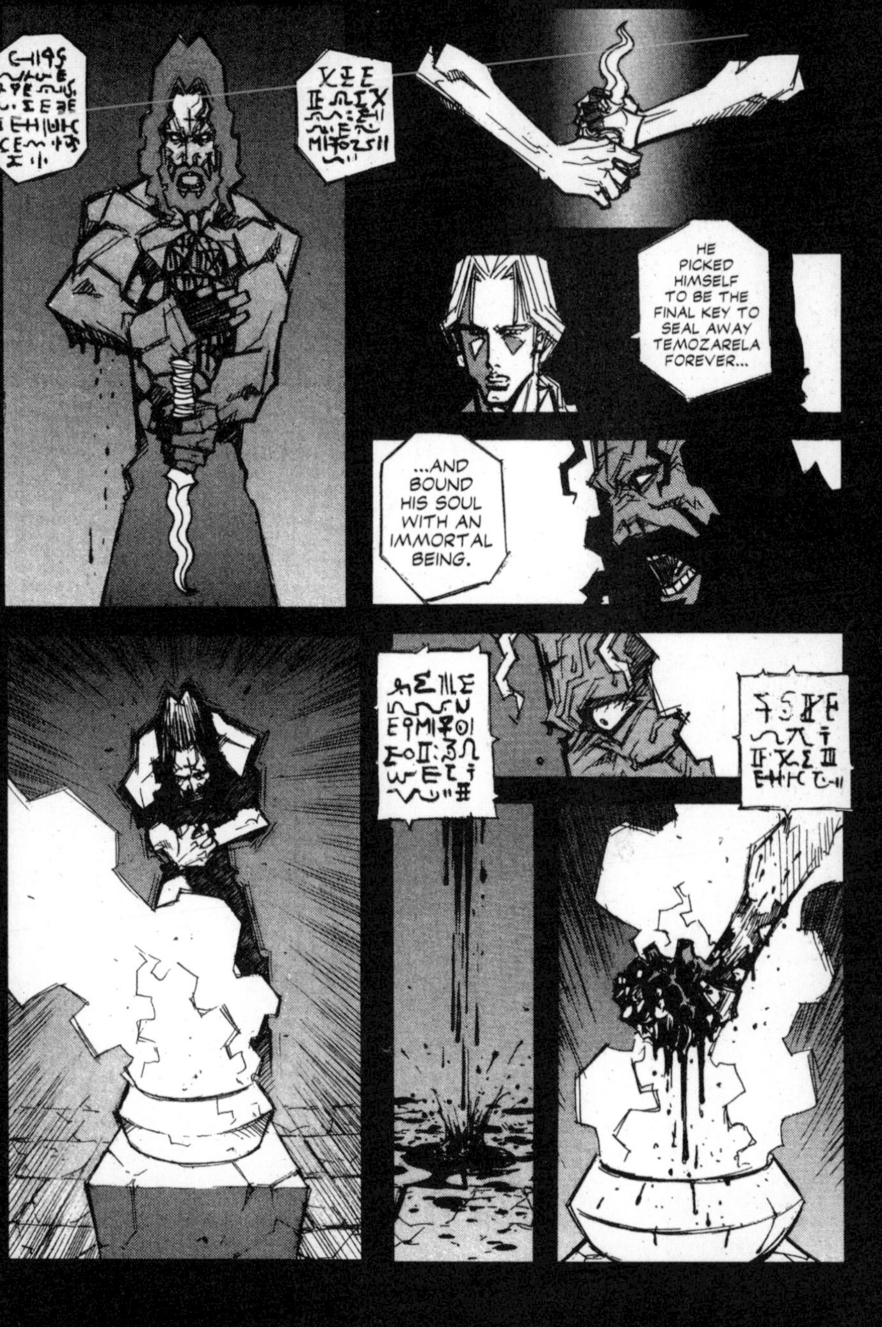

HE PICKED HIMSELF TO BE THE FINAL KEY TO SEAL AWAY TEMOZARELA FOREVER...
...AND BOUND HIS SOUL WITH AN IMMORTAL BEING.

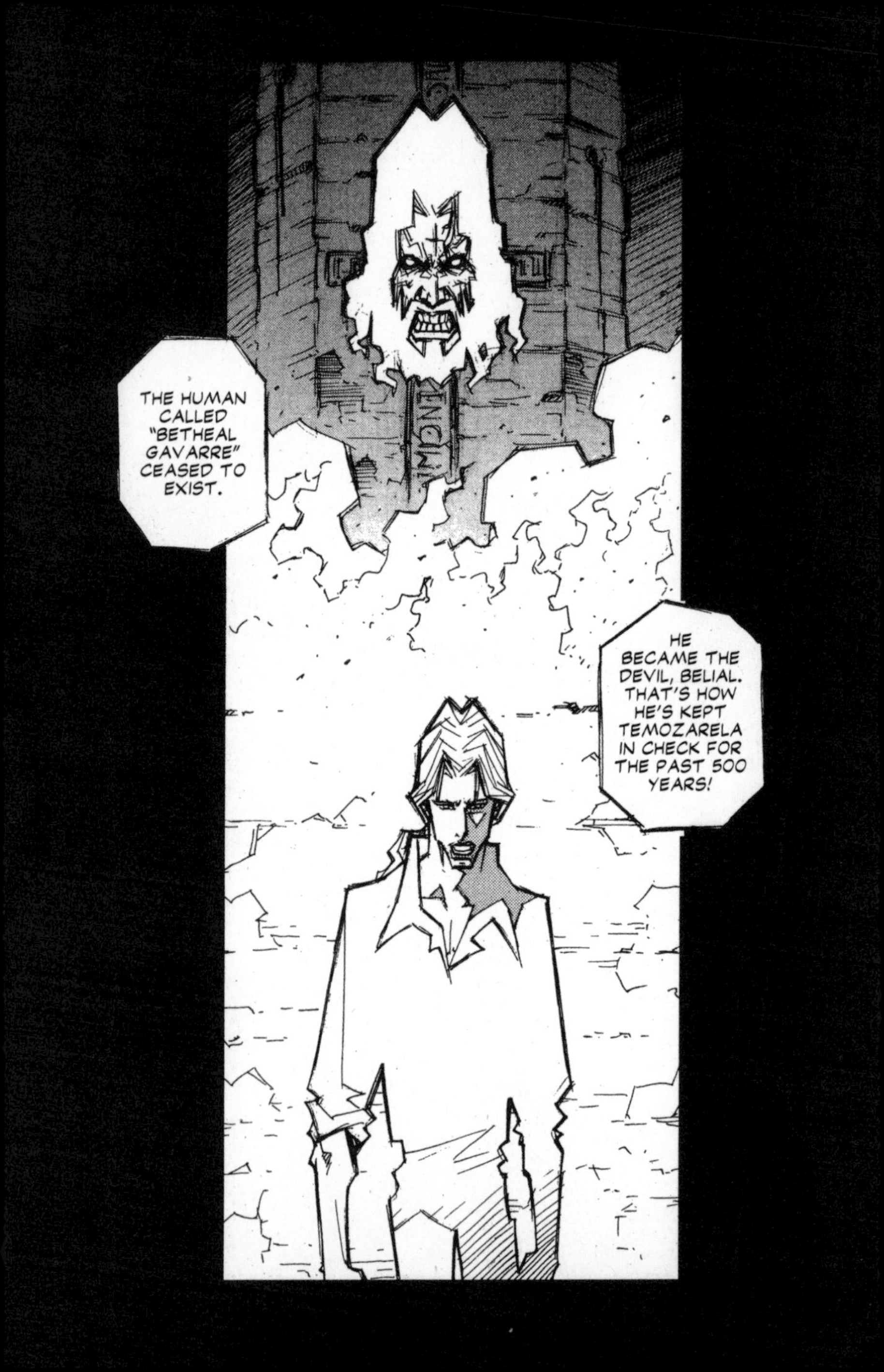
THE HUMAN CALLED "BETHEAL GAVARRE" CEASED TO EXIST.
HE BECAME THE DEVIL, BELIAL. THAT'S HOW HE'S KEPT TEMOZARELA IN CHECK FOR THE PAST 500 YEARS!

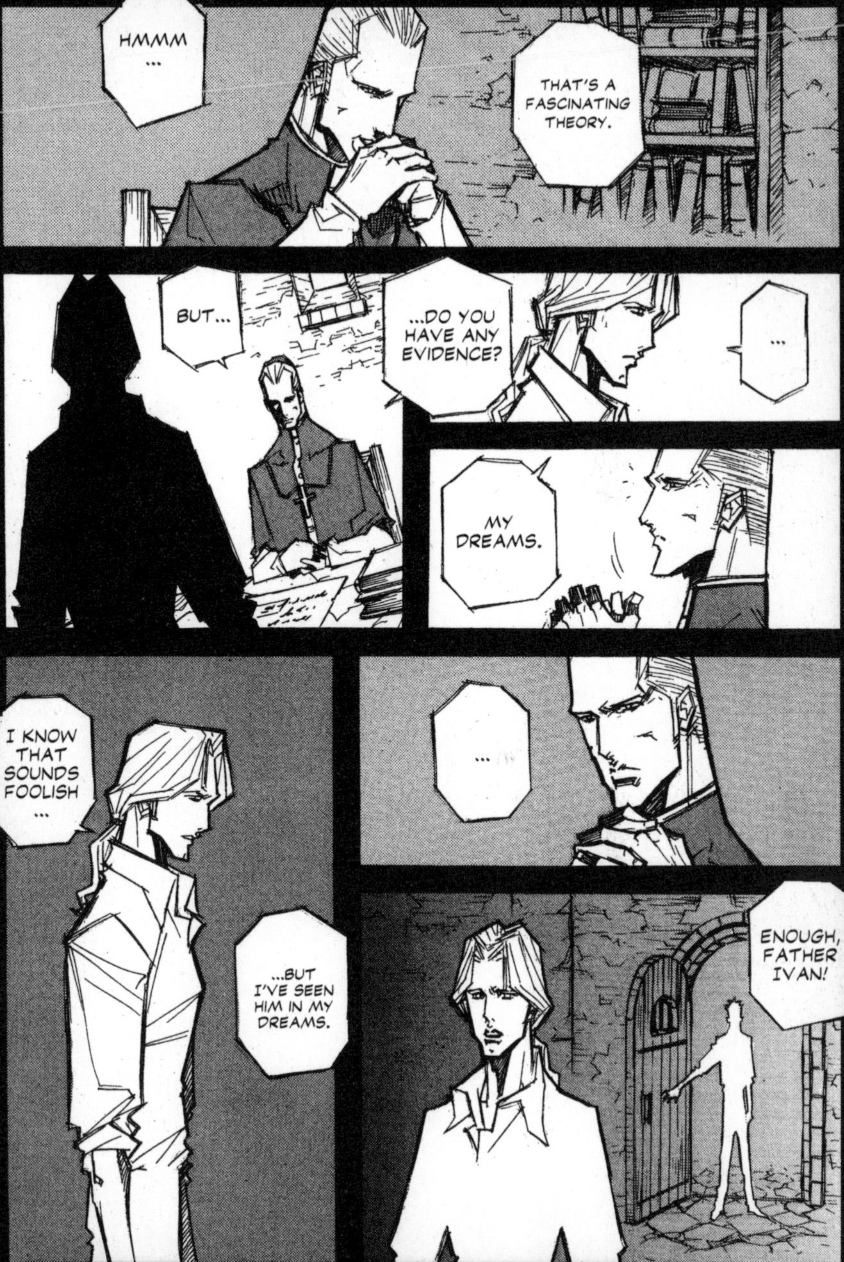
HMMM...
THAT'S A FASCINATING THEORY.
BUT...
...DO YOU HAVE ANY EVIDENCE?
...
MY DREAMS.
I KNOW THAT SOUNDS FOOLISH...
...BUT I'VE SEEN HIM IN MY DREAMS.
...
ENOUGH, FATHER IVAN!

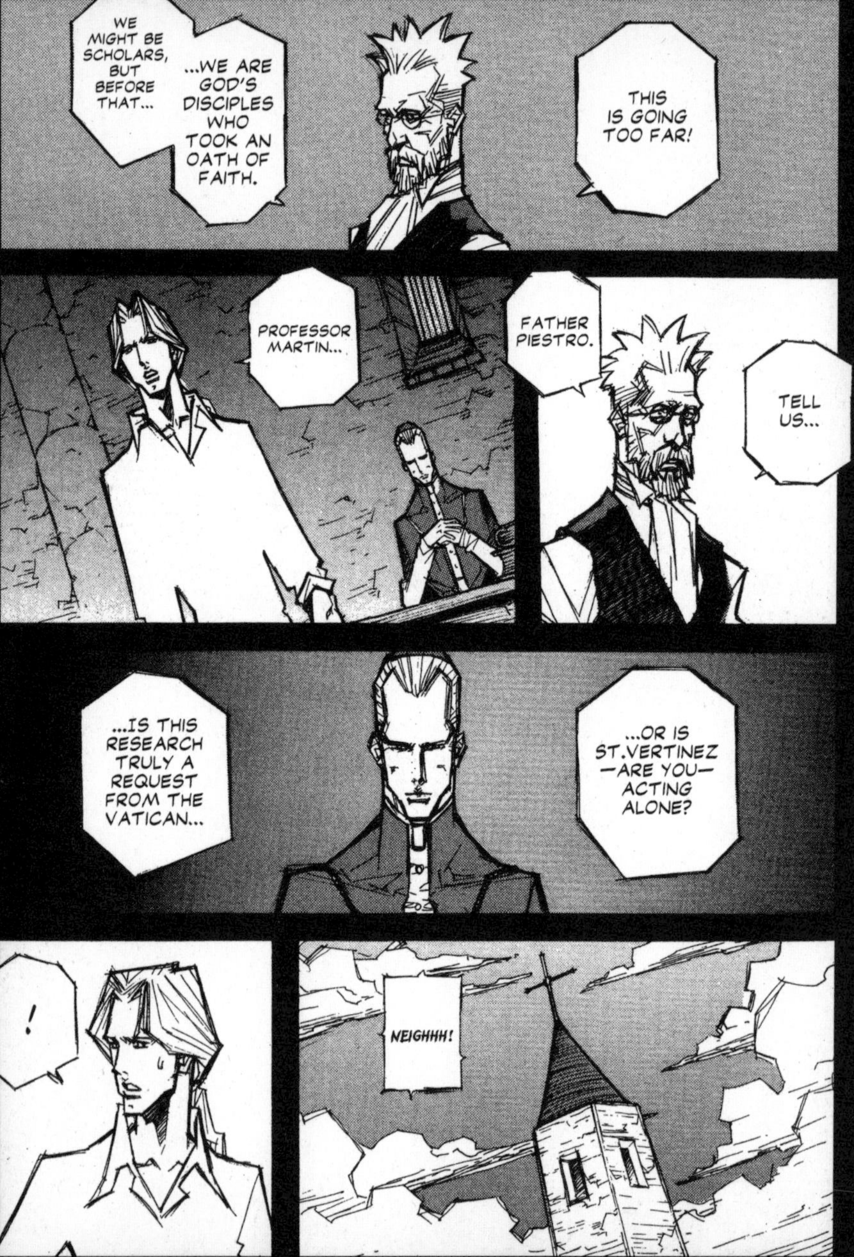
WE MIGHT BE SCHOLARS, BUT BEFORE THAT...
...WE ARE GOD'S DISCIPLES WHO TOOK AN OATH OF FAITH.
THIS IS GOING TOO FAR!
PROFESSOR MARTIN...
FATHER PIESTRO.
TELL US...
...IS THIS RESEARCH TRULY A REQUEST FROM THE VATICAN...
...OR IS ST.VERTINEZ —ARE YOU— ACTING ALONE?
!
NEIGHHH!

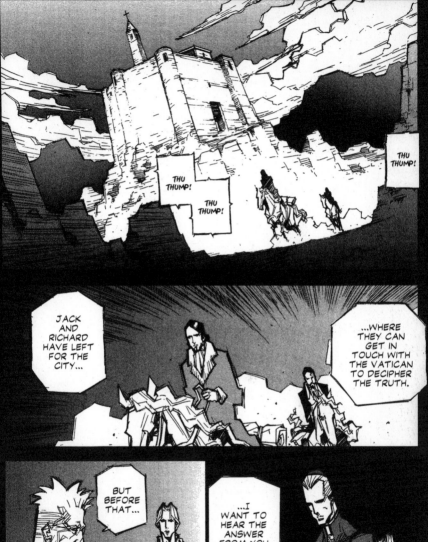

THU THUMP!

THU THUMP!

THU THUMP!

JACK AND RICHARD HAVE LEFT FOR THE CITY...

...WHERE THEY CAN GET IN TOUCH WITH THE VATICAN TO DECIPHER THE TRUTH.

BUT BEFORE THAT...

...I WANT TO HEAR THE ANSWER FROM YOU DIRECTLY.

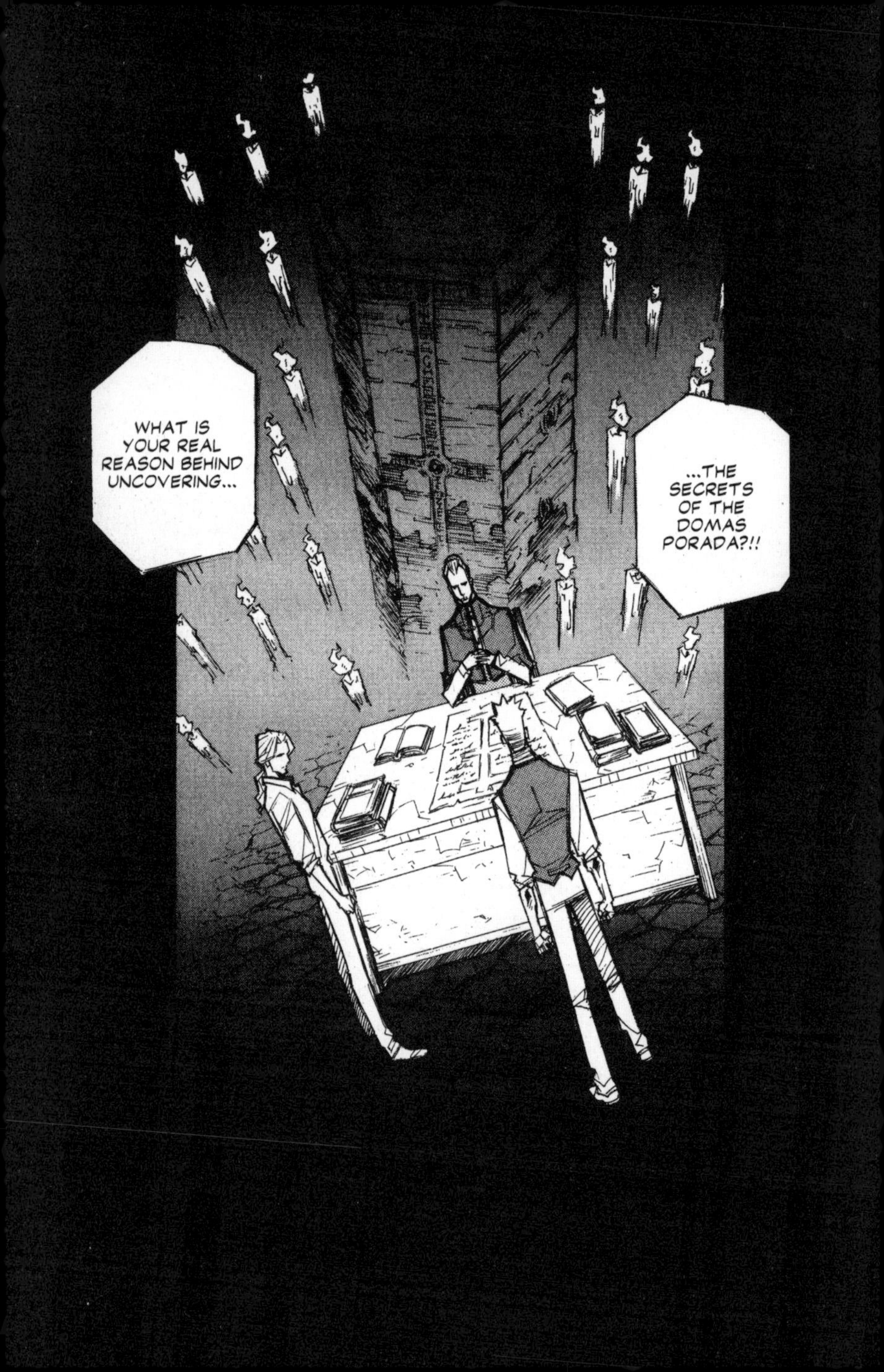
WHAT IS YOUR REAL REASON BEHIND UNCOVERING...
...THE SECRETS OF THE DOMAS PORADA?!!

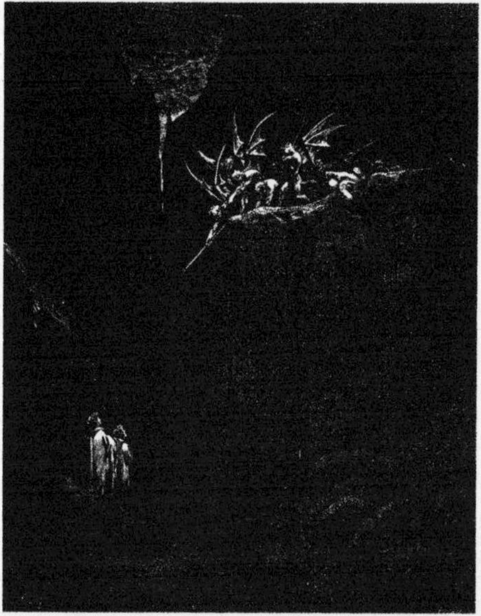

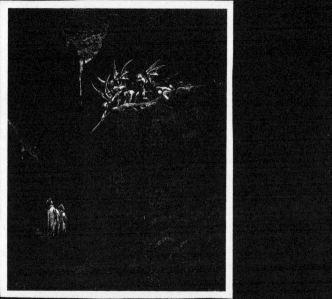

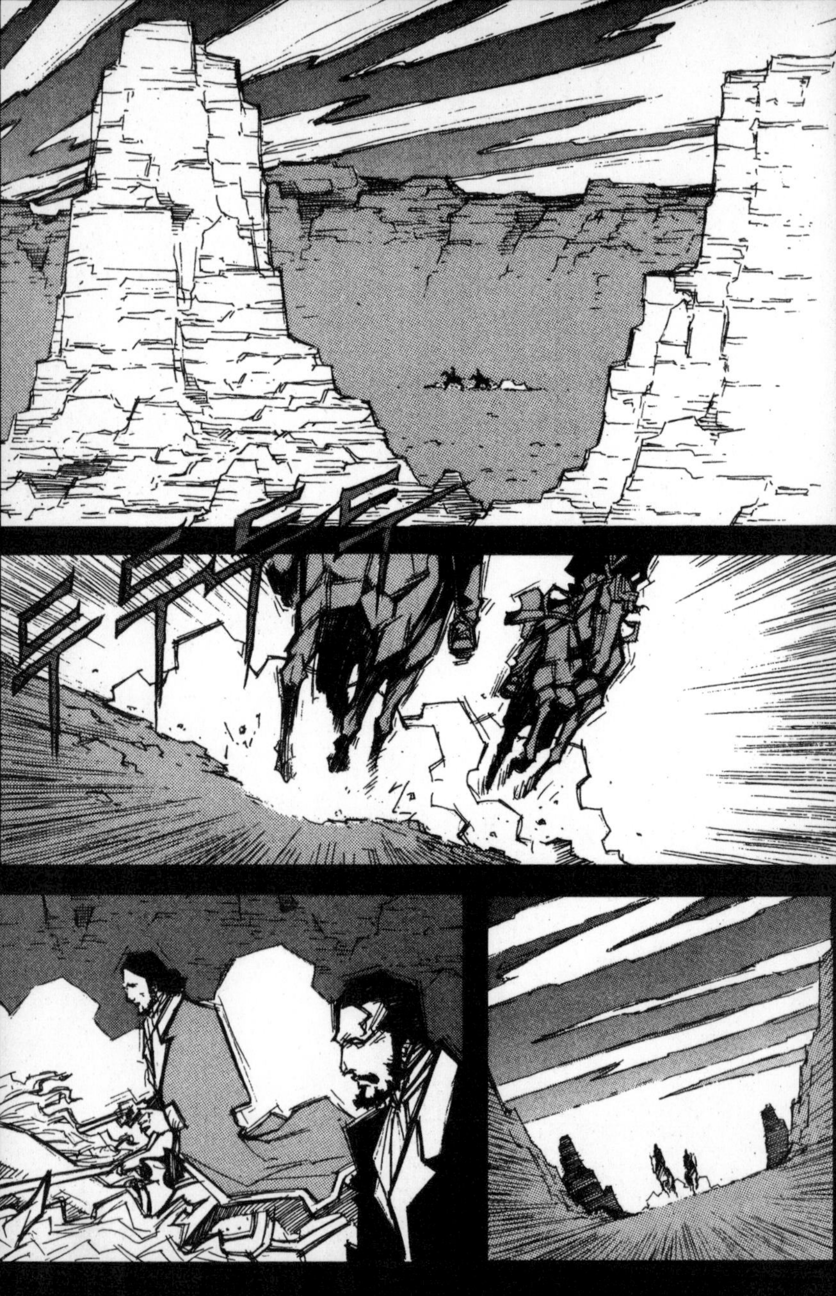

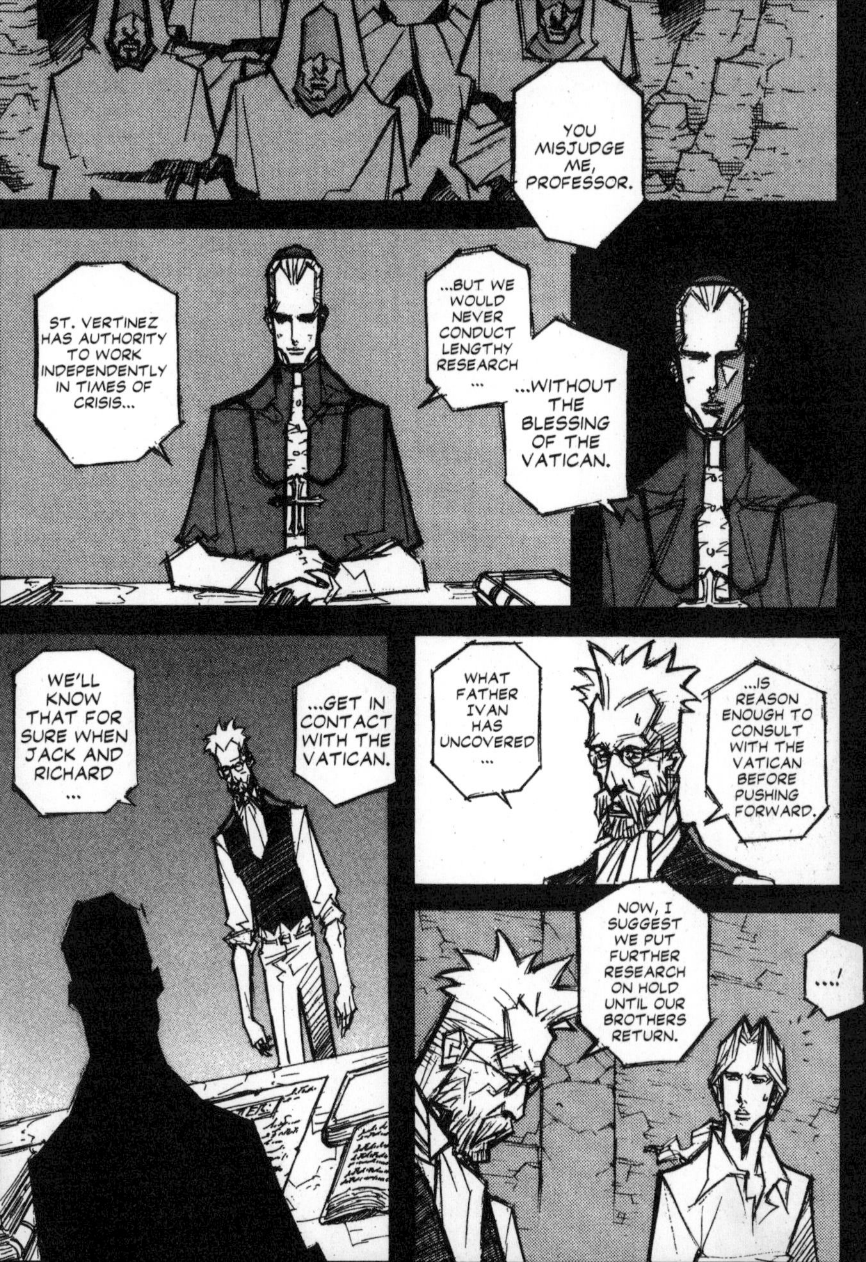
YOU MISJUDGE ME, PROFESSOR.
ST. VERTINEZ HAS AUTHORITY TO WORK INDEPENDENTLY IN TIMES OF CRISIS...
...BUT WE WOULD NEVER CONDUCT LENGTHY RESEARCH ...
...WITHOUT THE BLESSING OF THE VATICAN.
WE'LL KNOW THAT FOR SURE WHEN JACK AND RICHARD ...
...GET IN CONTACT WITH THE VATICAN.
WHAT FATHER IVAN HAS UNCOVERED ...
...IS REASON ENOUGH TO CONSULT WITH THE VATICAN BEFORE PUSHING FORWARD.
NOW, I SUGGEST WE PUT FURTHER RESEARCH ON HOLD UNTIL OUR BROTHERS RETURN.
...!

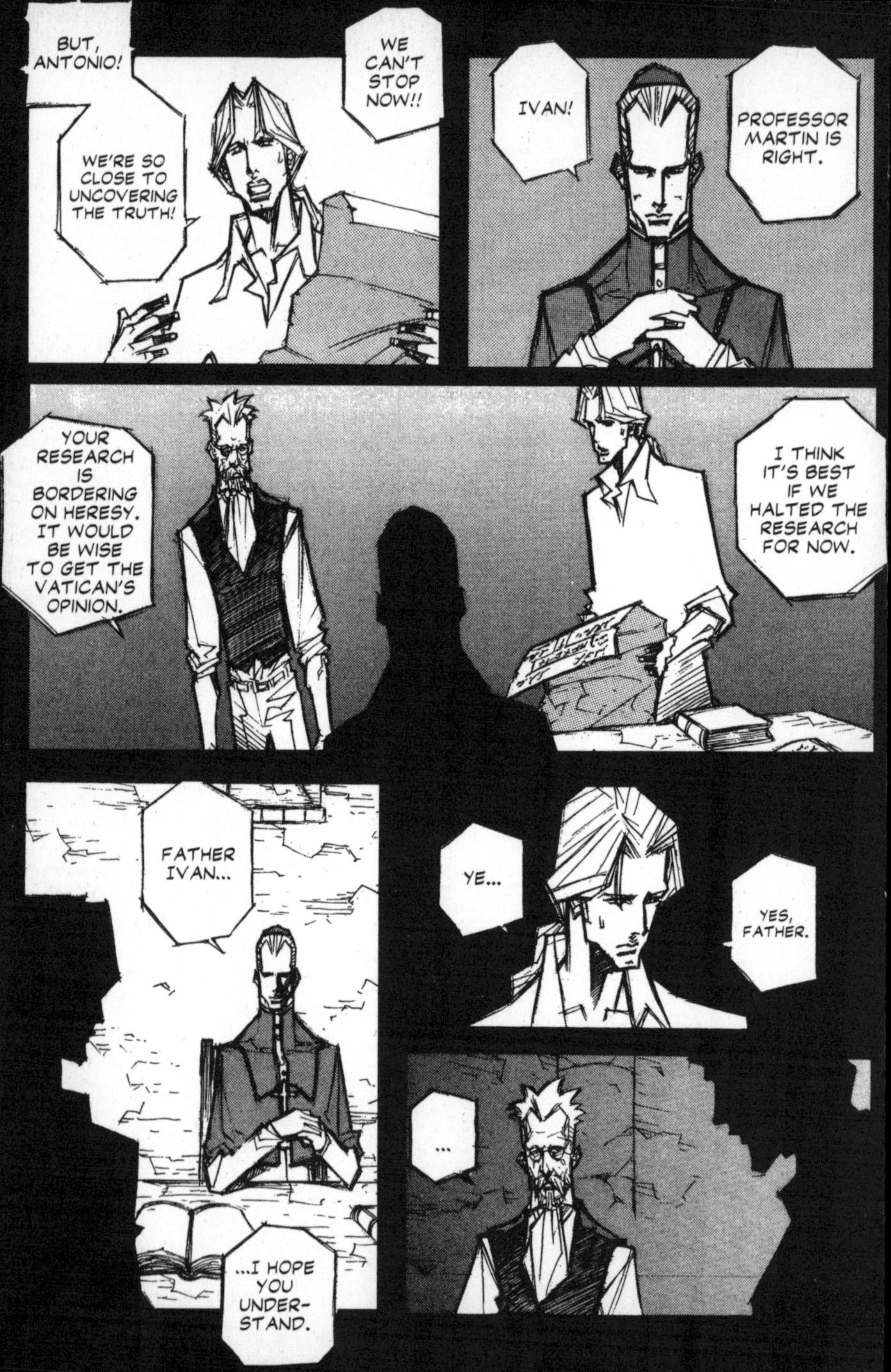
BUT, ANTONIO!
WE'RE SO CLOSE TO UNCOVERING THE TRUTH!
WE CAN'T STOP NOW!!
IVAN!
PROFESSOR MARTIN IS RIGHT.
YOUR RESEARCH IS BORDERING ON HERESY. IT WOULD BE WISE TO GET THE VATICAN'S OPINION.
I THINK IT'S BEST IF WE HALTED THE RESEARCH FOR NOW.
FATHER IVAN...
...I HOPE YOU UNDER-STAND.
YE...
YES, FATHER.
...

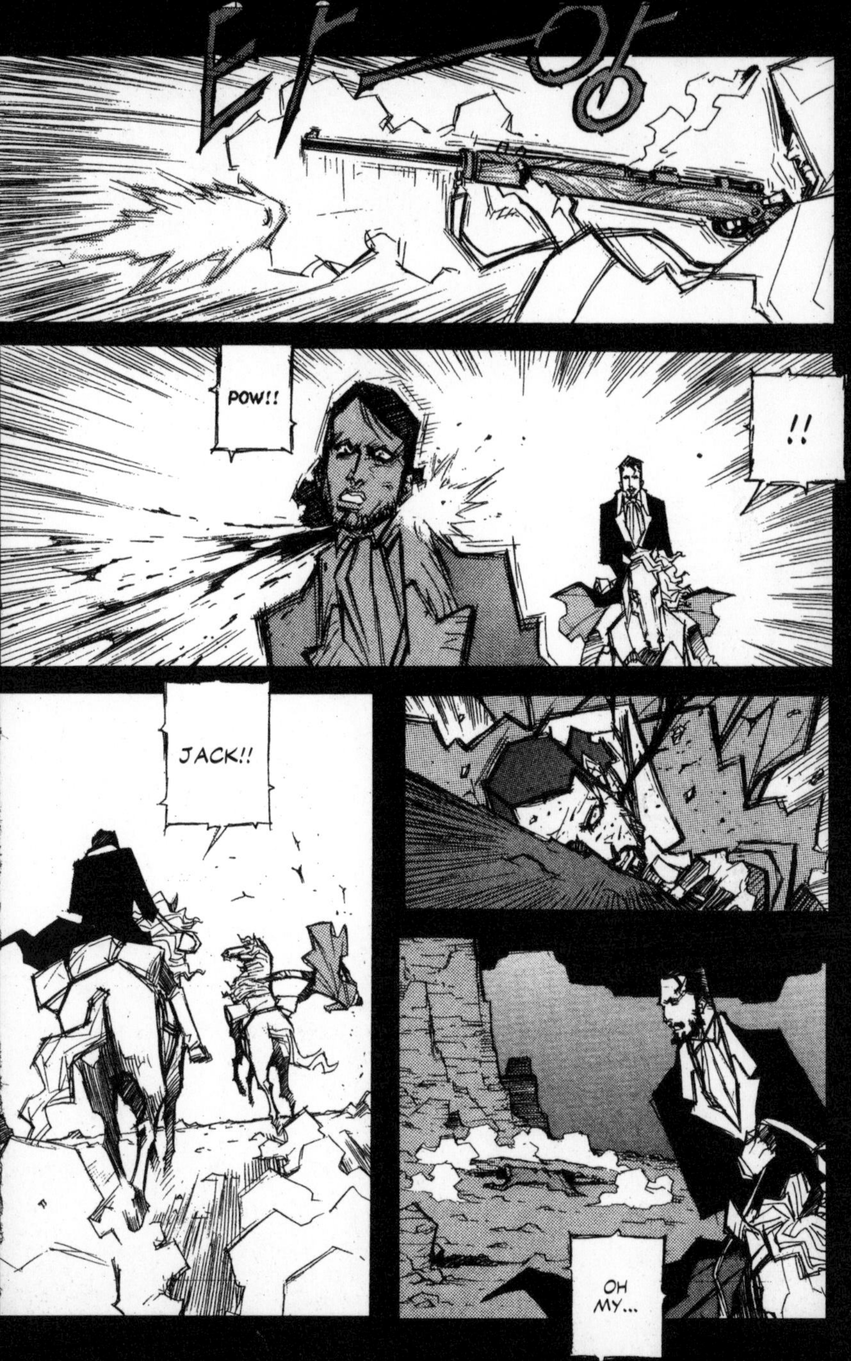

타—앙
POW!!
!!
JACK!!
OH MY...

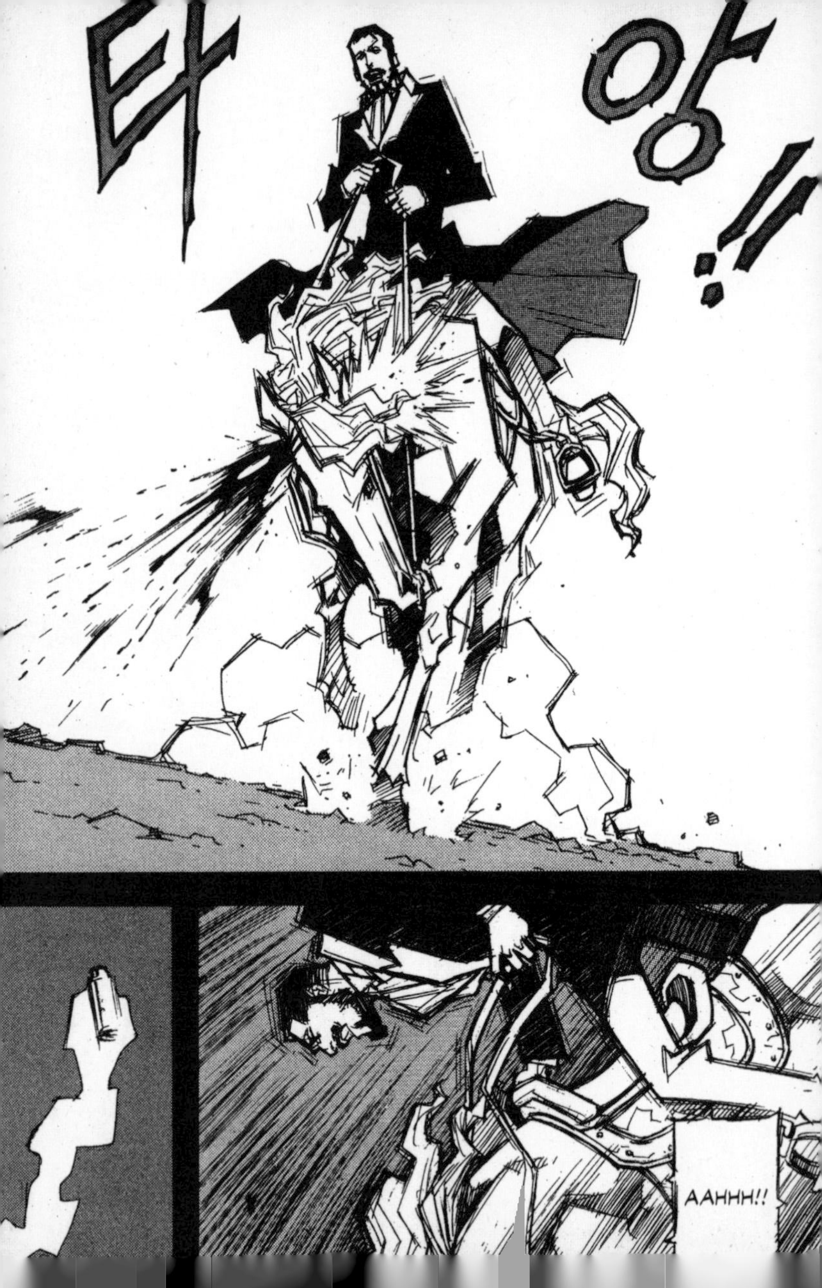
터엉!!
AAHHH!!

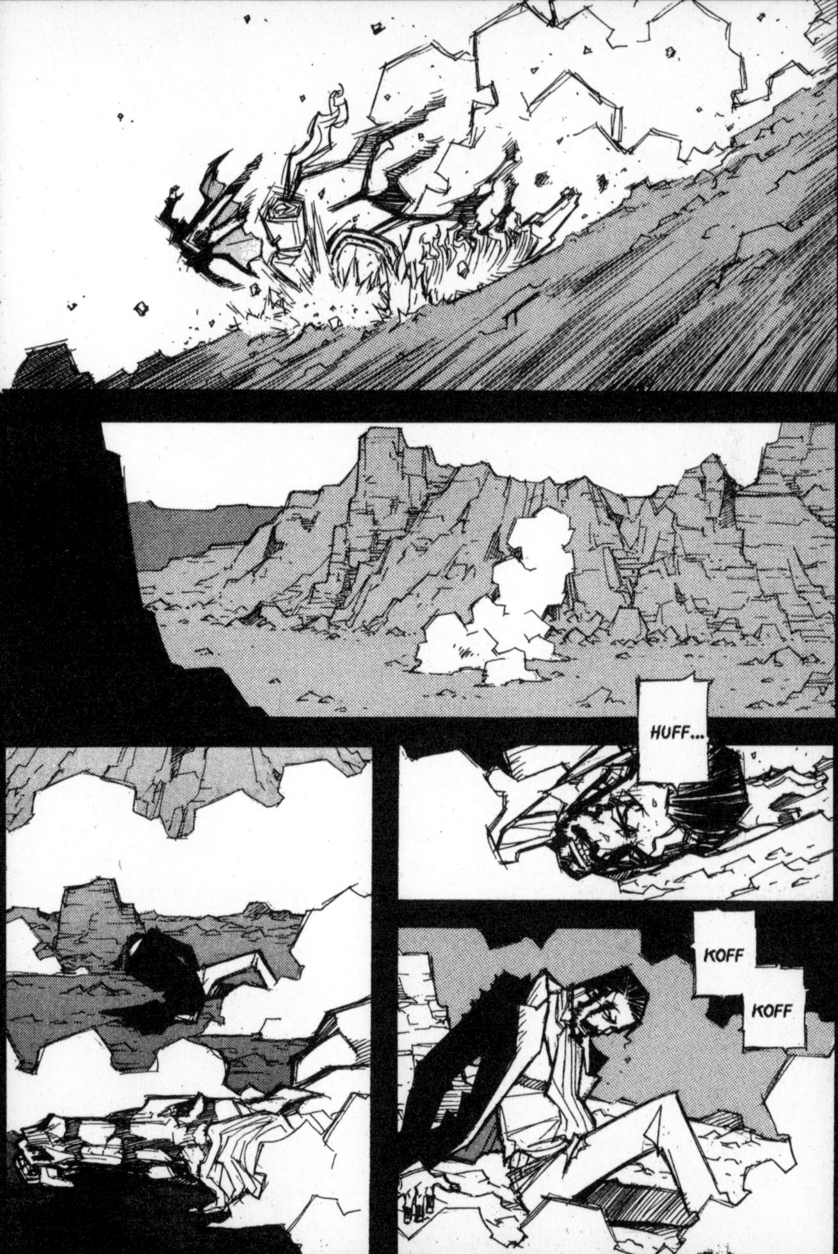
HUFF...
KOFF
KOFF

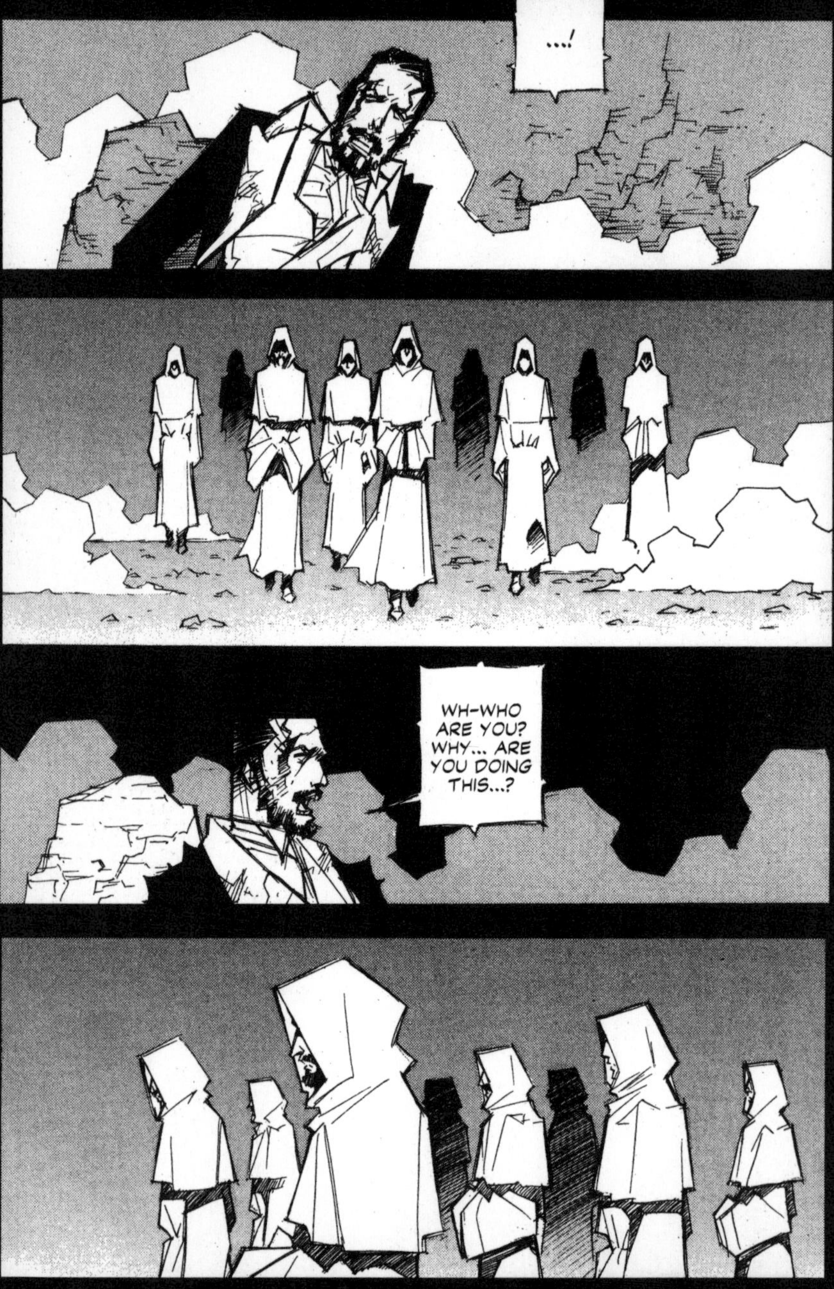
...!
WH-WHO ARE YOU? WHY... ARE YOU DOING THIS...?

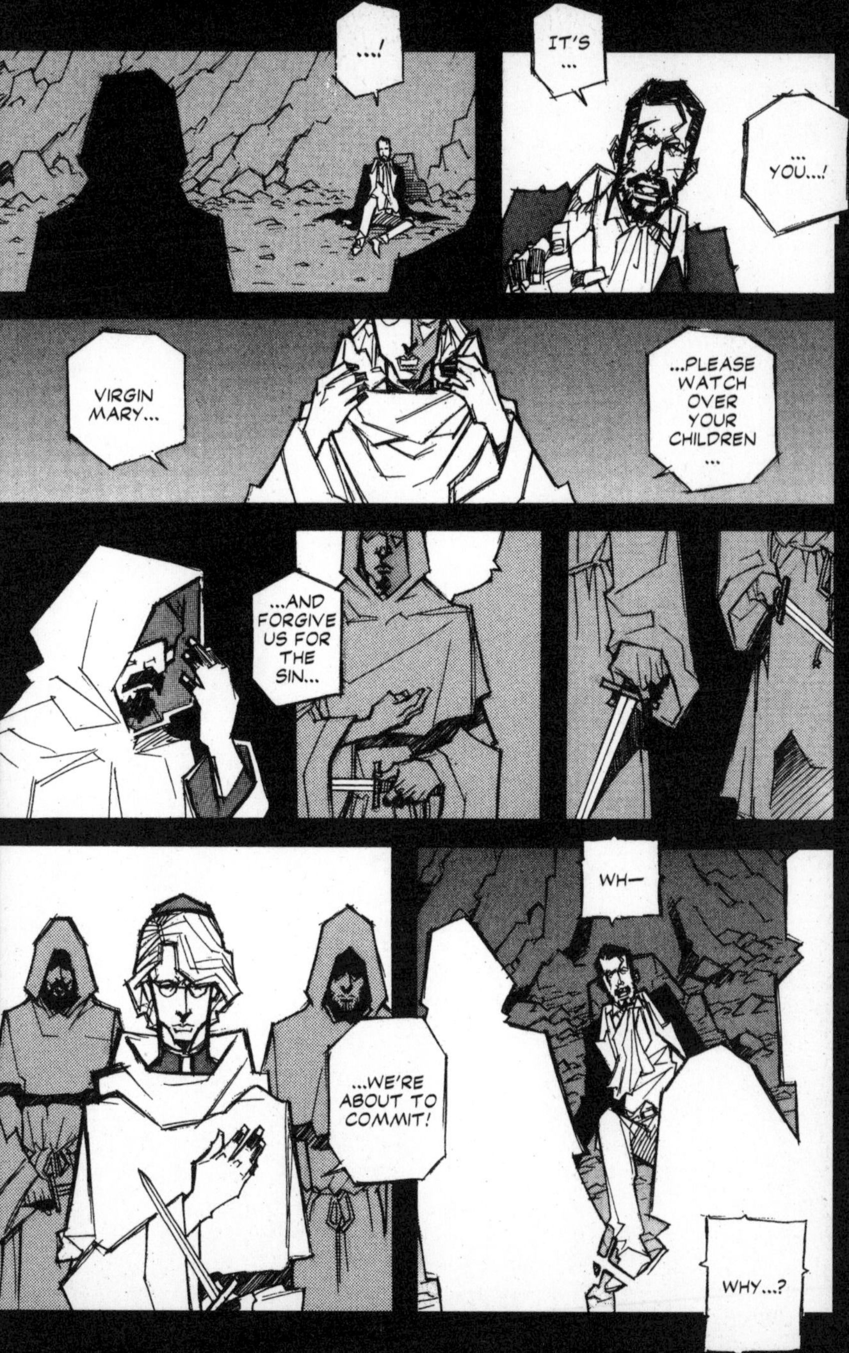
....!
IT'S ...
... YOU...!
VIRGIN MARY...
...PLEASE WATCH OVER YOUR CHILDREN ...
...AND FORGIVE US FOR THE SIN...
...WE'RE ABOUT TO COMMIT!
WH—
WHY...?

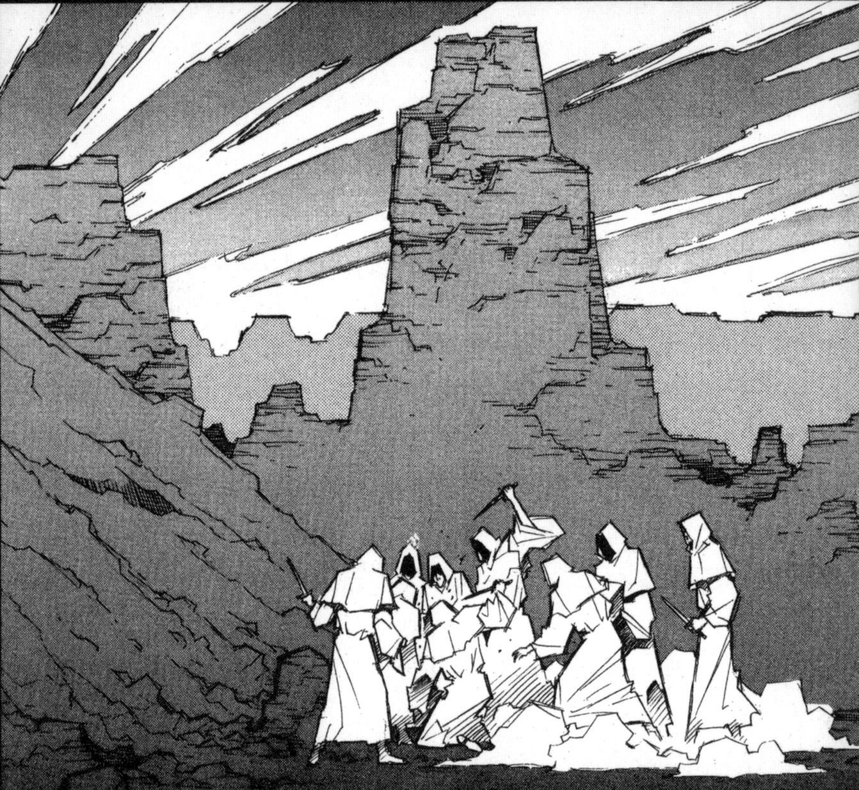

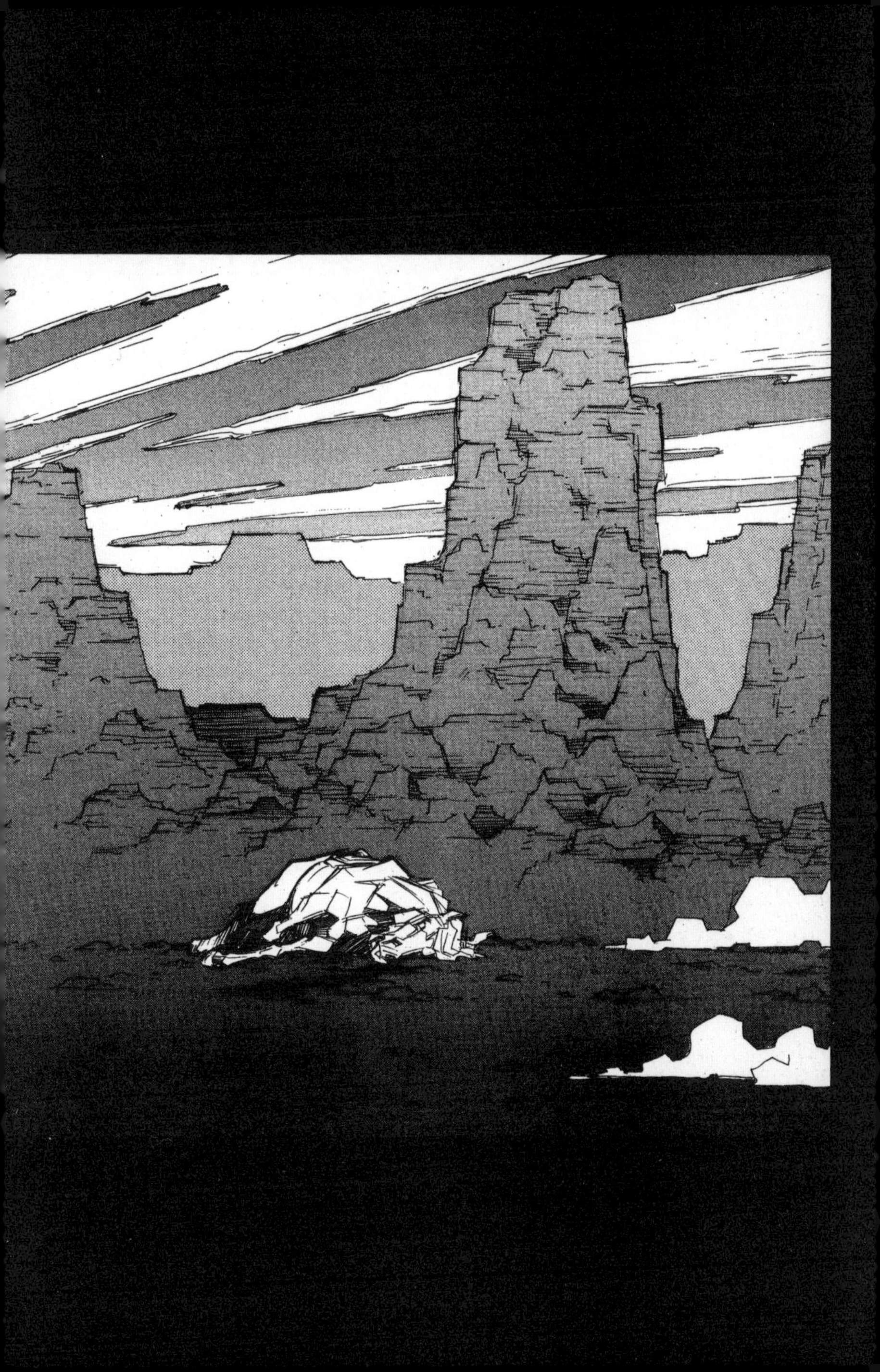

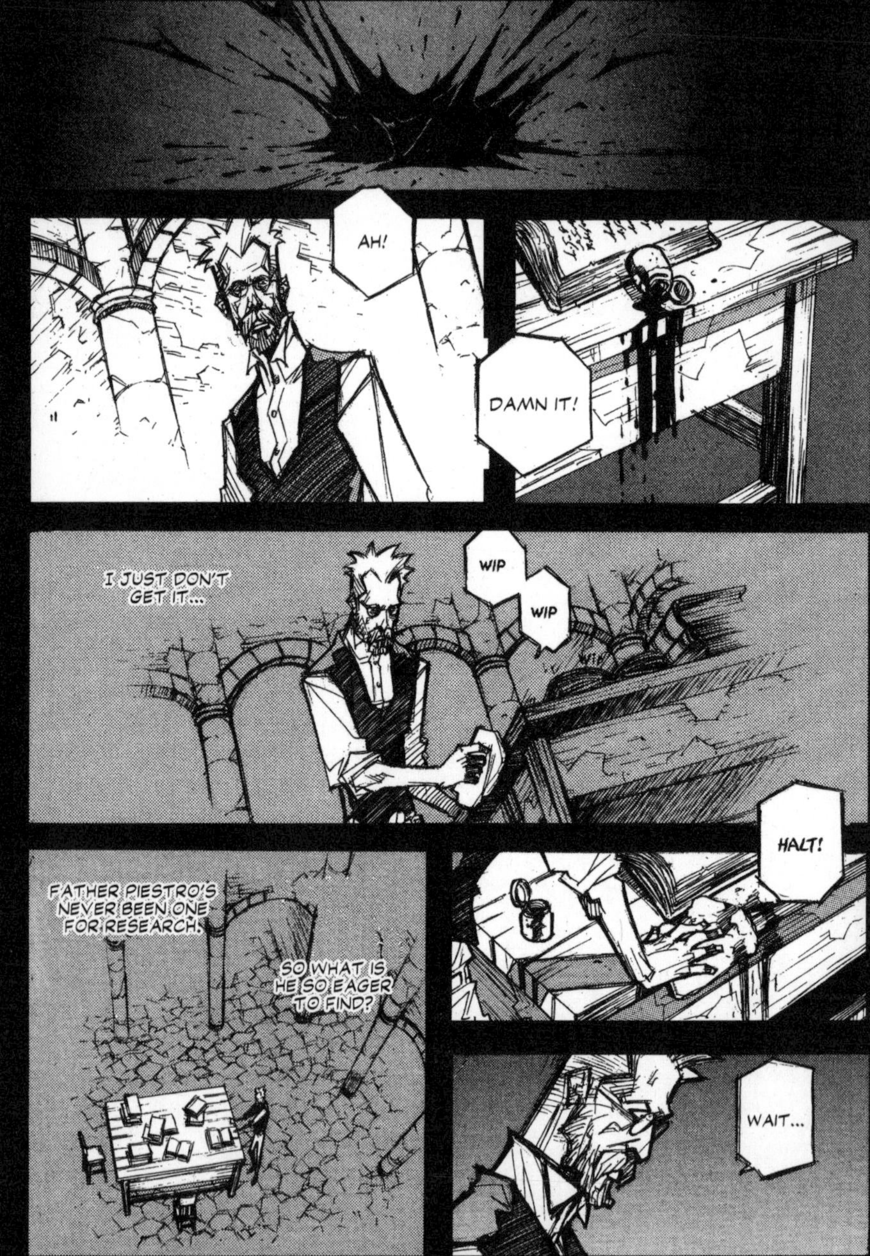
AH!
DAMN IT!
I JUST DON'T GET IT...
WIP
WIP
FATHER PIESTRO'S NEVER BEEN ONE FOR RESEARCH.
SO WHAT IS HE SO EAGER TO FIND?
HALT!
WAIT...

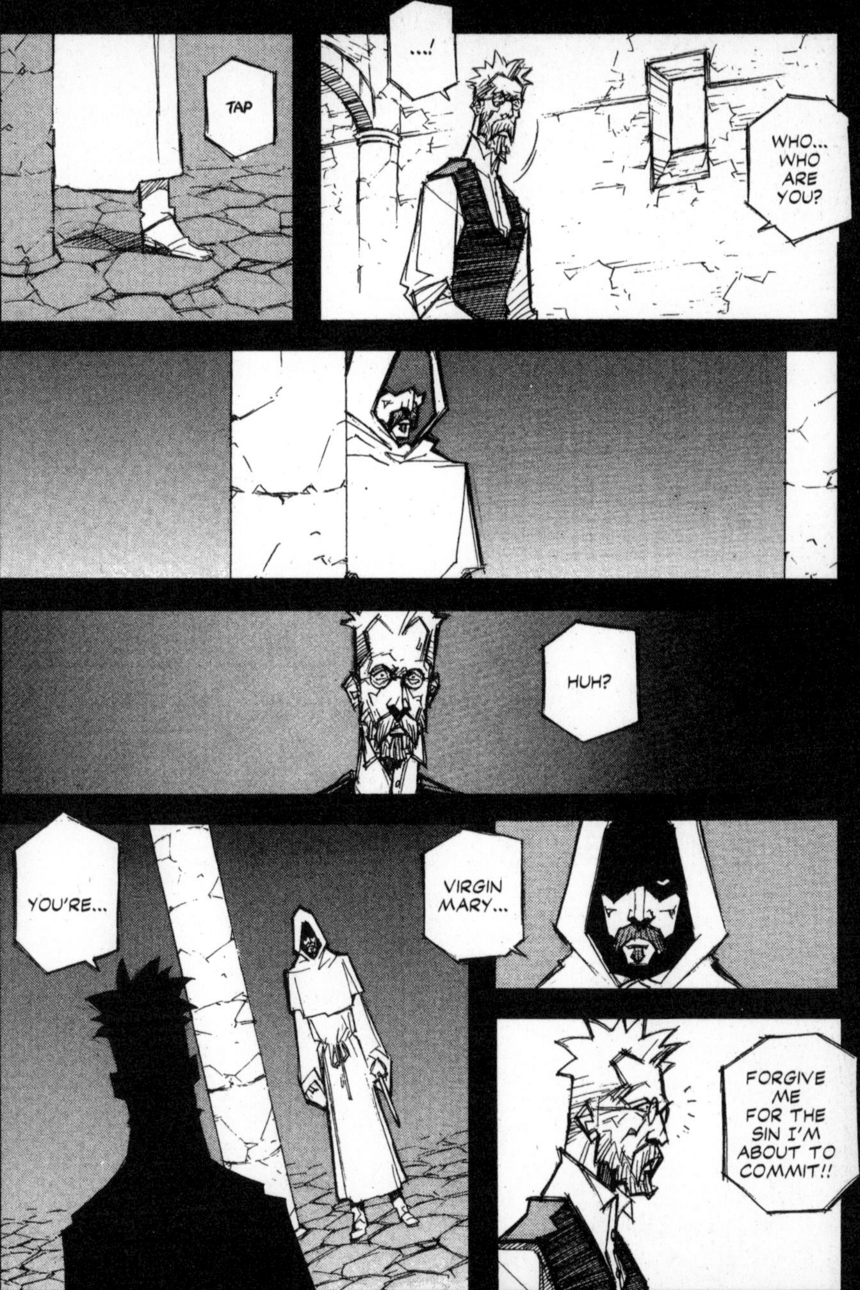
TAP
....!
WHO... WHO ARE YOU?
HUH?
YOU'RE...
VIRGIN MARY...
FORGIVE ME FOR THE SIN I'M ABOUT TO COMMIT!!

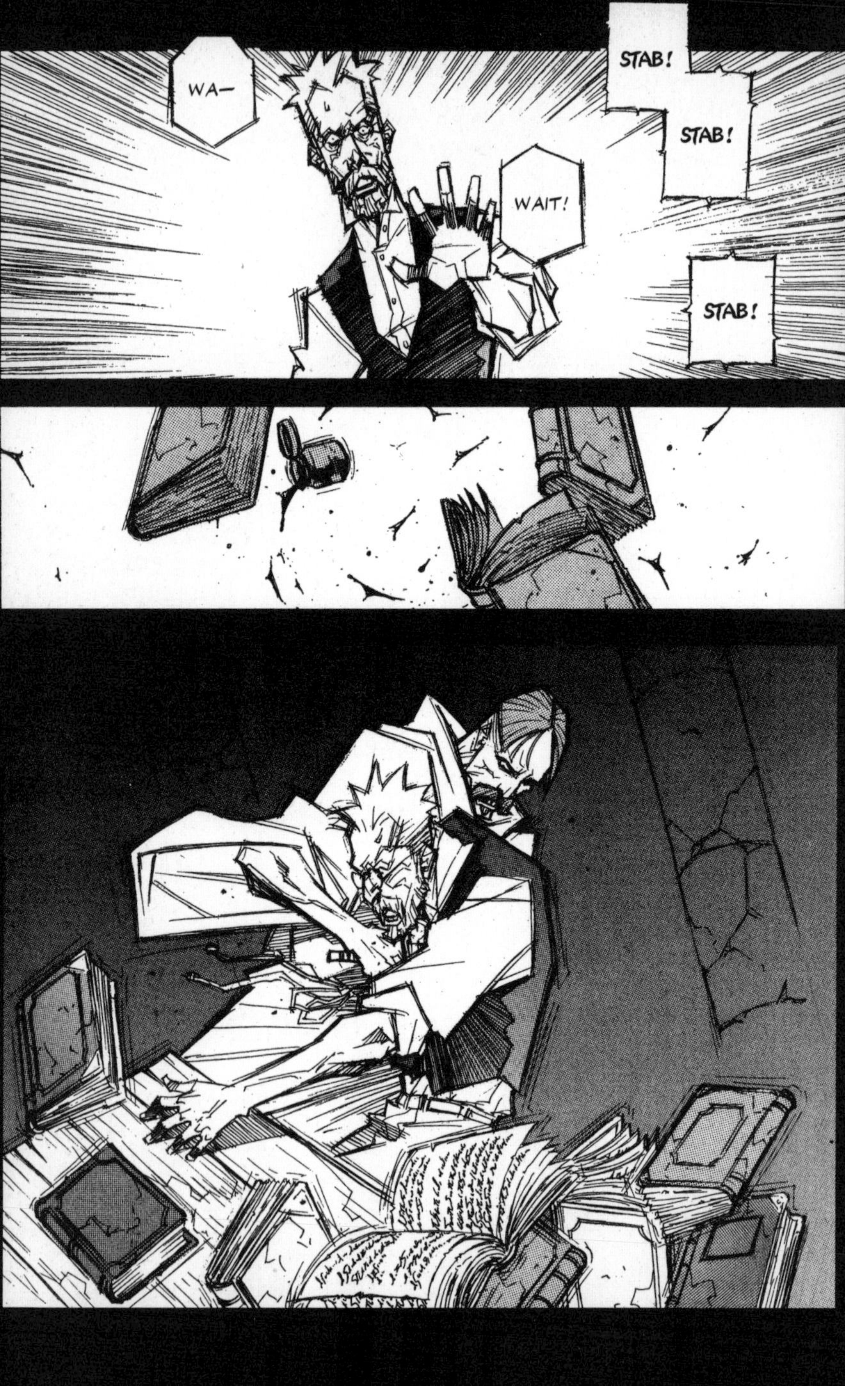
WA—
STAB!
STAB!
WAIT!
STAB!

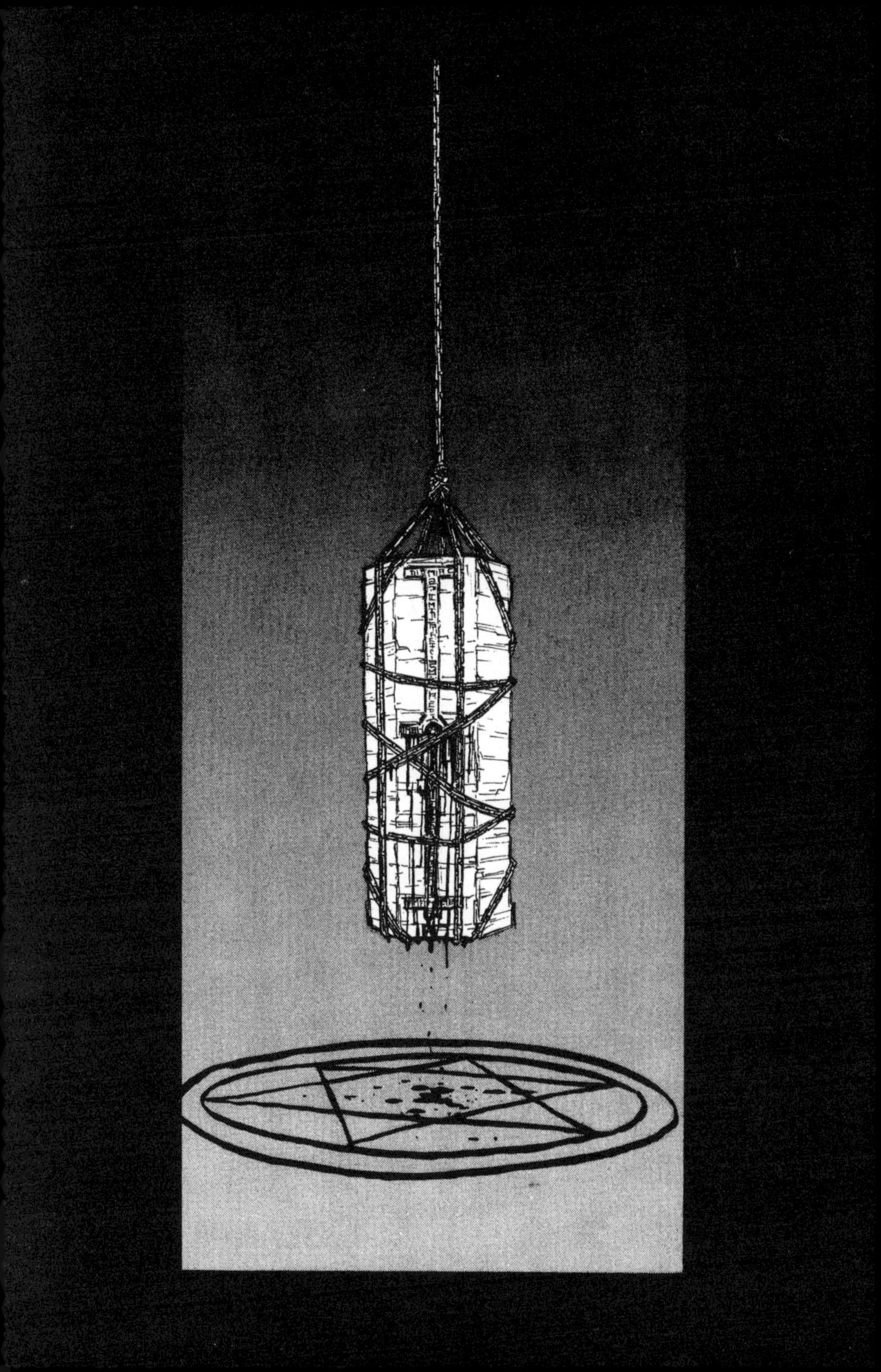

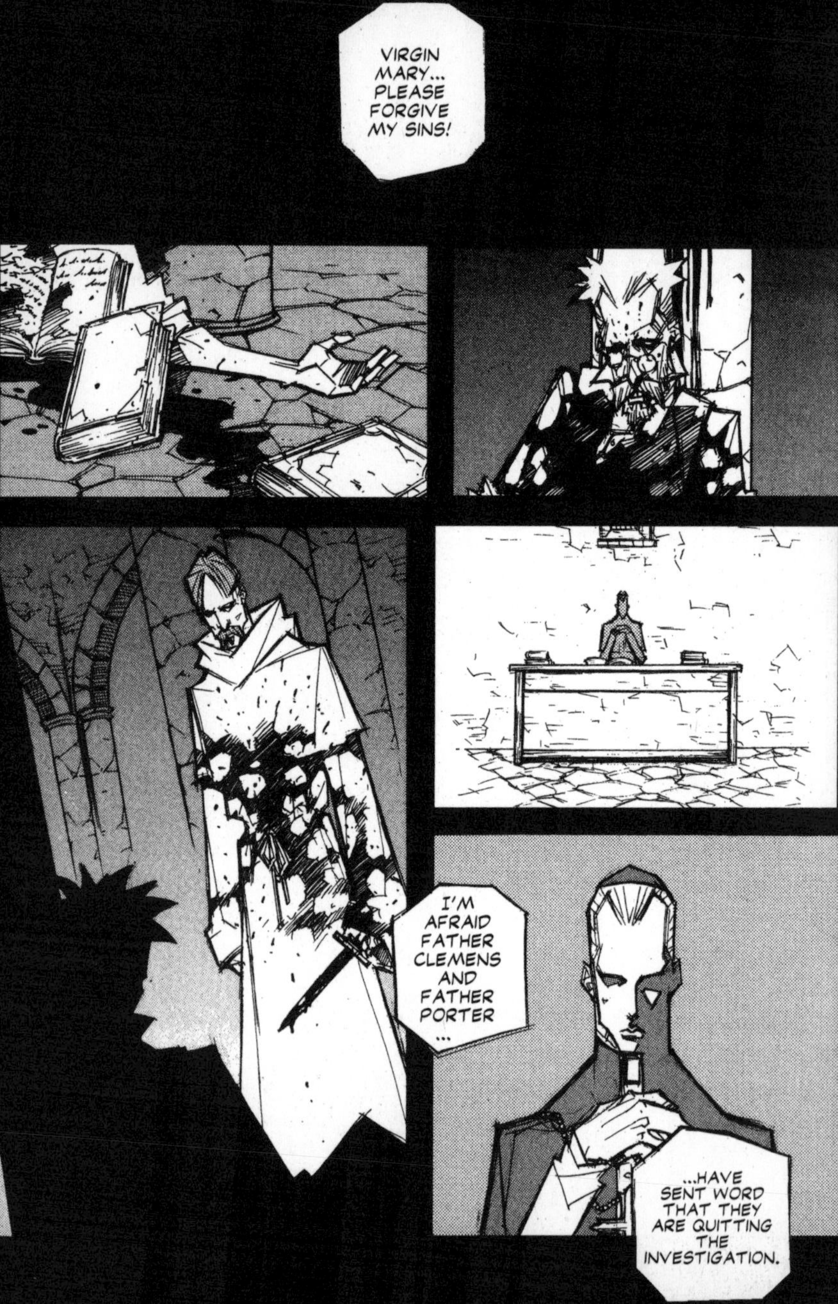
VIRGIN MARY... PLEASE FORGIVE MY SINS!
I'M AFRAID FATHER CLEMENS AND FATHER PORTER ...
...HAVE SENT WORD THAT THEY ARE QUITTING THE INVESTIGATION.

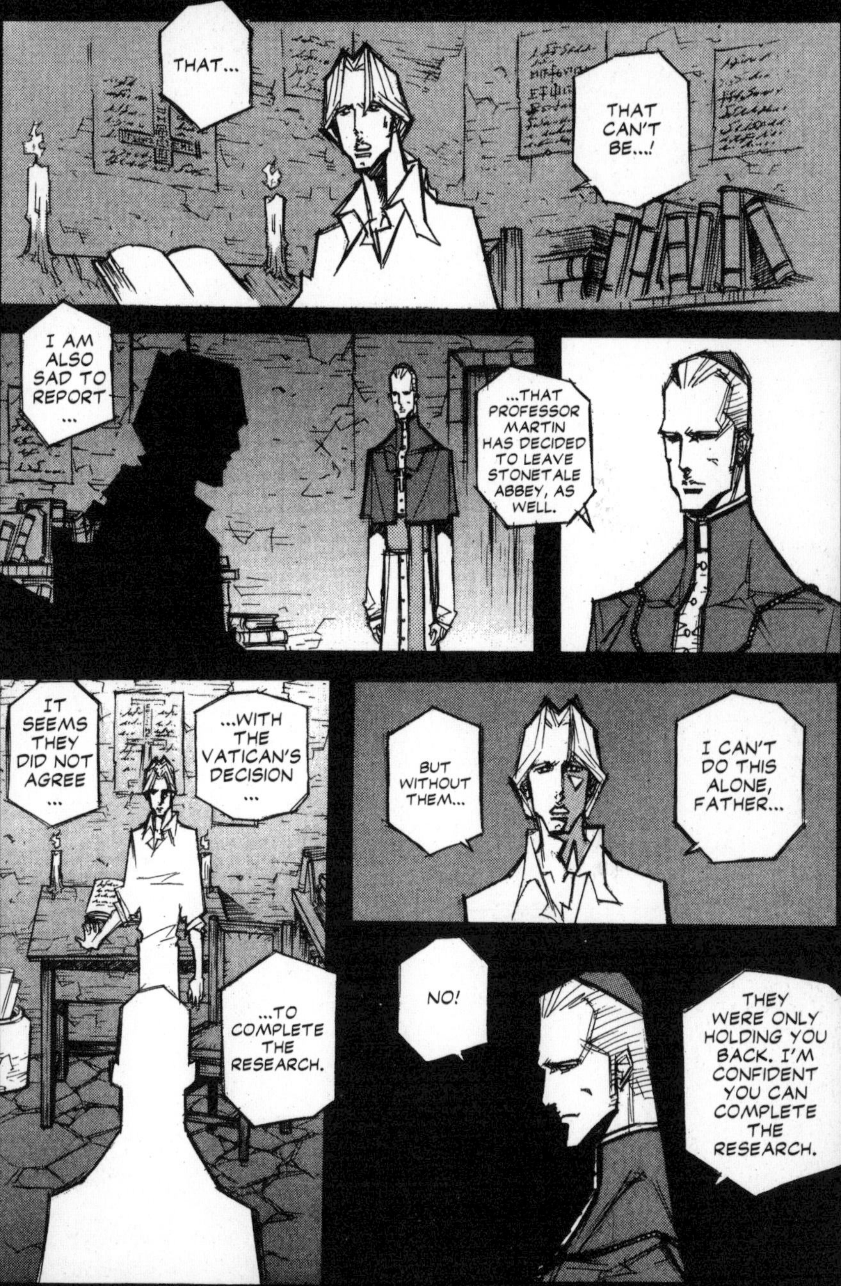
THAT...
THAT CAN'T BE...!
I AM ALSO SAD TO REPORT ...
...THAT PROFESSOR MARTIN HAS DECIDED TO LEAVE STONETALE ABBEY, AS WELL.
IT SEEMS THEY DID NOT AGREE ...
...WITH THE VATICAN'S DECISION ...
...TO COMPLETE THE RESEARCH.
BUT WITHOUT THEM...
I CAN'T DO THIS ALONE, FATHER...
NO!
THEY WERE ONLY HOLDING YOU BACK. I'M CONFIDENT YOU CAN COMPLETE THE RESEARCH.

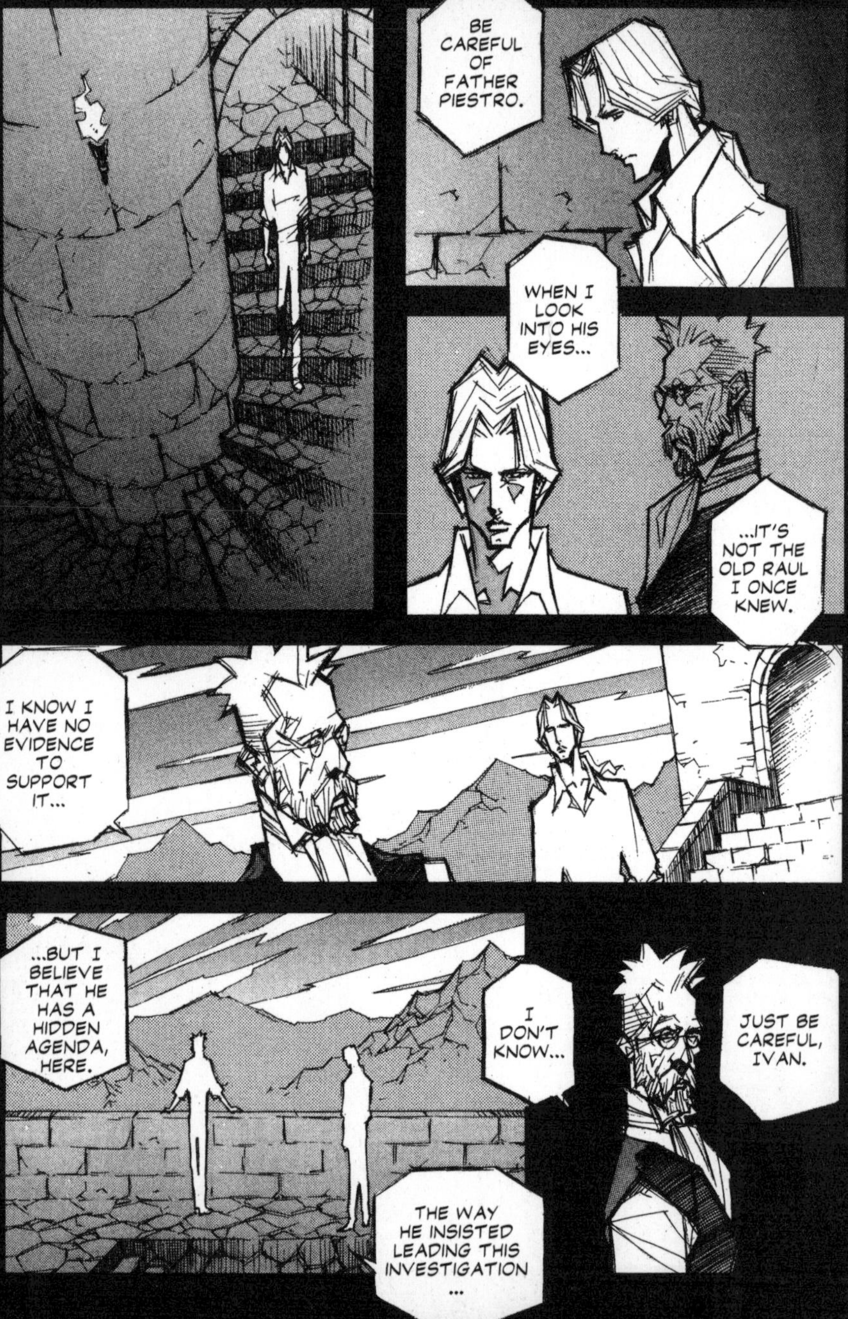

BE CAREFUL OF FATHER PIESTRO.
WHEN I LOOK INTO HIS EYES...
...IT'S NOT THE OLD RAUL I ONCE KNEW.
I KNOW I HAVE NO EVIDENCE TO SUPPORT IT...
...BUT I BELIEVE THAT HE HAS A HIDDEN AGENDA, HERE.
THE WAY HE INSISTED LEADING THIS INVESTIGATION ...
I DON'T KNOW...
JUST BE CAREFUL, IVAN.

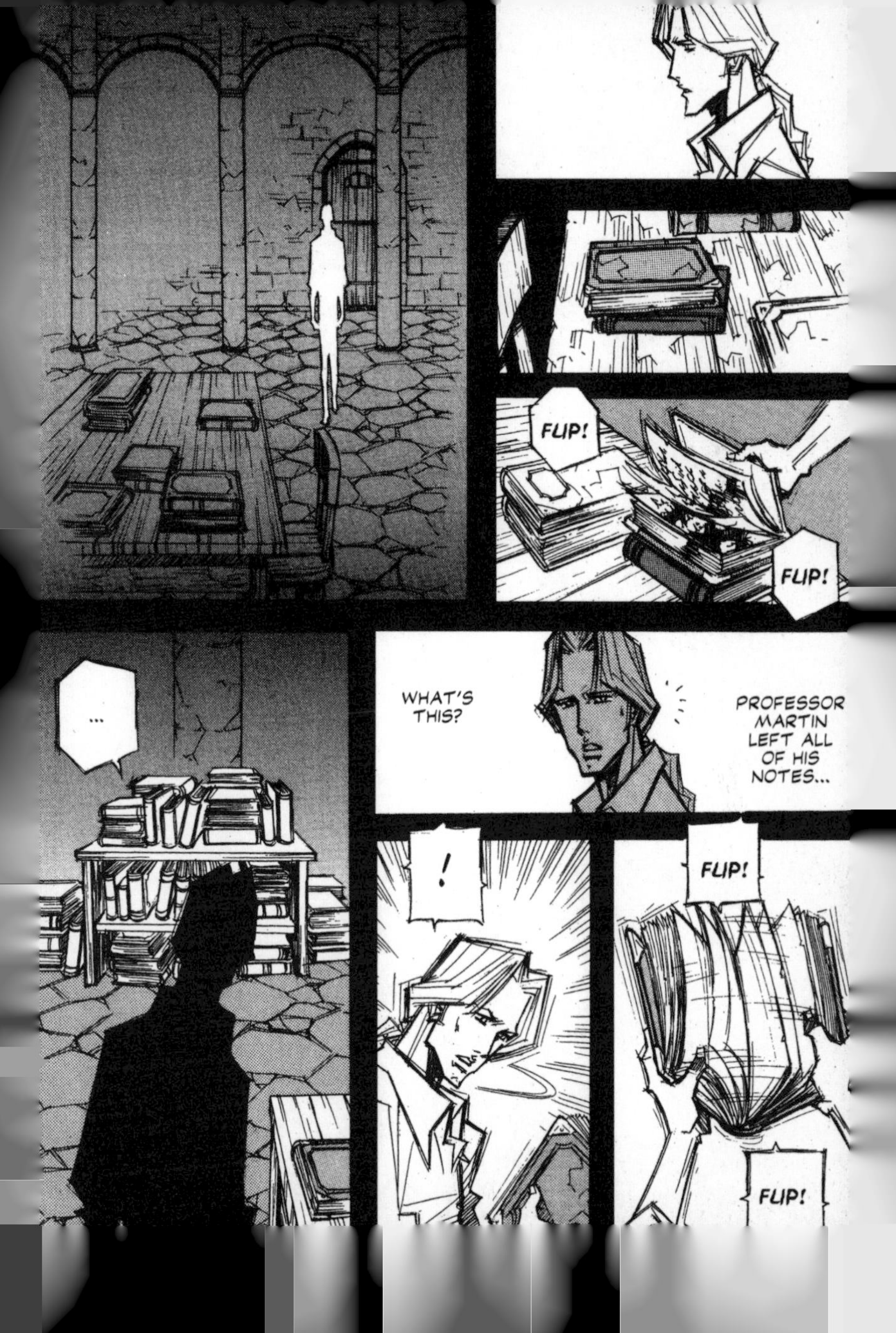

FLIP!
FLIP!
...
WHAT'S THIS?
PROFESSOR MARTIN LEFT ALL OF HIS NOTES...
!
FLIP!
FLIP!

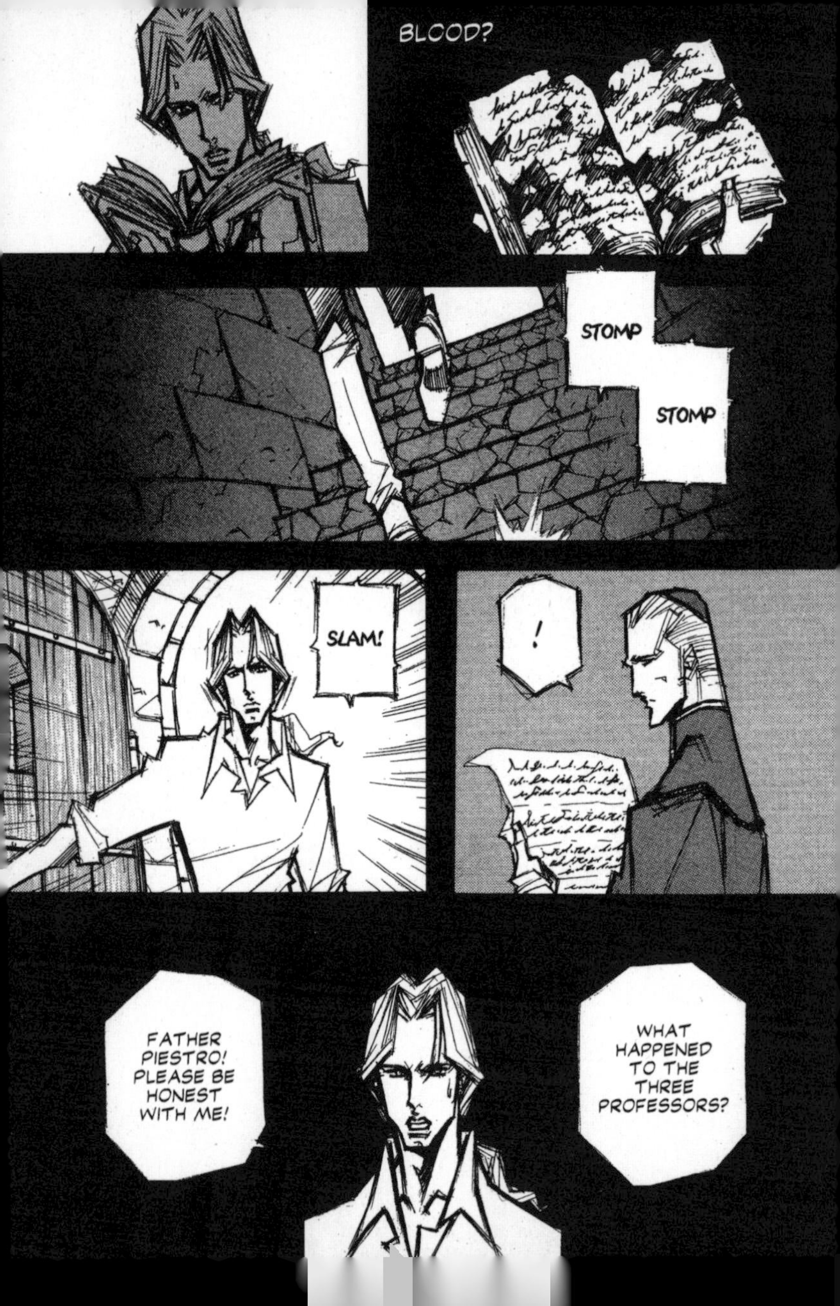
BLOOD?
STOMP
STOMP
SLAM!
!
FATHER PIESTRO! PLEASE BE HONEST WITH ME!
WHAT HAPPENED TO THE THREE PROFESSORS?

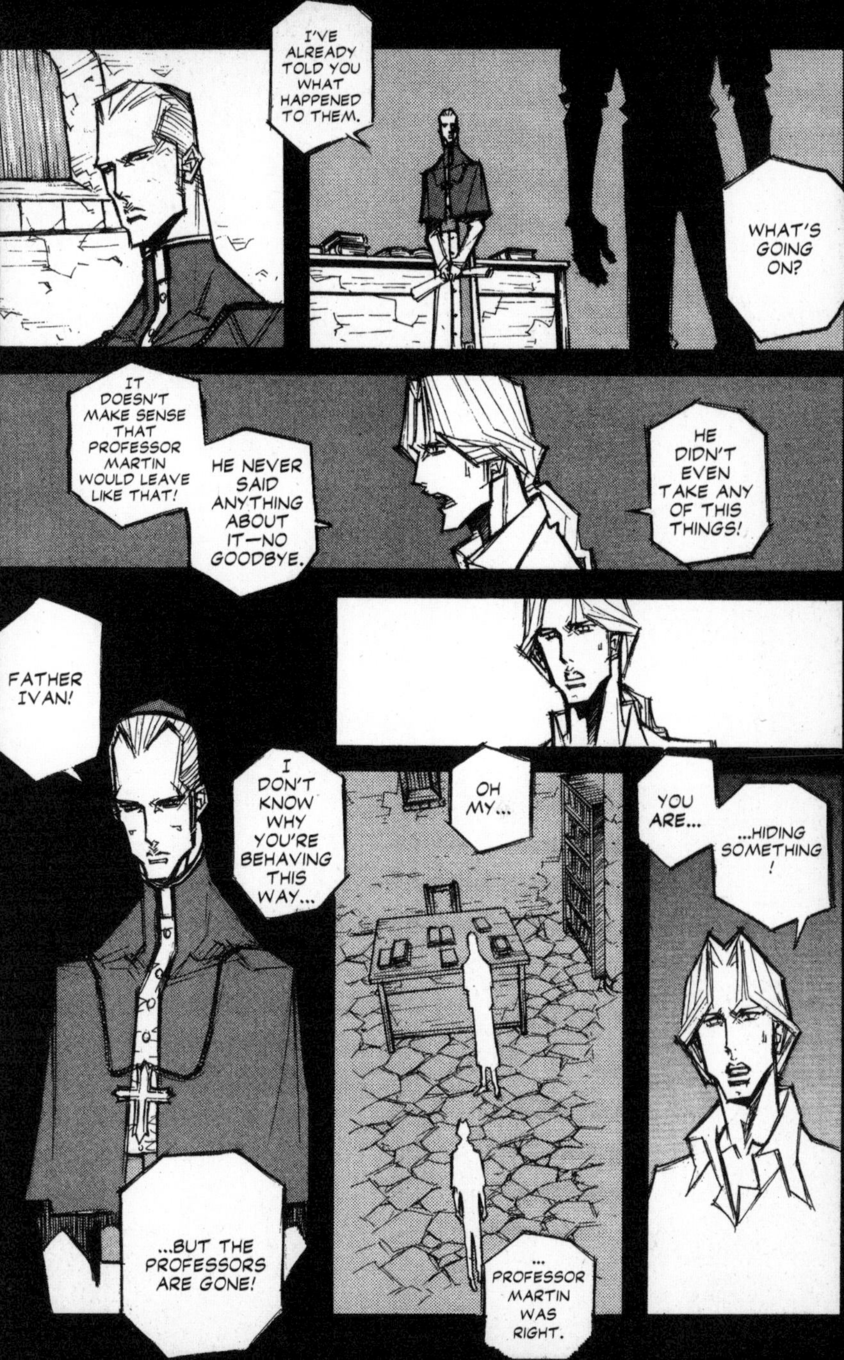
I'VE ALREADY TOLD YOU WHAT HAPPENED TO THEM.
WHAT'S GOING ON?
IT DOESN'T MAKE SENSE THAT PROFESSOR MARTIN WOULD LEAVE LIKE THAT!
HE NEVER SAID ANYTHING ABOUT IT—NO GOODBYE.
HE DIDN'T EVEN TAKE ANY OF THIS THINGS!
FATHER IVAN!
I DON'T KNOW WHY YOU'RE BEHAVING THIS WAY...
...BUT THE PROFESSORS ARE GONE!
OH MY...
... PROFESSOR MARTIN WAS RIGHT.
YOU ARE...
...HIDING SOMETHING!

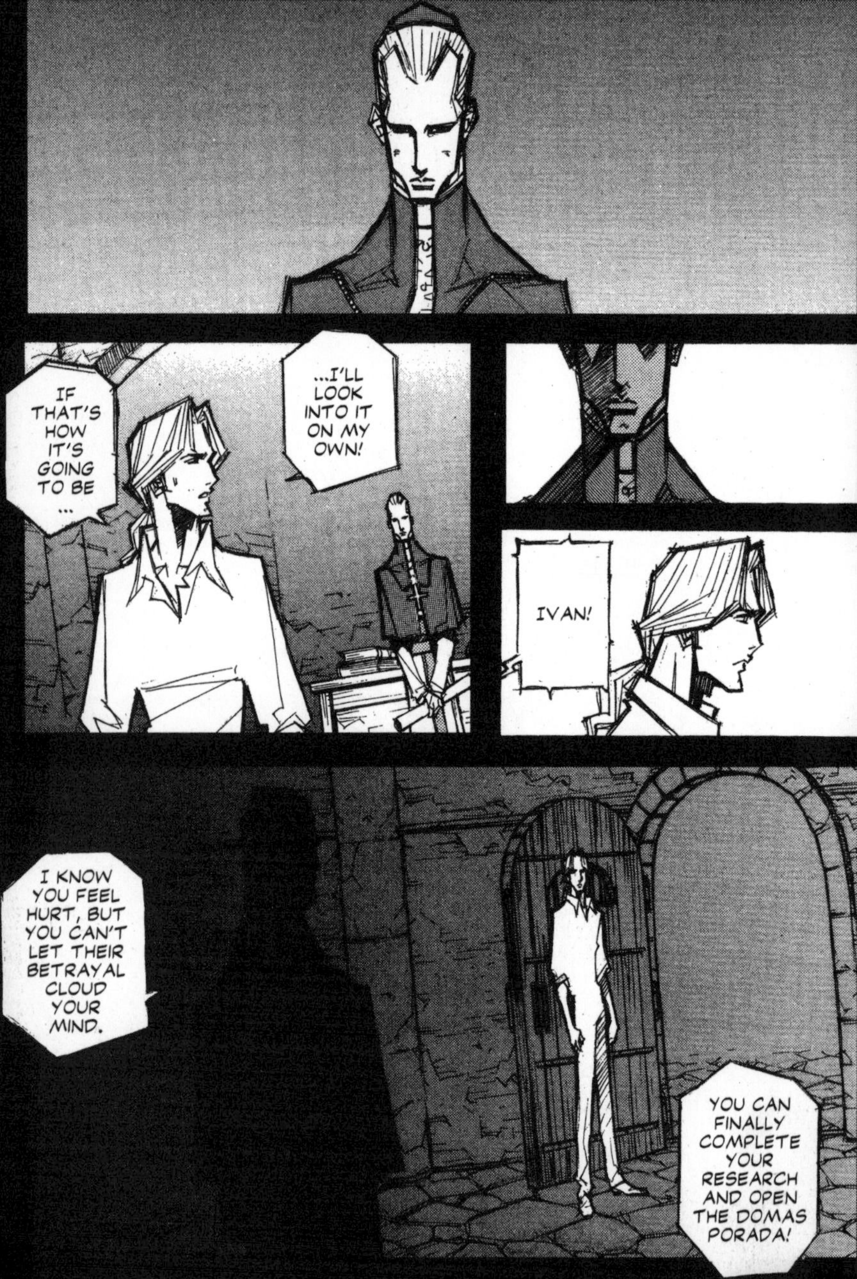
IF THAT'S HOW IT'S GOING TO BE ...
...I'LL LOOK INTO IT ON MY OWN!
IVAN!
I KNOW YOU FEEL HURT, BUT YOU CAN'T LET THEIR BETRAYAL CLOUD YOUR MIND.
YOU CAN FINALLY COMPLETE YOUR RESEARCH AND OPEN THE DOMAS PORADA!

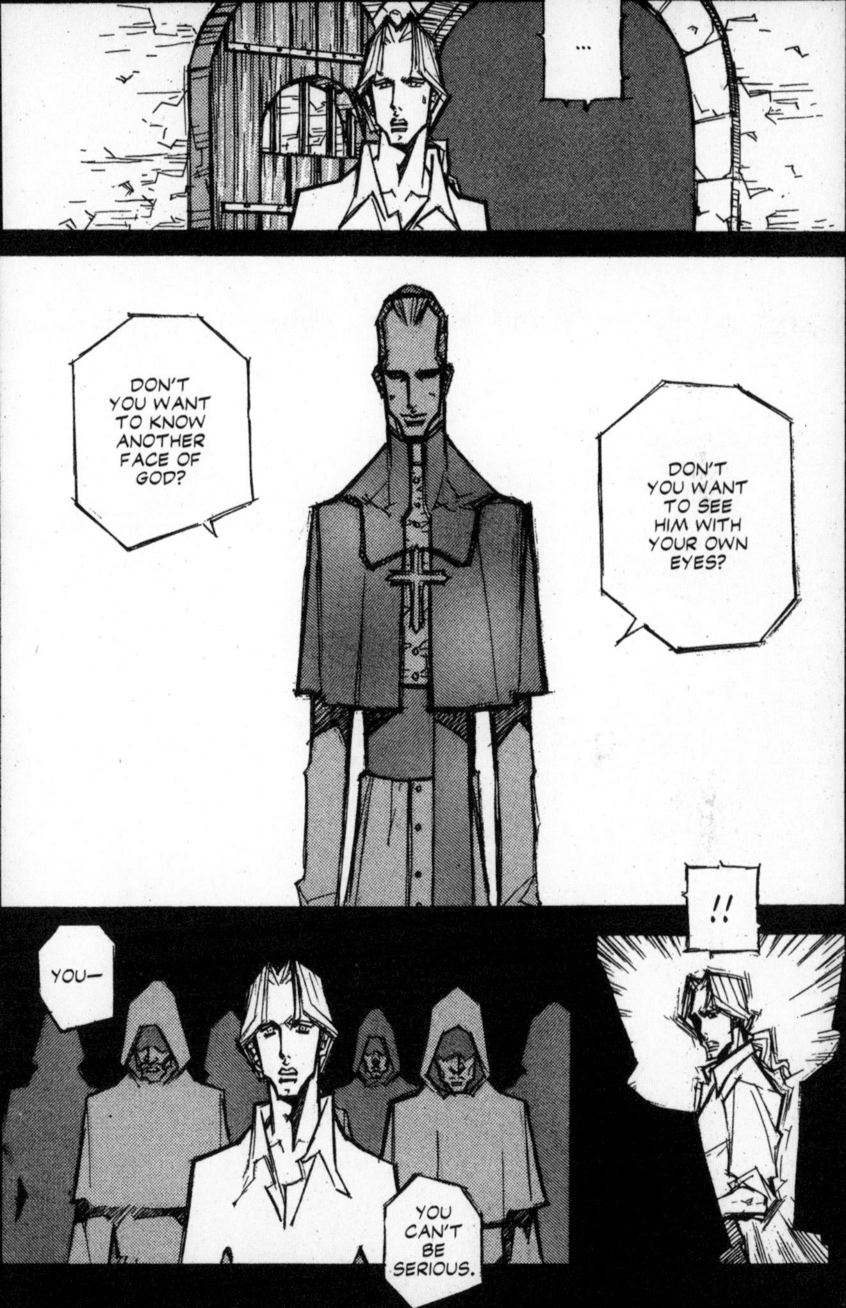
...
DON'T YOU WANT TO KNOW ANOTHER FACE OF GOD?
DON'T YOU WANT TO SEE HIM WITH YOUR OWN EYES?
YOU—
YOU CAN'T BE SERIOUS.
!!

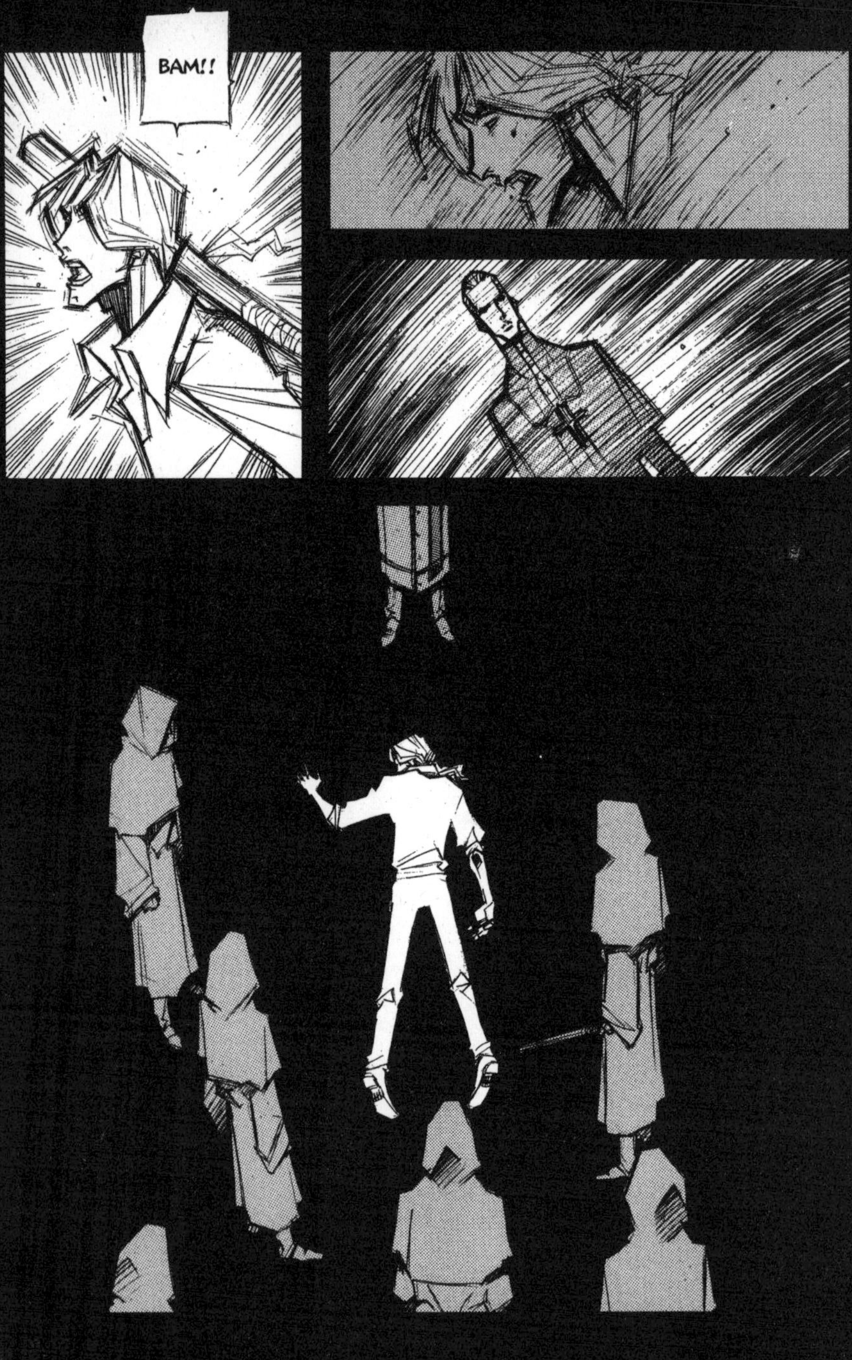
BAM!!

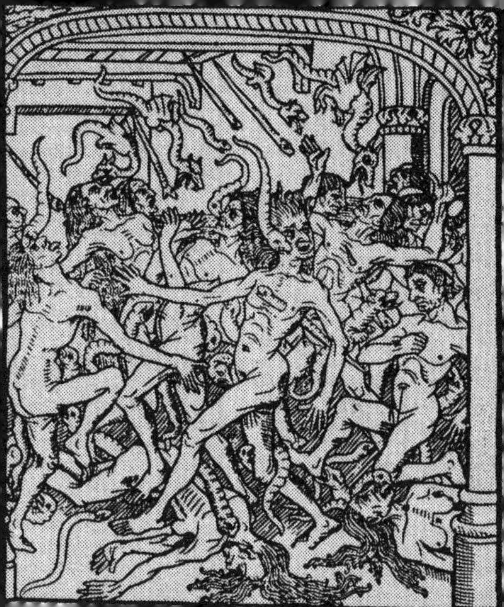

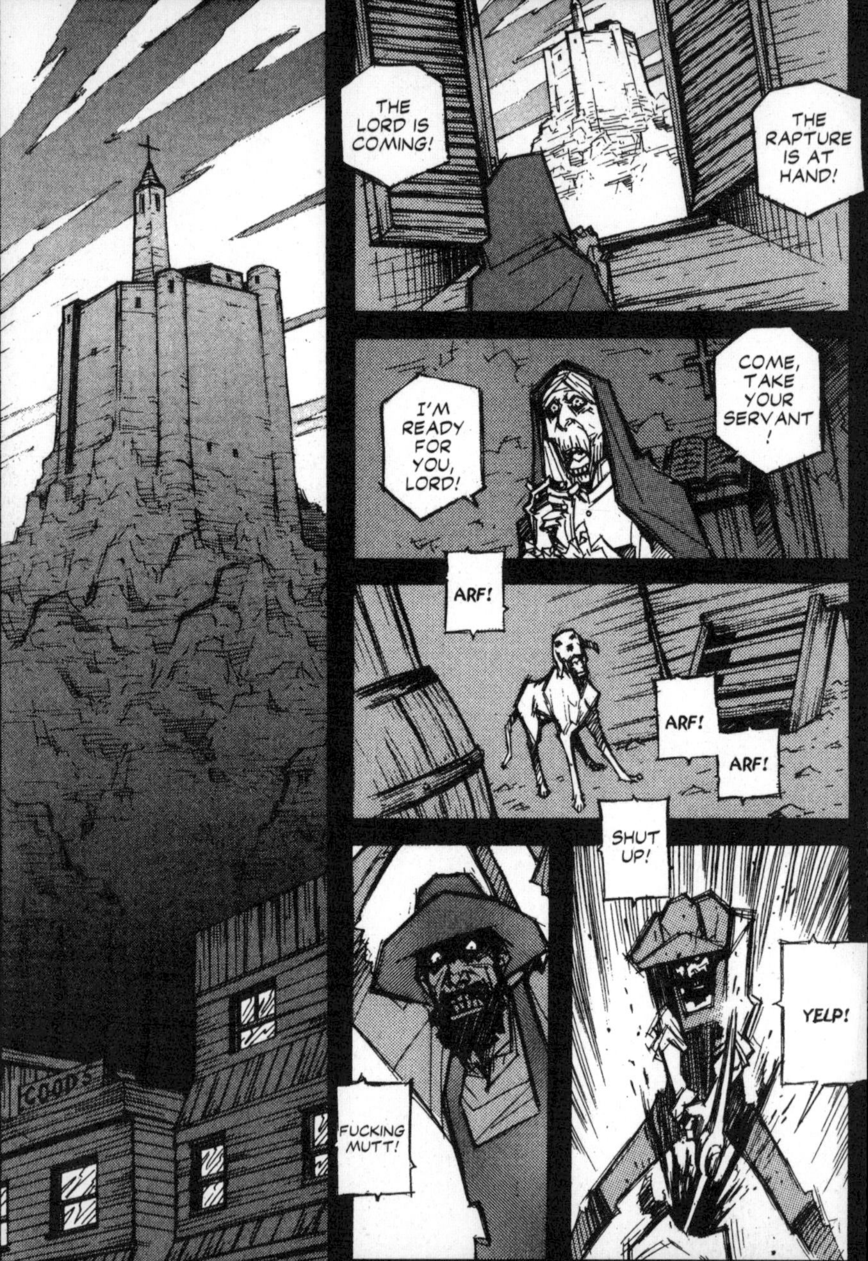
THE LORD IS COMING!
THE RAPTURE IS AT HAND!
I'M READY FOR YOU, LORD!
COME, TAKE YOUR SERVANT!
ARF!
ARF!
ARF!
SHUT UP!
FUCKING MUTT!
YELP!

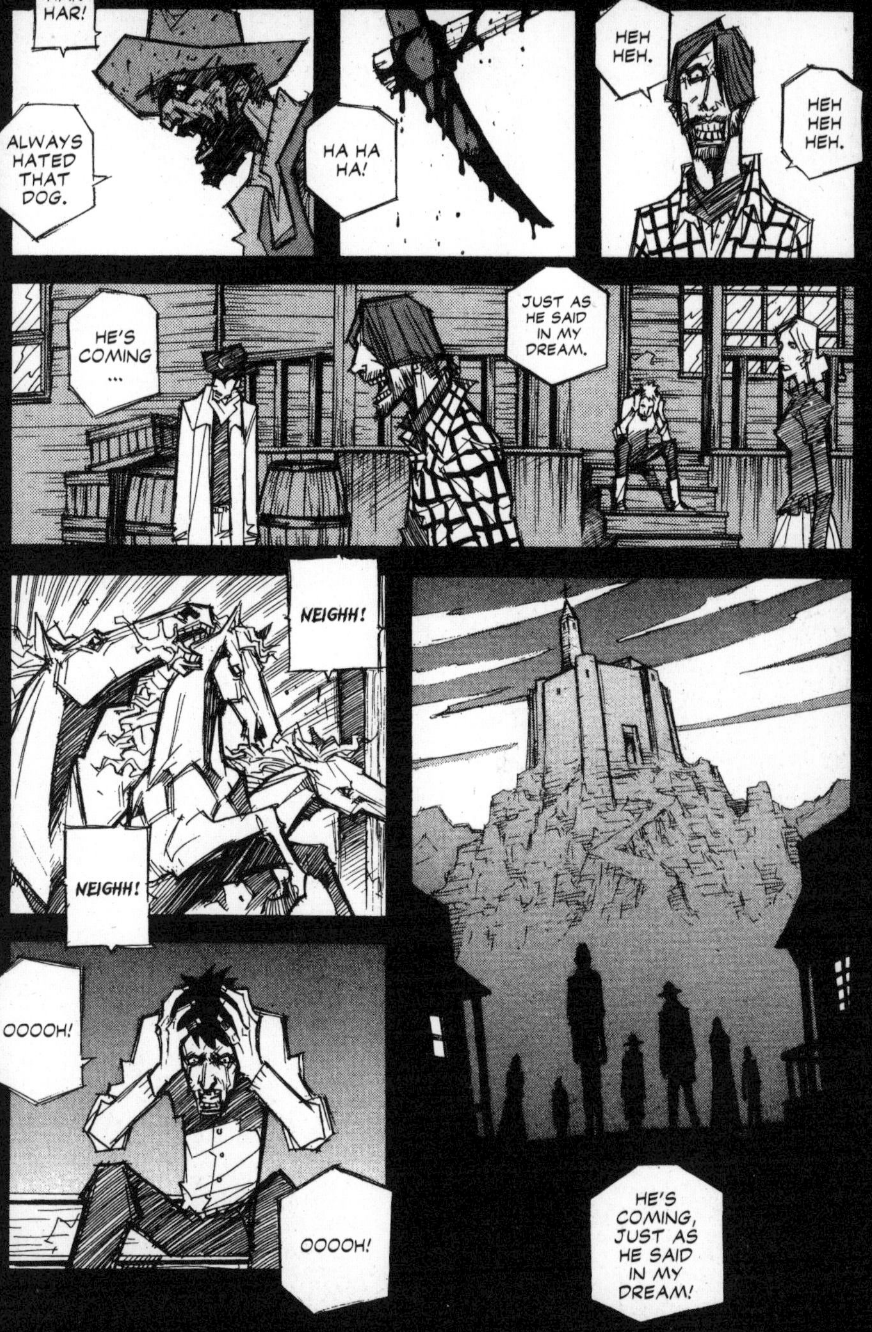
HAR HAR!
ALWAYS HATED THAT DOG.
HA HA HA!
HEH HEH.
HEH HEH HEH.
HE'S COMING ...
JUST AS HE SAID IN MY DREAM.
NEIGHH!
NEIGHH!
OOOOH!
OOOOH!
HE'S COMING, JUST AS HE SAID IN MY DREAM!

THE SIGNS OF HIS COMING HAVE BEEN THERE ALL ALONG...

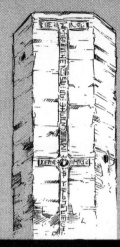

...BUT THE CHURCH CHOSE TO IGNORE THEM!

WE'VE BEEN HIDING BEHIND OUR OLD WAYS...

... UNABLE TO ACCEPT THAT GOD HAS A NEW PLAN!

JUST AS HE SENT HIS SON 18 CENTURIES AGO...

...HE SENDS A NEW MESSIAH.

WHAT ?!

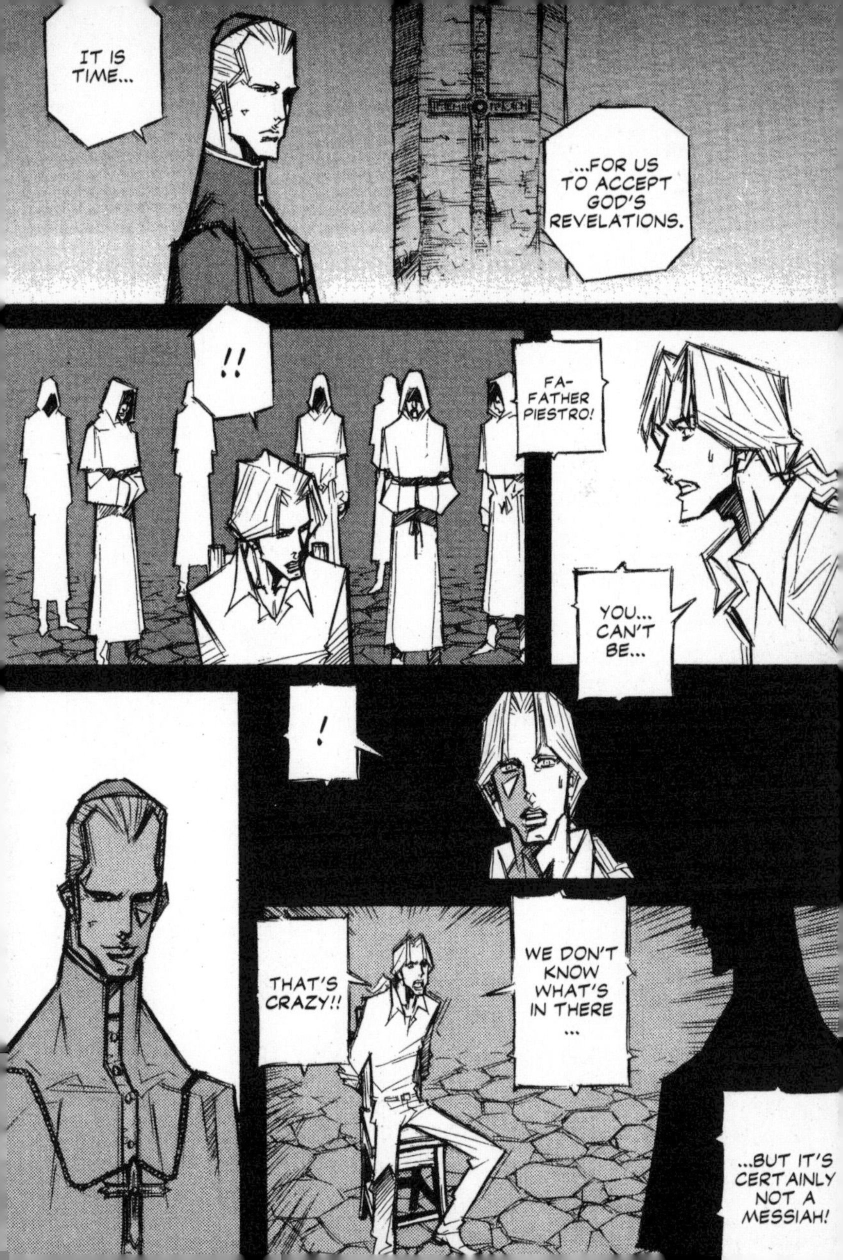
IT IS TIME...
...FOR US TO ACCEPT GOD'S REVELATIONS.
!!
FA-FATHER PIESTRO!
YOU... CAN'T BE...
!
THAT'S CRAZY!!
WE DON'T KNOW WHAT'S IN THERE ...
...BUT IT'S CERTAINLY NOT A MESSIAH!

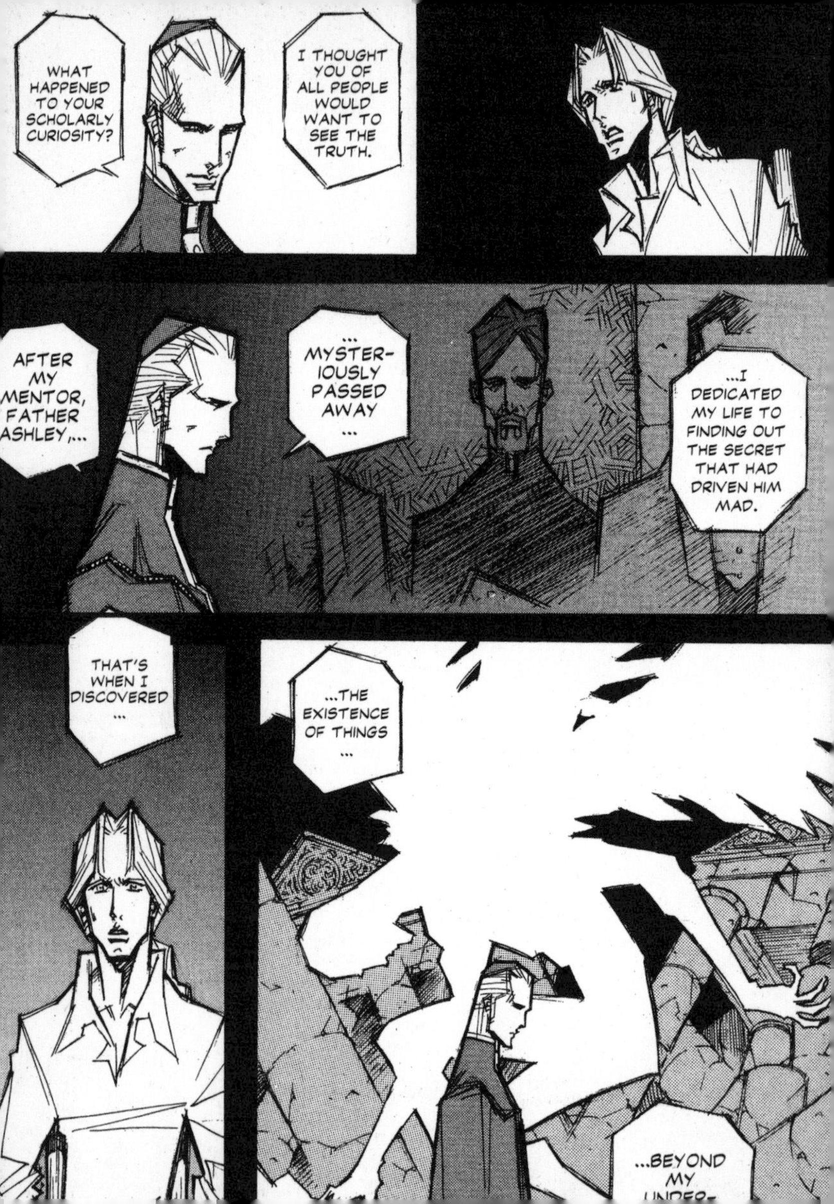
WHAT HAPPENED TO YOUR SCHOLARLY CURIOSITY?
I THOUGHT YOU OF ALL PEOPLE WOULD WANT TO SEE THE TRUTH.
AFTER MY MENTOR, FATHER ASHLEY,...
...MYSTERIOUSLY PASSED AWAY...
...I DEDICATED MY LIFE TO FINDING OUT THE SECRET THAT HAD DRIVEN HIM MAD.
THAT'S WHEN I DISCOVERED...
...THE EXISTENCE OF THINGS...
...BEYOND MY

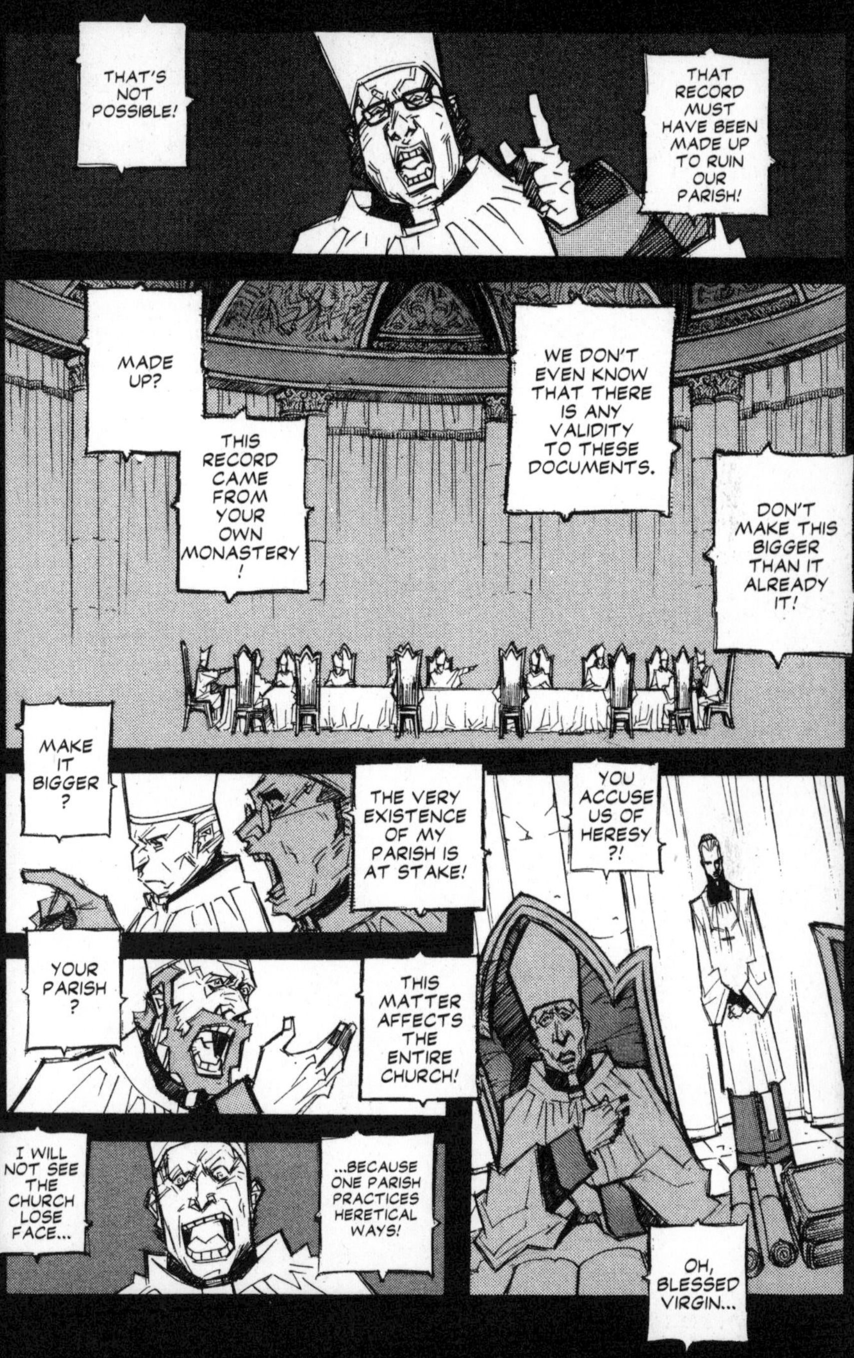
THAT'S NOT POSSIBLE!
THAT RECORD MUST HAVE BEEN MADE UP TO RUIN OUR PARISH!
MADE UP?
THIS RECORD CAME FROM YOUR OWN MONASTERY!
WE DON'T EVEN KNOW THAT THERE IS ANY VALIDITY TO THESE DOCUMENTS.
DON'T MAKE THIS BIGGER THAN IT ALREADY IT!
MAKE IT BIGGER?
THE VERY EXISTENCE OF MY PARISH IS AT STAKE!
YOUR PARISH?
THIS MATTER AFFECTS THE ENTIRE CHURCH!
I WILL NOT SEE THE CHURCH LOSE FACE...
...BECAUSE ONE PARISH PRACTICES HERETICAL WAYS!
YOU ACCUSE US OF HERESY?!
OH, BLESSED VIRGIN...

WORKING IN THE VATICAN, I SAW JUST HOW MUCH THE CHURCH HAD BEEN CONSUMED...

...BY BUREAUCRACY AND EARTHLY AFFAIRS.

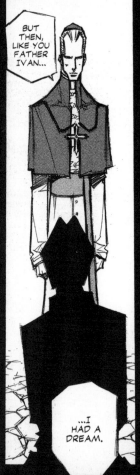

BUT THEN, LIKE YOU FATHER IVAN...

...I HAD A DREAM.

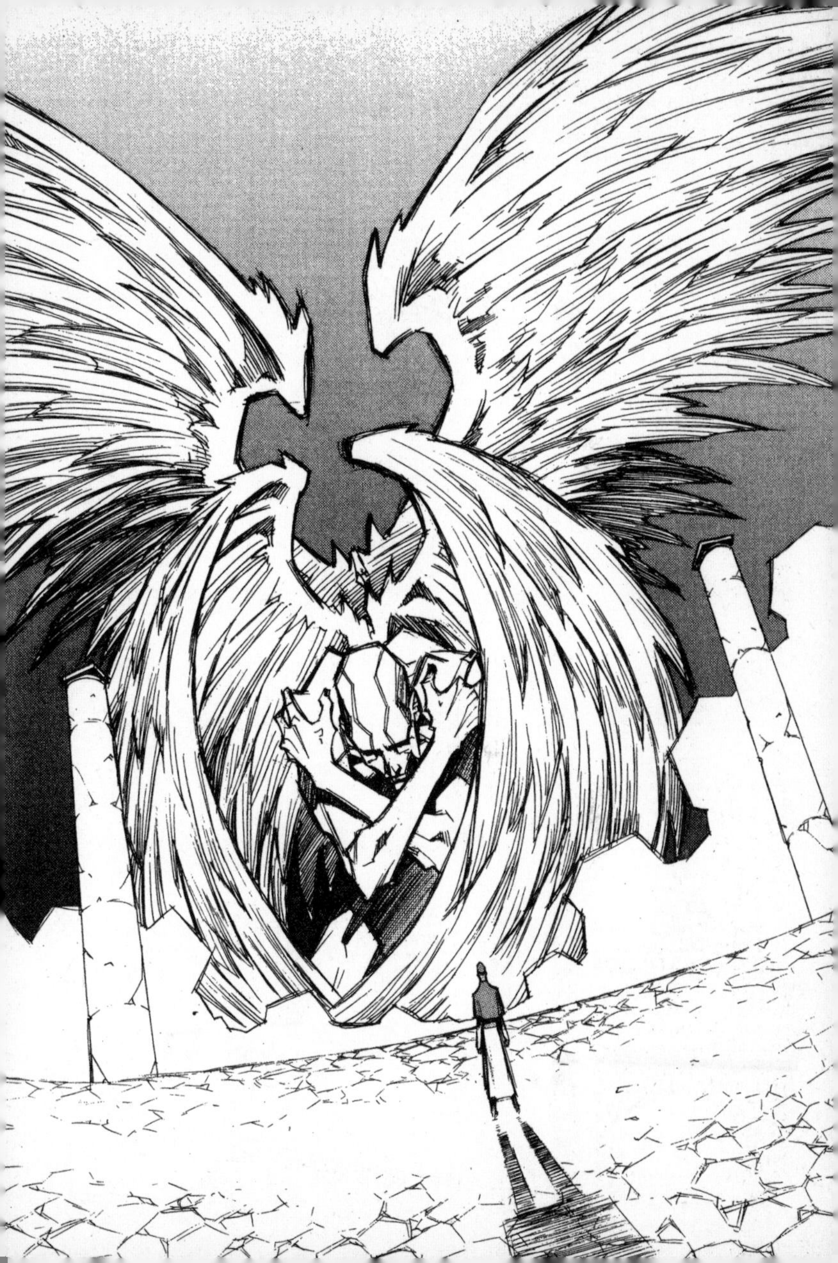

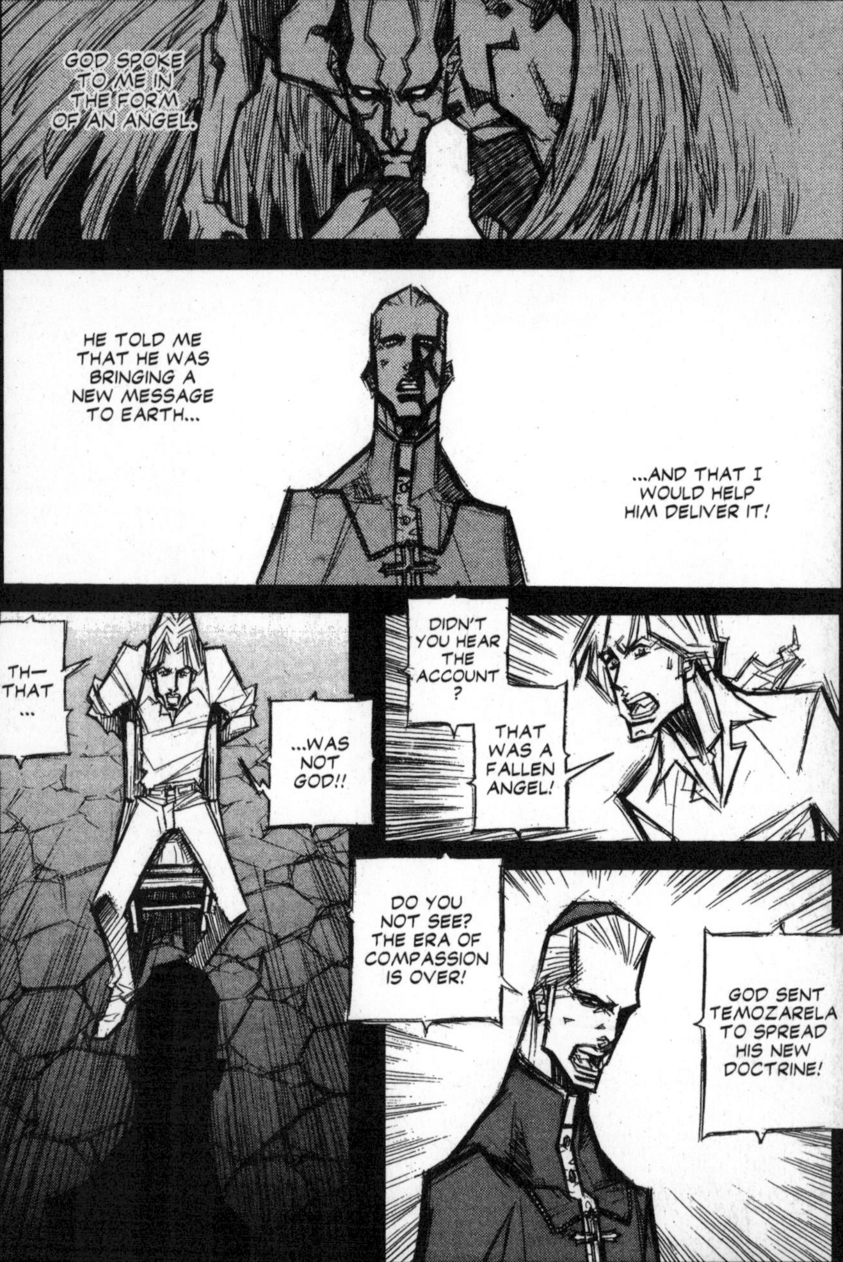
GOD SPOKE TO ME IN THE FORM OF AN ANGEL.
HE TOLD ME THAT HE WAS BRINGING A NEW MESSAGE TO EARTH...
...AND THAT I WOULD HELP HIM DELIVER IT!
TH— THAT ...
...WAS NOT GOD!!
DIDN'T YOU HEAR THE ACCOUNT ?
THAT WAS A FALLEN ANGEL!
DO YOU NOT SEE? THE ERA OF COMPASSION IS OVER!
GOD SENT TEMOZARELA TO SPREAD HIS NEW DOCTRINE!

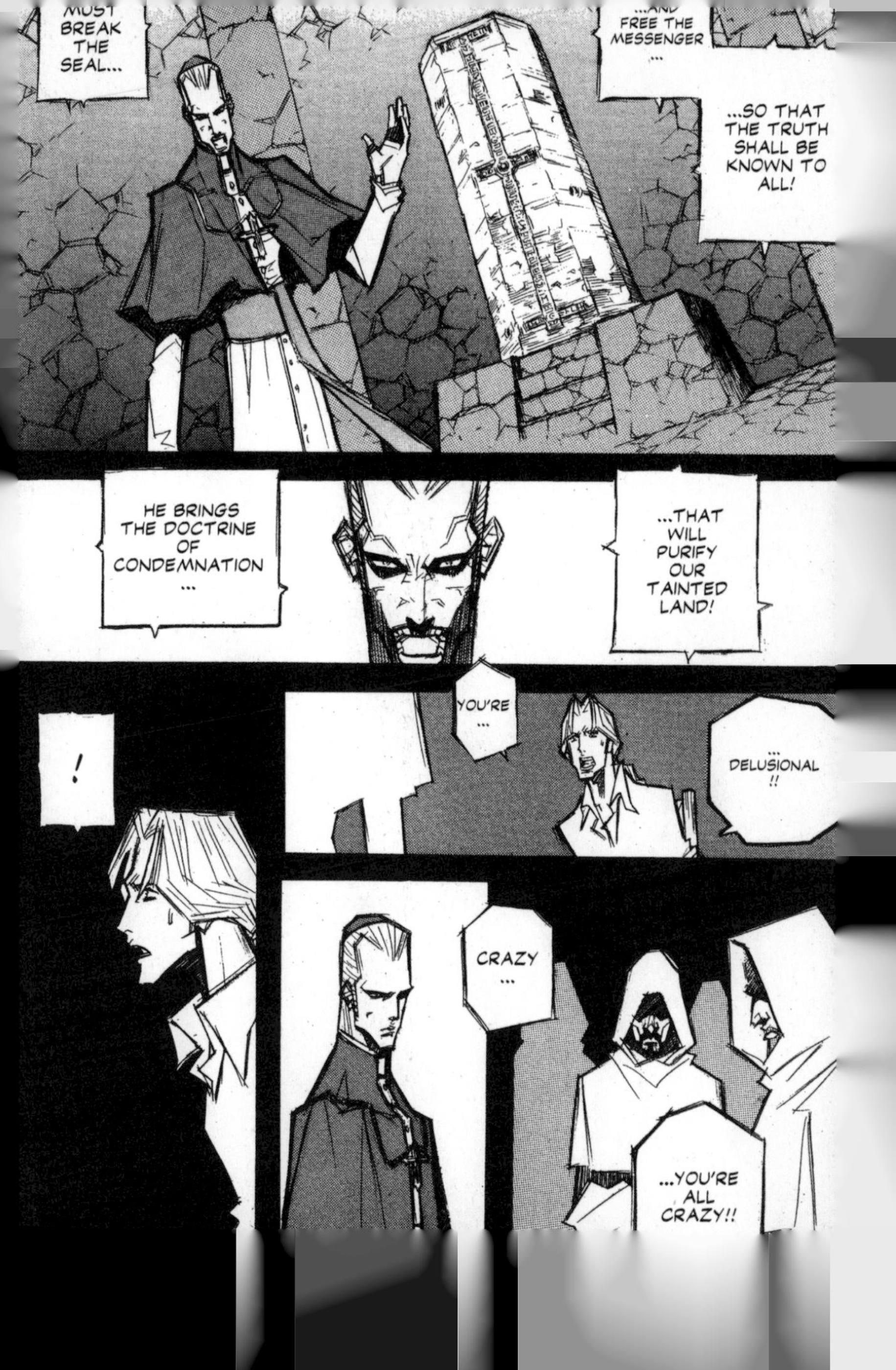
MUST BREAK THE SEAL...
...AND FREE THE MESSENGER ...
...SO THAT THE TRUTH SHALL BE KNOWN TO ALL!
HE BRINGS THE DOCTRINE OF CONDEMNATION ...
...THAT WILL PURIFY OUR TAINTED LAND!
!
YOU'RE ...
... DELUSIONAL !!
CRAZY ...
...YOU'RE ALL CRAZY!!

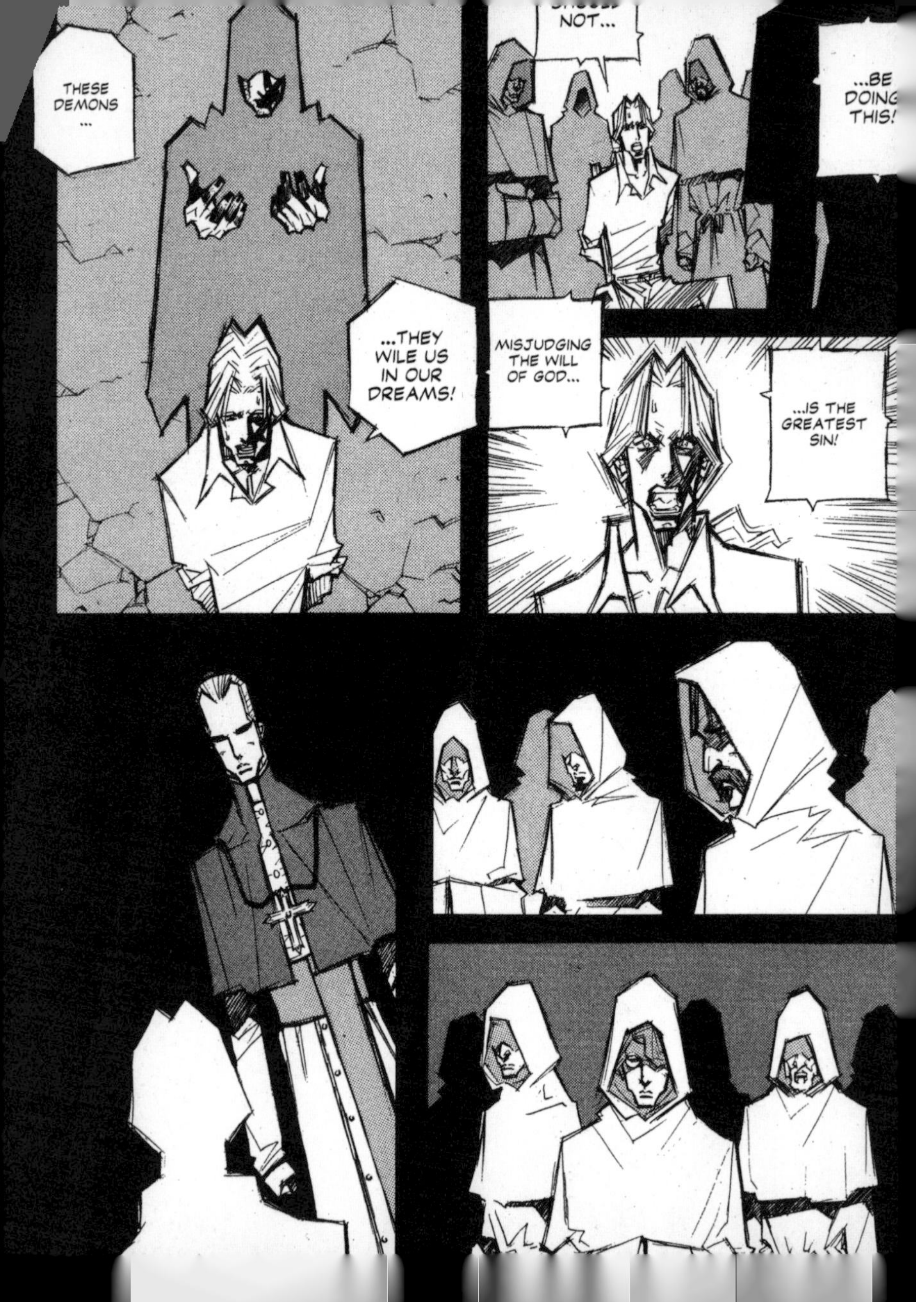
THESE DEMONS ...
...THEY WILE US IN OUR DREAMS!
NOT...
...BE DOING THIS!
MISJUDGING THE WILL OF GOD...
...IS THE GREATEST SIN!

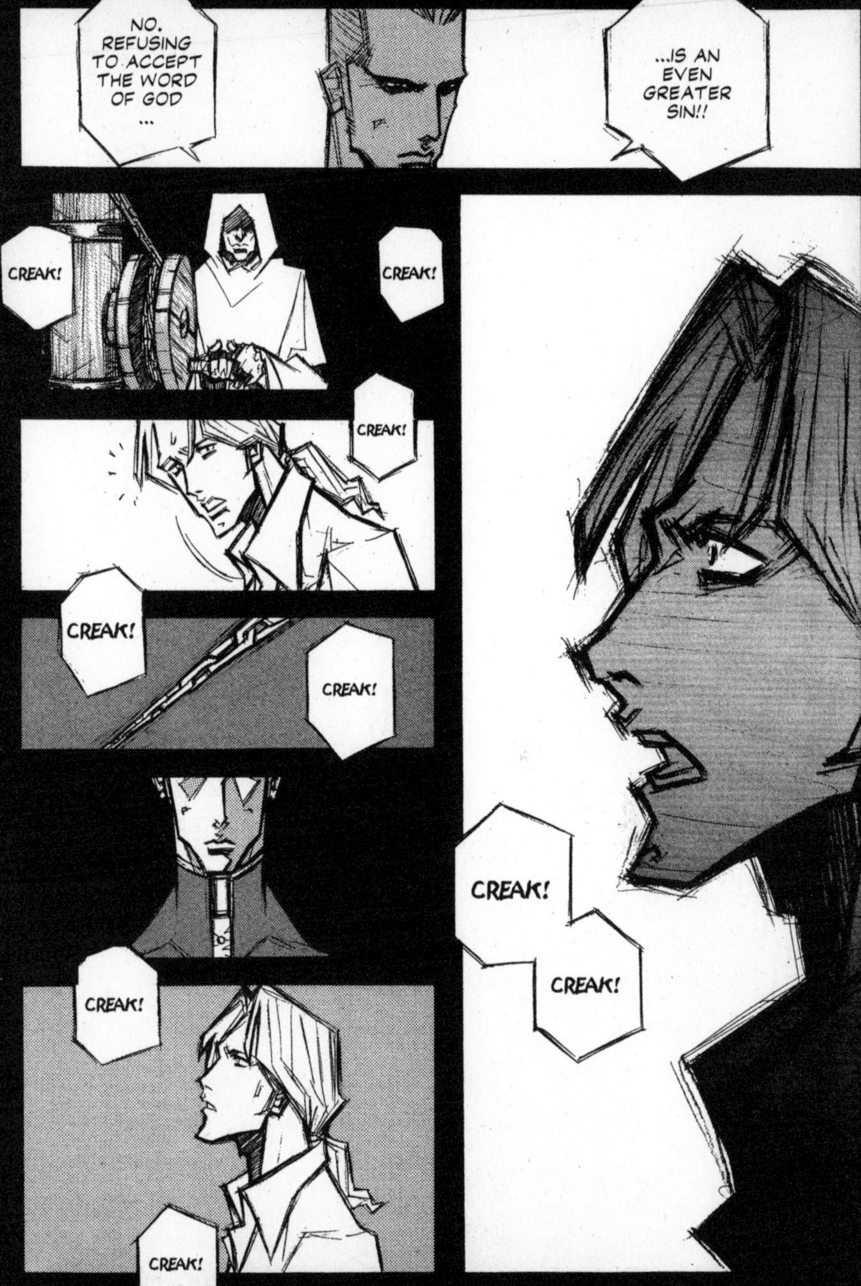
NO. REFUSING TO ACCEPT THE WORD OF GOD ...
...IS AN EVEN GREATER SIN!!
CREAK!
CREAK!
CREAK!
CREAK!
CREAK!
CREAK!
CREAK!
CREAK!
CREAK!

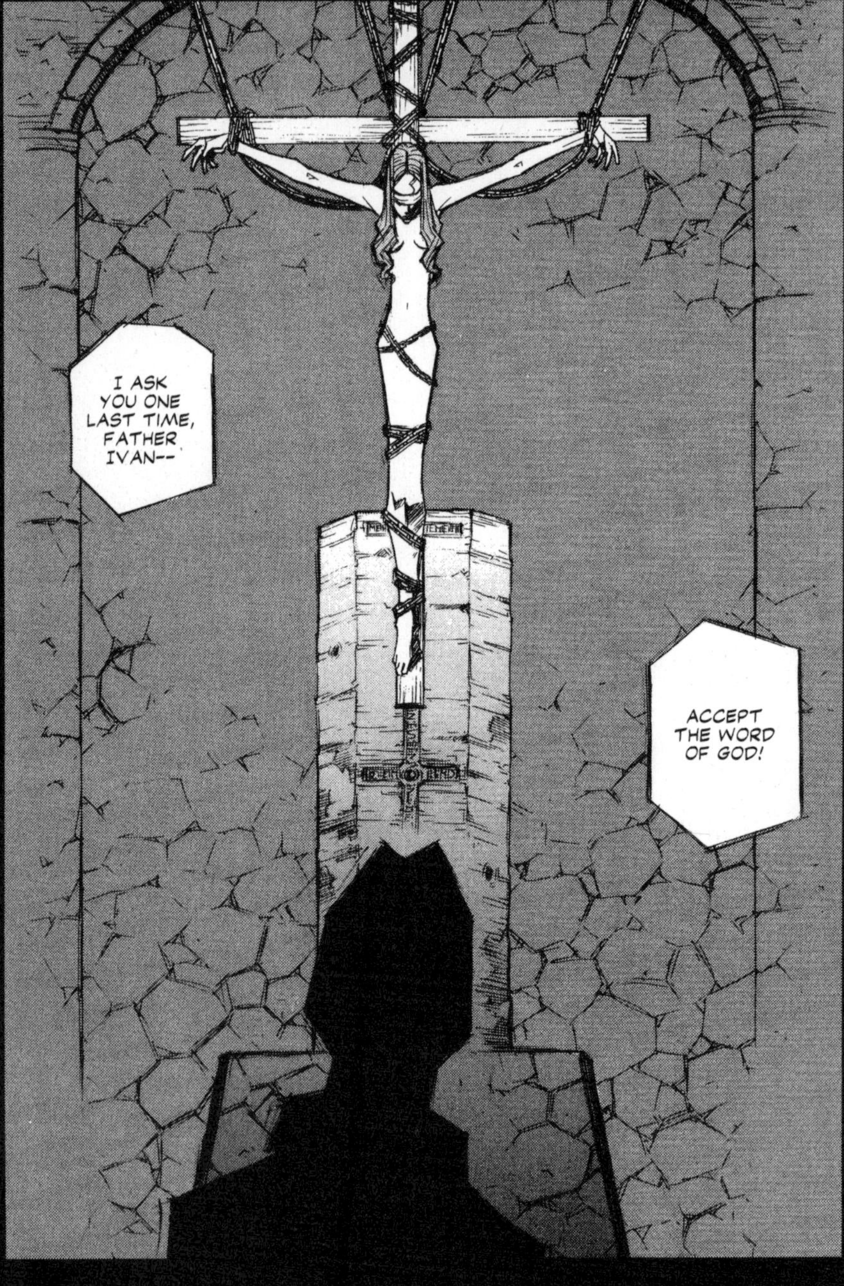
I ASK YOU ONE LAST TIME, FATHER IVAN--
ACCEPT THE WORD OF GOD!

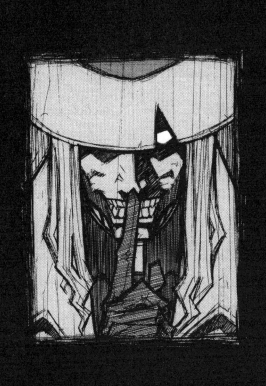

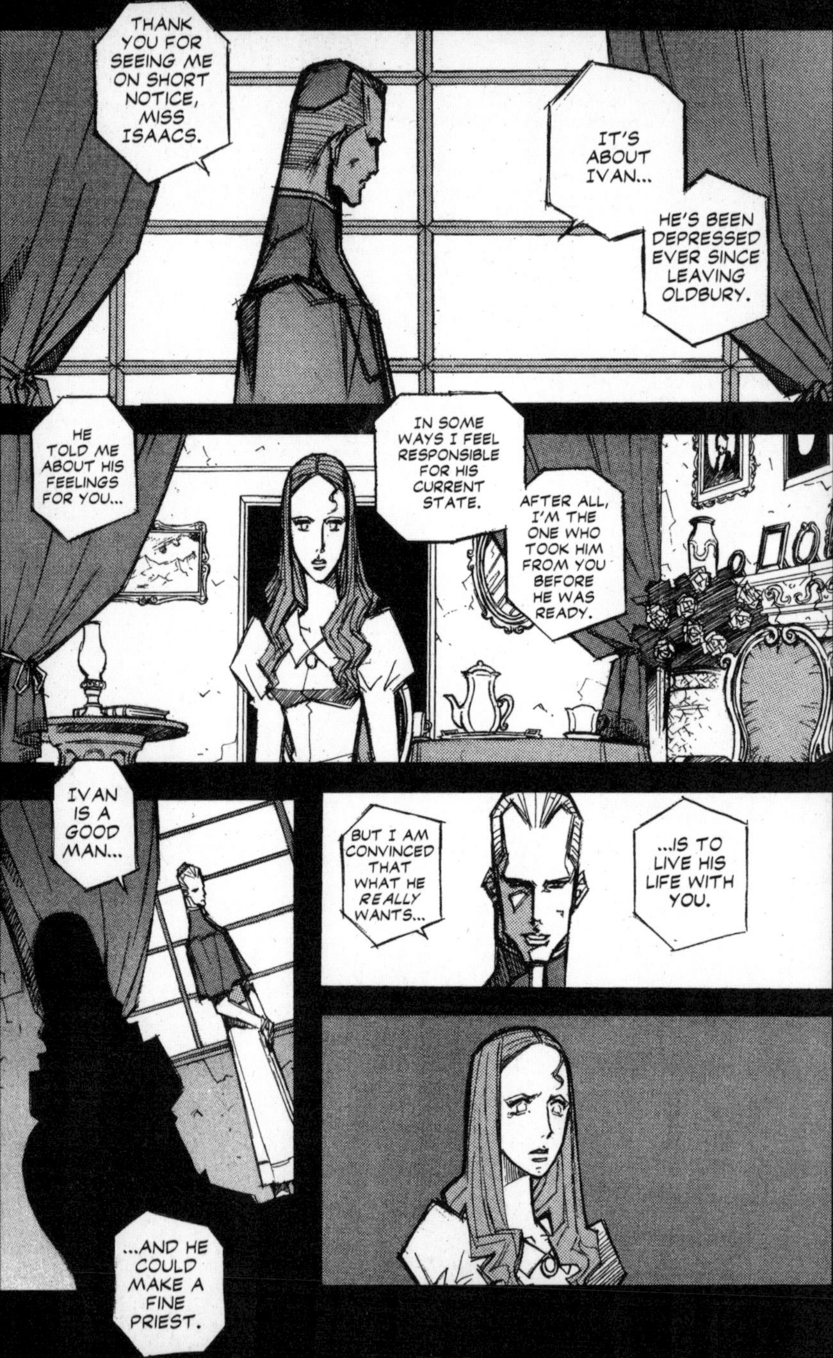
THANK YOU FOR SEEING ME ON SHORT NOTICE, MISS ISAACS.
IT'S ABOUT IVAN...
HE'S BEEN DEPRESSED EVER SINCE LEAVING OLDBURY.
HE TOLD ME ABOUT HIS FEELINGS FOR YOU...
IN SOME WAYS I FEEL RESPONSIBLE FOR HIS CURRENT STATE.
AFTER ALL, I'M THE ONE WHO TOOK HIM FROM YOU BEFORE HE WAS READY.
IVAN IS A GOOD MAN...
...AND HE COULD MAKE A FINE PRIEST.
BUT I AM CONVINCED THAT WHAT HE *REALLY* WANTS...
...IS TO LIVE HIS LIFE WITH YOU.

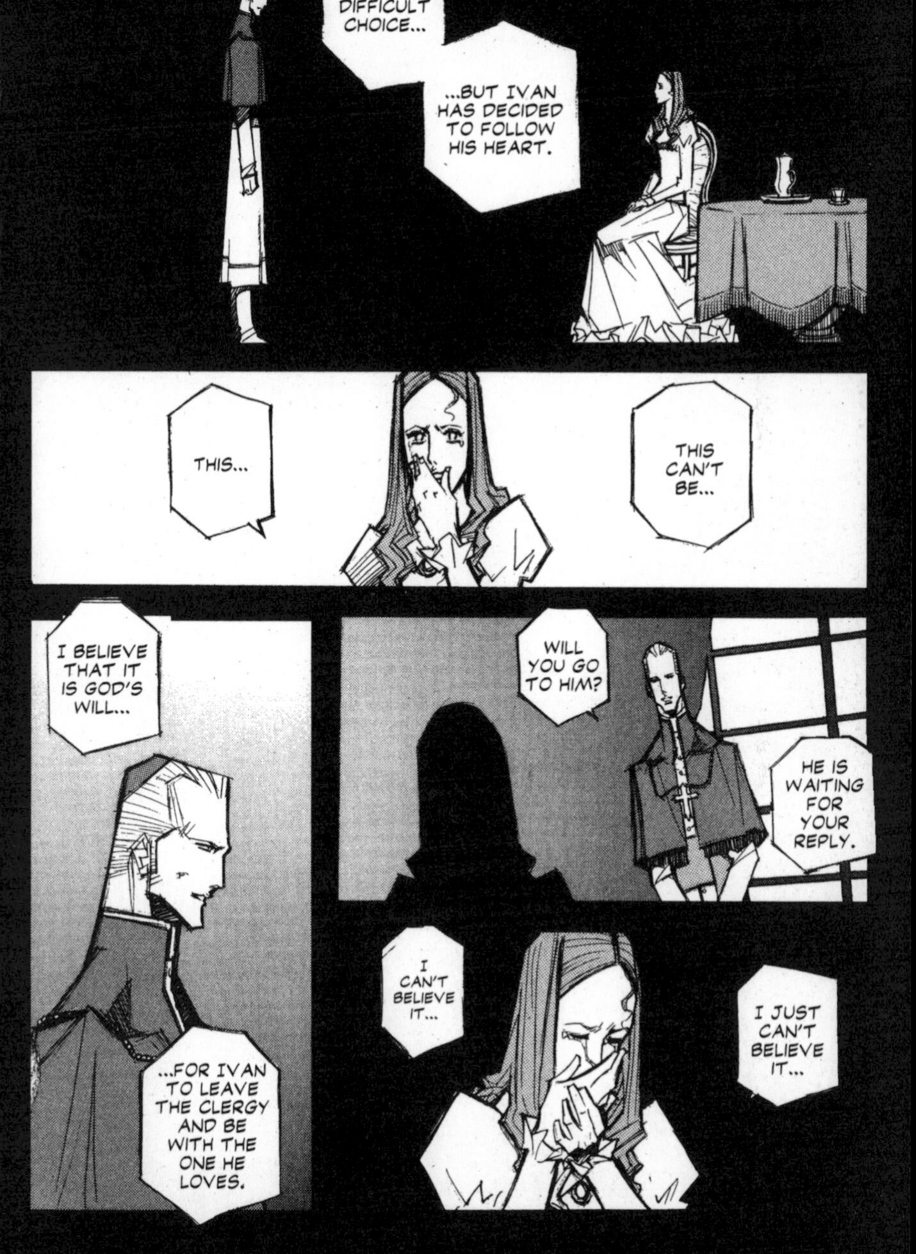
DIFFICULT CHOICE...
...BUT IVAN HAS DECIDED TO FOLLOW HIS HEART.
THIS...
THIS CAN'T BE...
I BELIEVE THAT IT IS GOD'S WILL...
...FOR IVAN TO LEAVE THE CLERGY AND BE WITH THE ONE HE LOVES.
WILL YOU GO TO HIM?
HE IS WAITING FOR YOUR REPLY.
I CAN'T BELIEVE IT...
I JUST CAN'T BELIEVE IT...

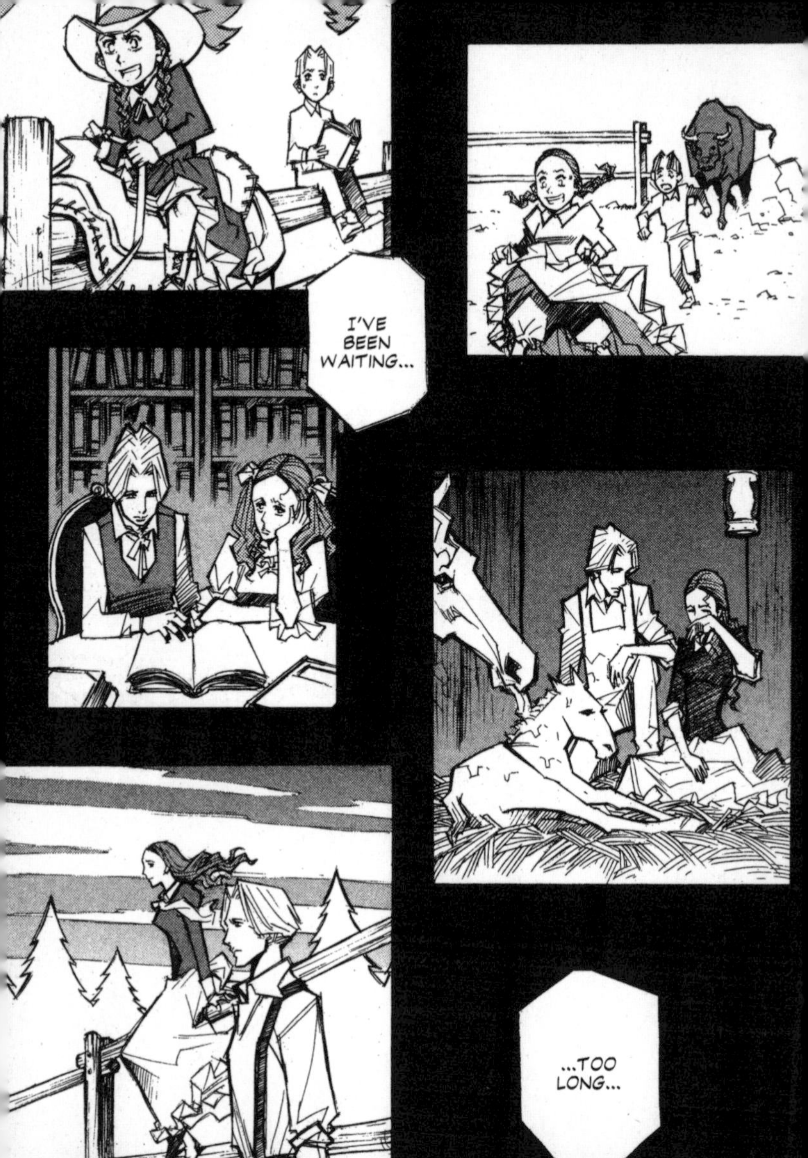
I'VE BEEN WAITING...
...TOO LONG...

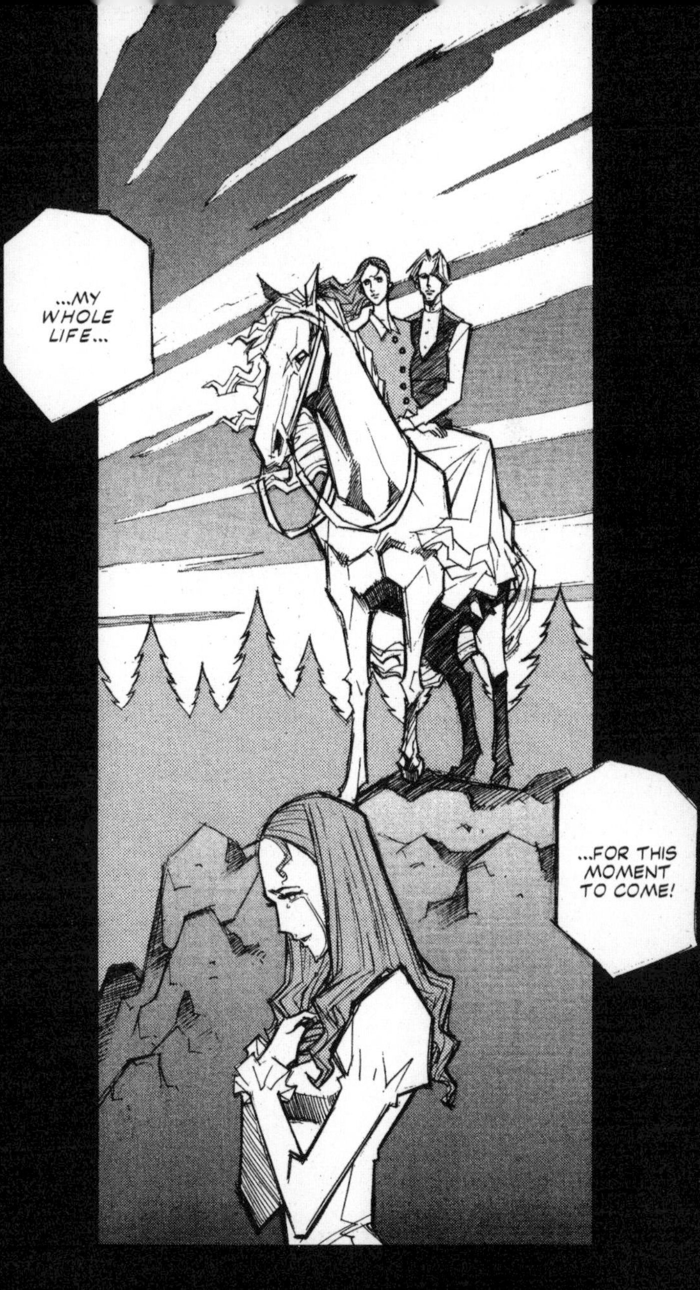
...MY WHOLE LIFE...
...FOR THIS MOMENT TO COME!

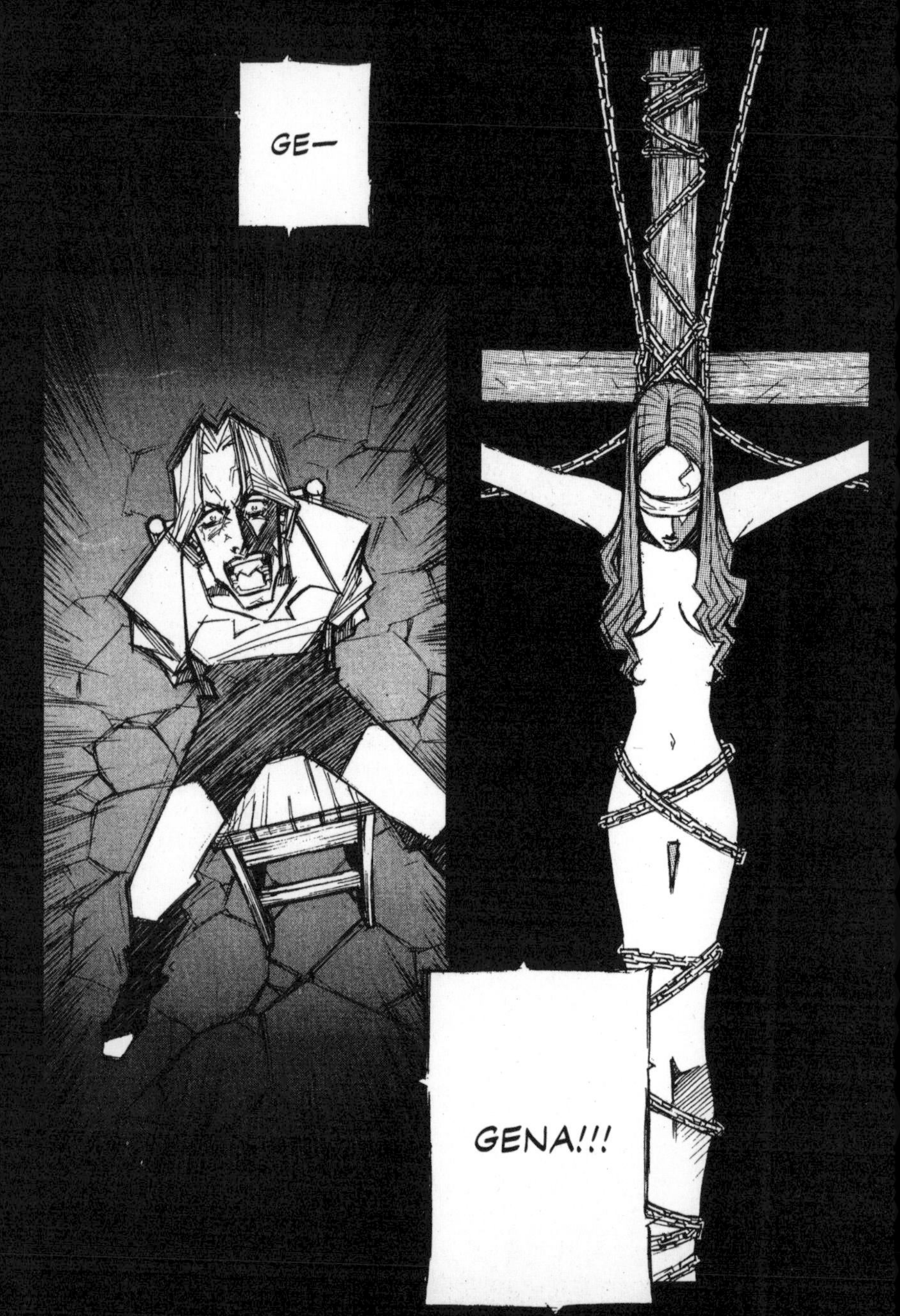
GE—
GENA!!!

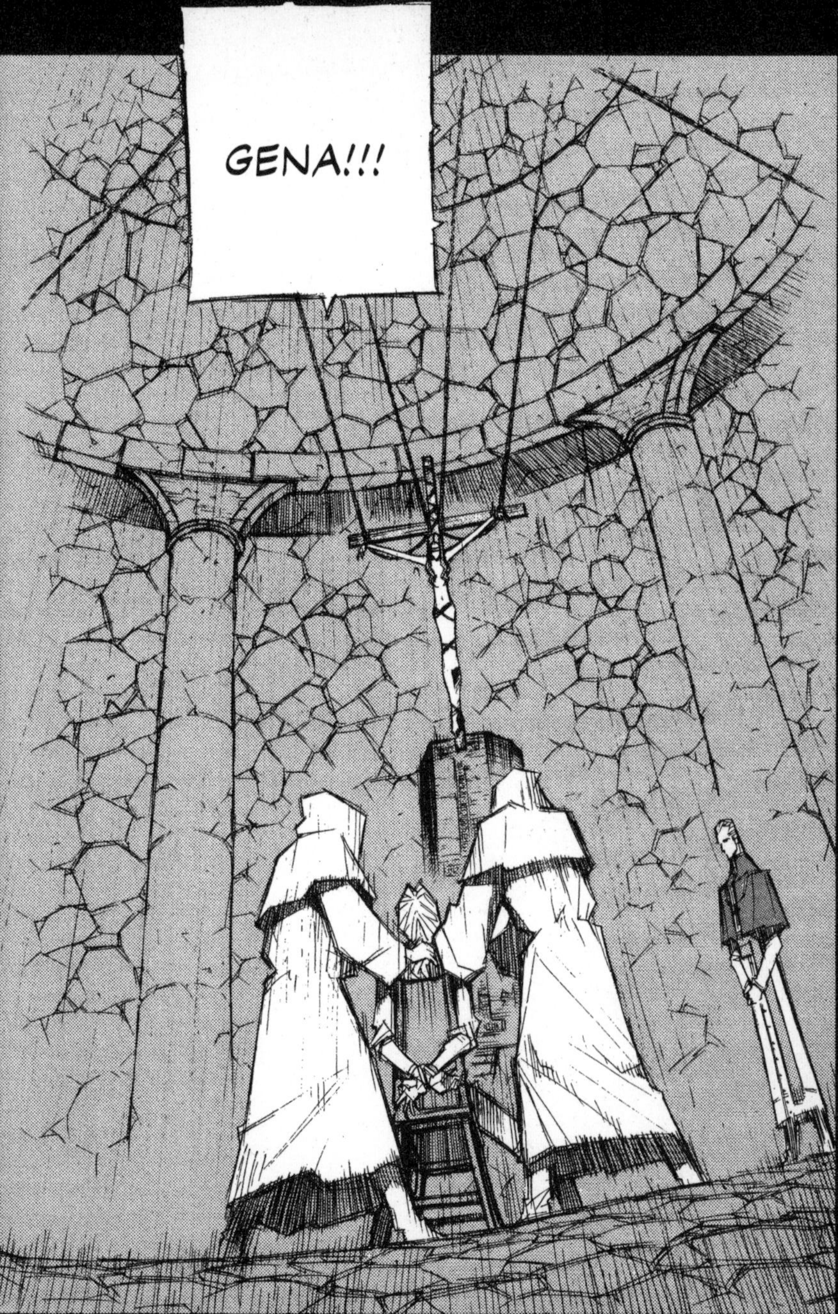
GENA!!!

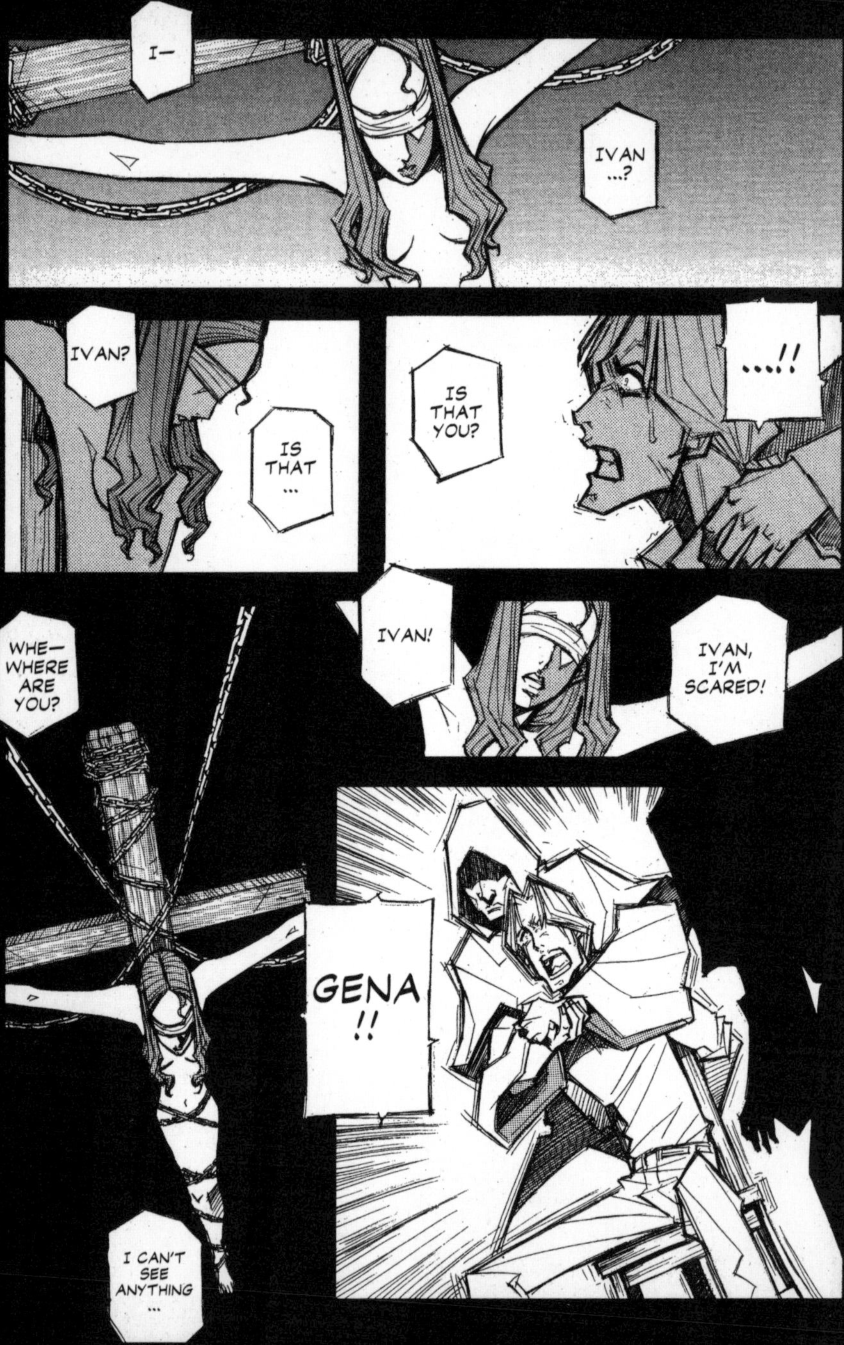
I—
IVAN ...?
IVAN?
IS THAT ...
IS THAT YOU?
...!!
WHE— WHERE ARE YOU?
I CAN'T SEE ANYTHING ...
IVAN!
IVAN, I'M SCARED!
GENA !!

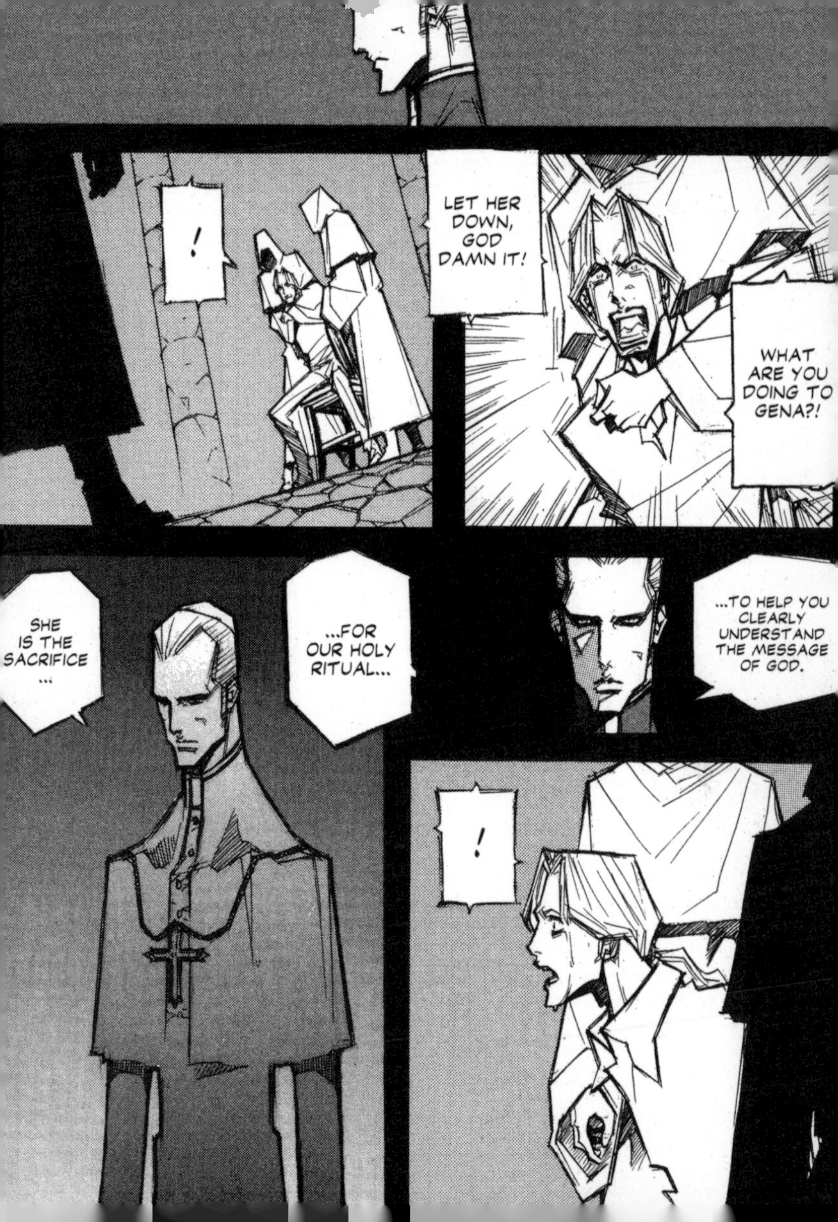
!
LET HER DOWN, GOD DAMN IT!
WHAT ARE YOU DOING TO GENA?!
SHE IS THE SACRIFICE ...
...FOR OUR HOLY RITUAL...
...TO HELP YOU CLEARLY UNDERSTAND THE MESSAGE OF GOD.
!

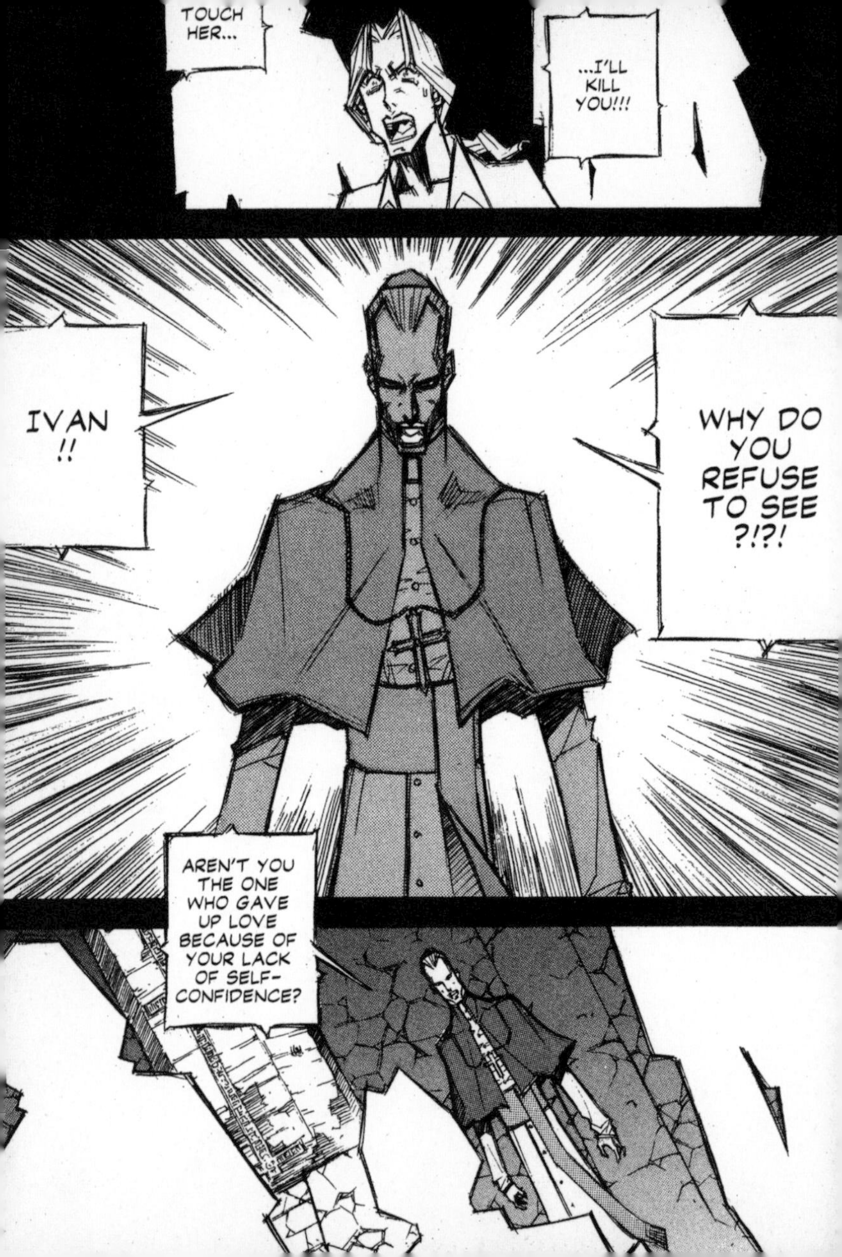
TOUCH HER...
...I'LL KILL YOU!!!
IVAN !!
WHY DO YOU REFUSE TO SEE ?!?!
AREN'T YOU THE ONE WHO GAVE UP LOVE BECAUSE OF YOUR LACK OF SELF-CONFIDENCE?

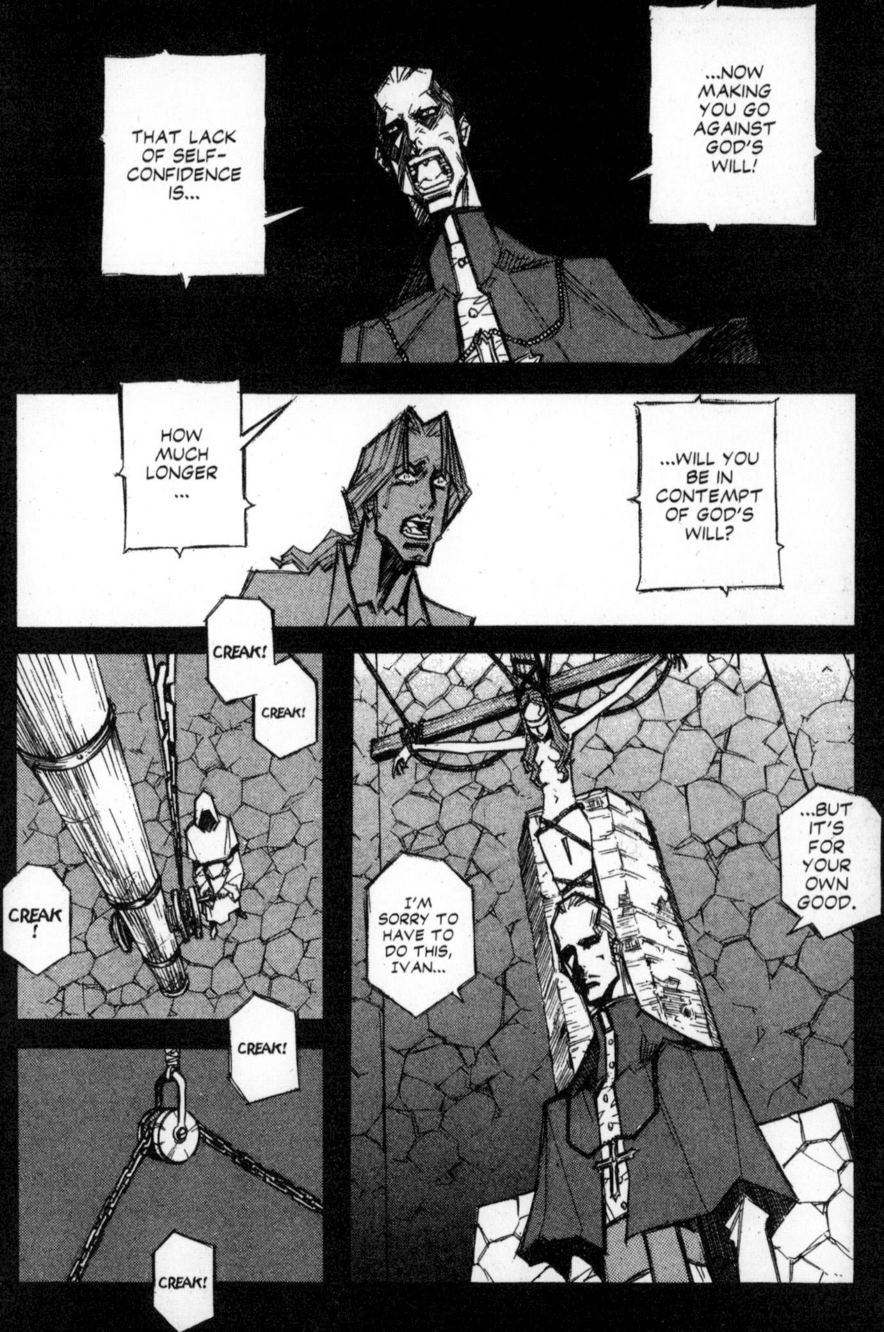
THAT LACK OF SELF-CONFIDENCE IS...
...NOW MAKING YOU GO AGAINST GOD'S WILL!
HOW MUCH LONGER ...
...WILL YOU BE IN CONTEMPT OF GOD'S WILL?
CREAK!
CREAK!
CREAK!
CREAK!
CREAK!
I'M SORRY TO HAVE TO DO THIS, IVAN...
...BUT IT'S FOR YOUR OWN GOOD.

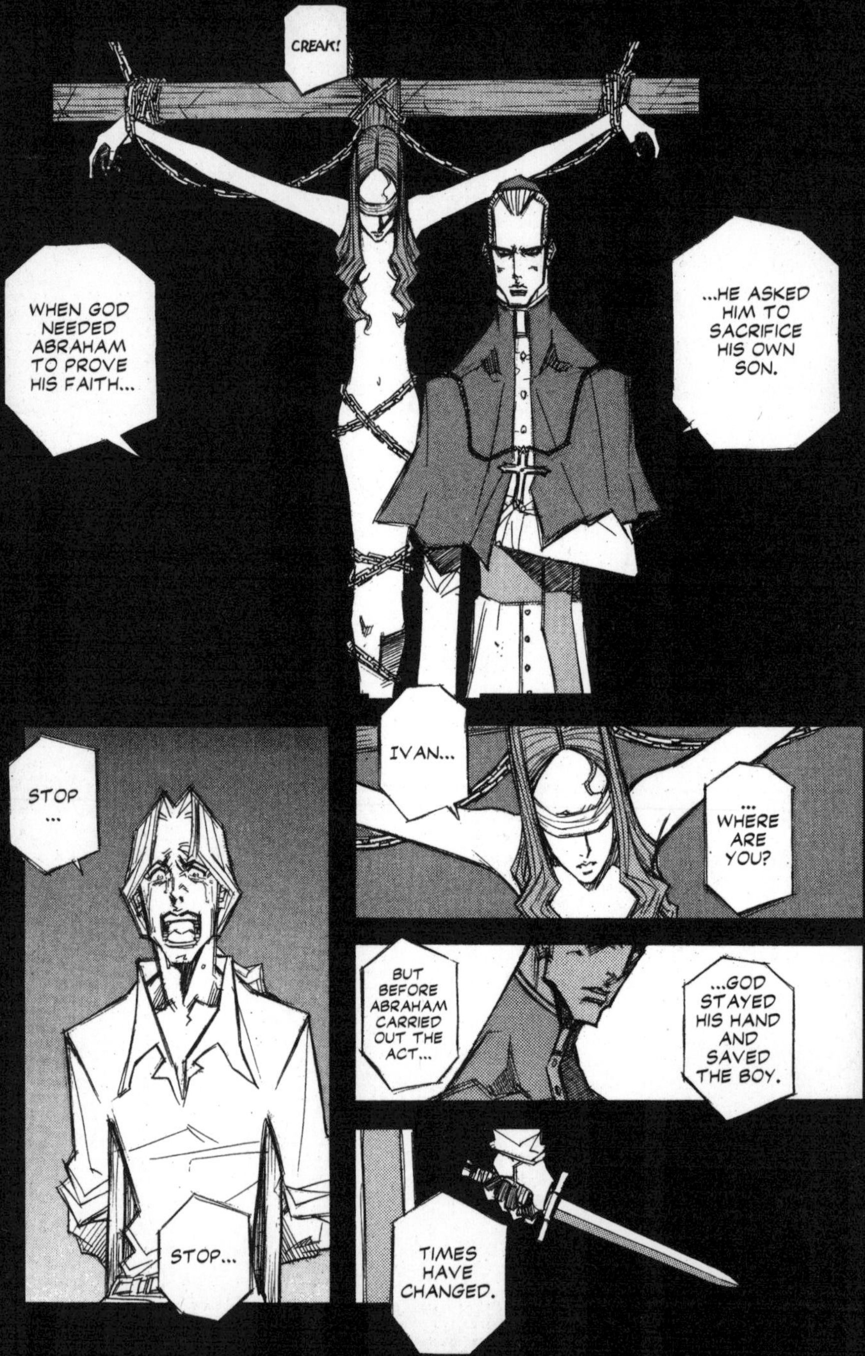
CREAK!
WHEN GOD NEEDED ABRAHAM TO PROVE HIS FAITH...
...HE ASKED HIM TO SACRIFICE HIS OWN SON.
STOP ...
STOP...
IVAN...
... WHERE ARE YOU?
BUT BEFORE ABRAHAM CARRIED OUT THE ACT...
...GOD STAYED HIS HAND AND SAVED THE BOY.
TIMES HAVE CHANGED.

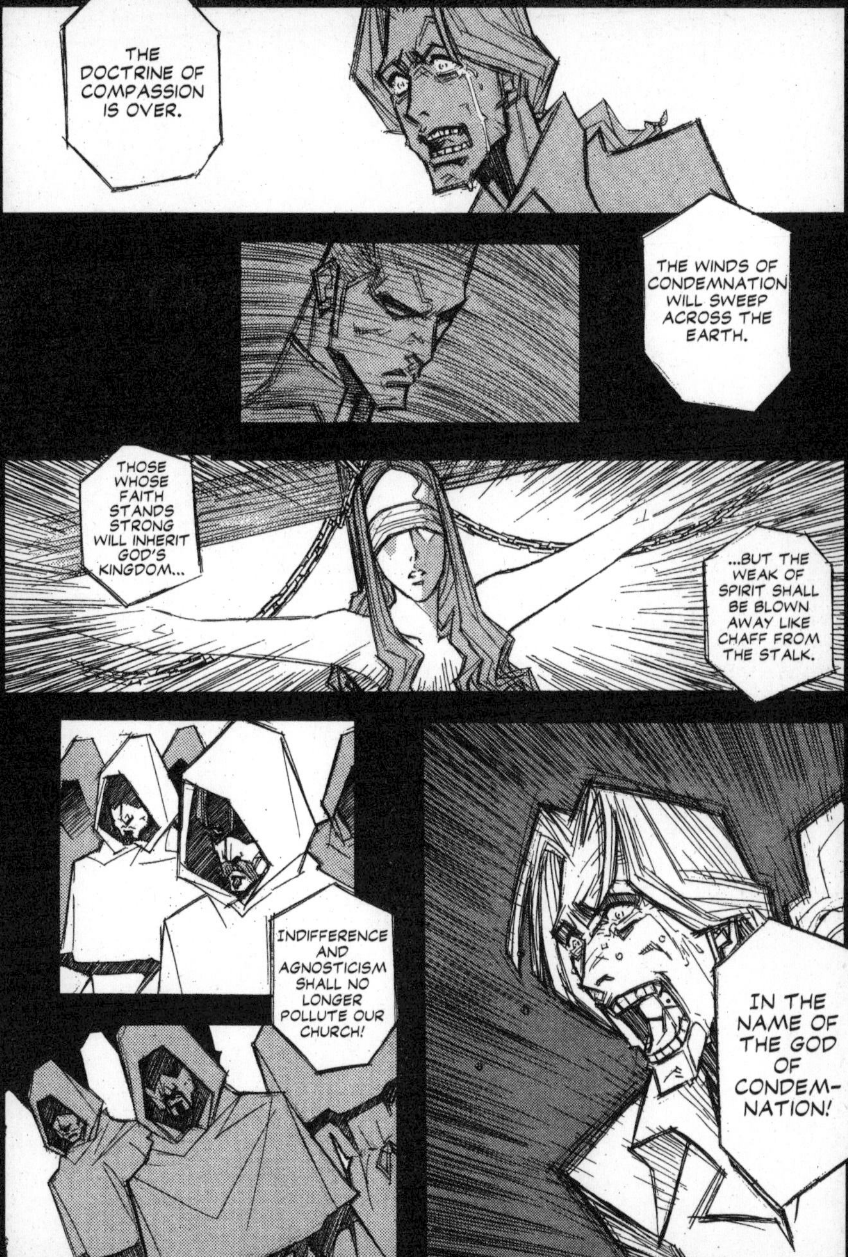
THE DOCTRINE OF COMPASSION IS OVER.
THE WINDS OF CONDEMNATION WILL SWEEP ACROSS THE EARTH.
THOSE WHOSE FAITH STANDS STRONG WILL INHERIT GOD'S KINGDOM...
...BUT THE WEAK OF SPIRIT SHALL BE BLOWN AWAY LIKE CHAFF FROM THE STALK.
INDIFFERENCE AND AGNOSTICISM SHALL NO LONGER POLLUTE OUR CHURCH!
IN THE NAME OF THE GOD OF CONDEM-NATION!

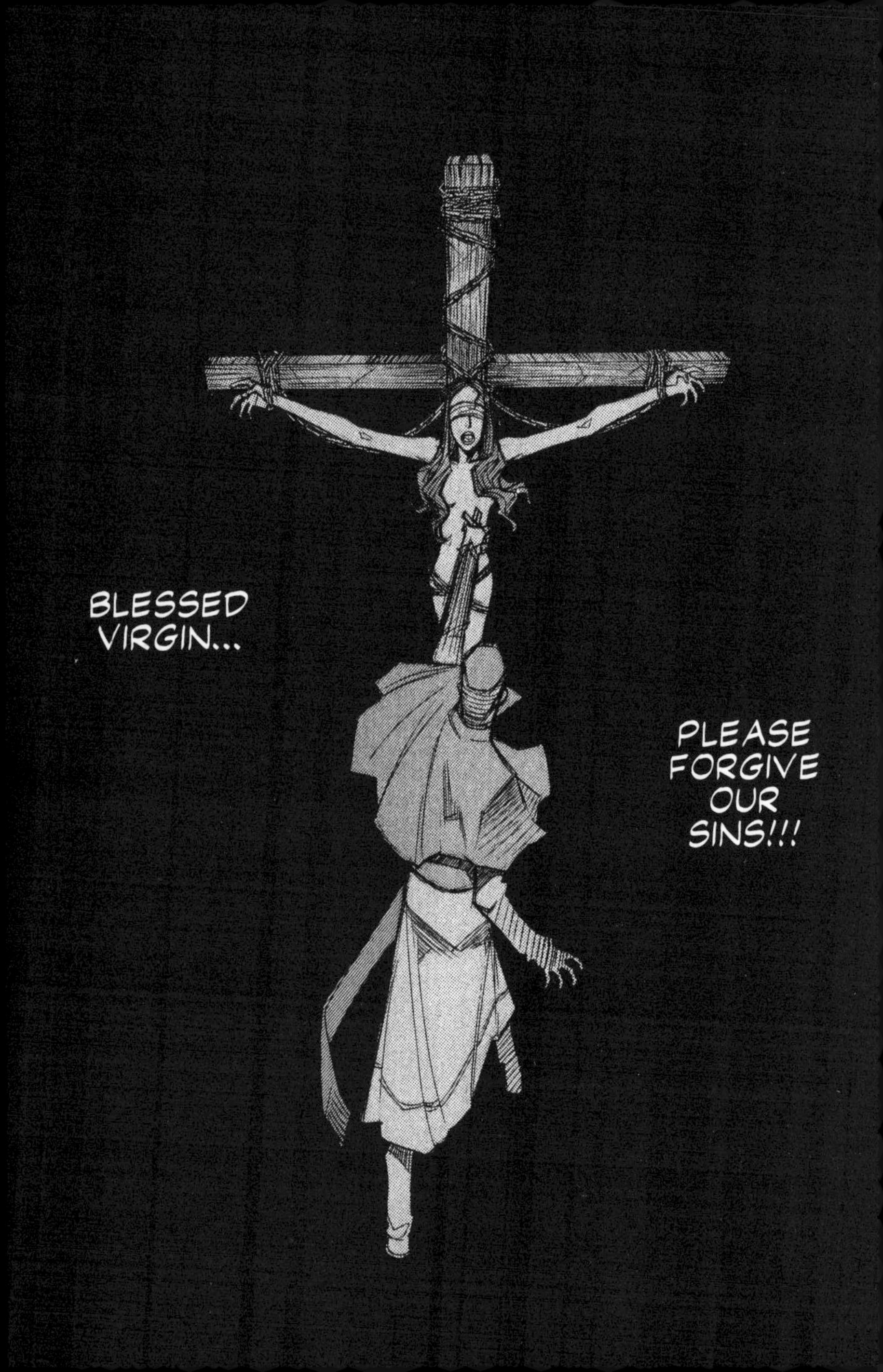
BLESSED VIRGIN...
PLEASE FORGIVE OUR SINS!!!

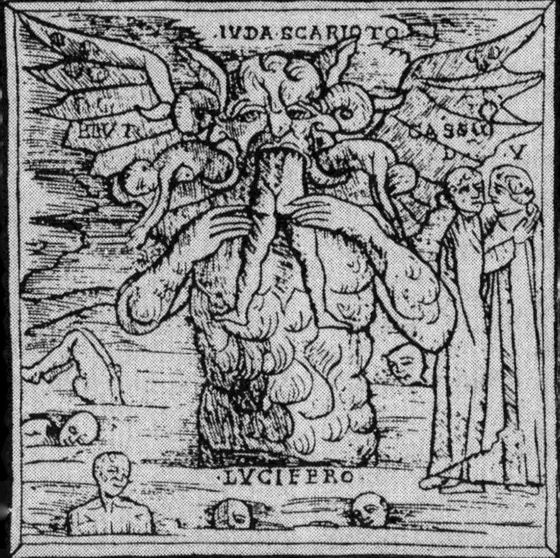
IVDA SCARIOTO
LVCIFERO

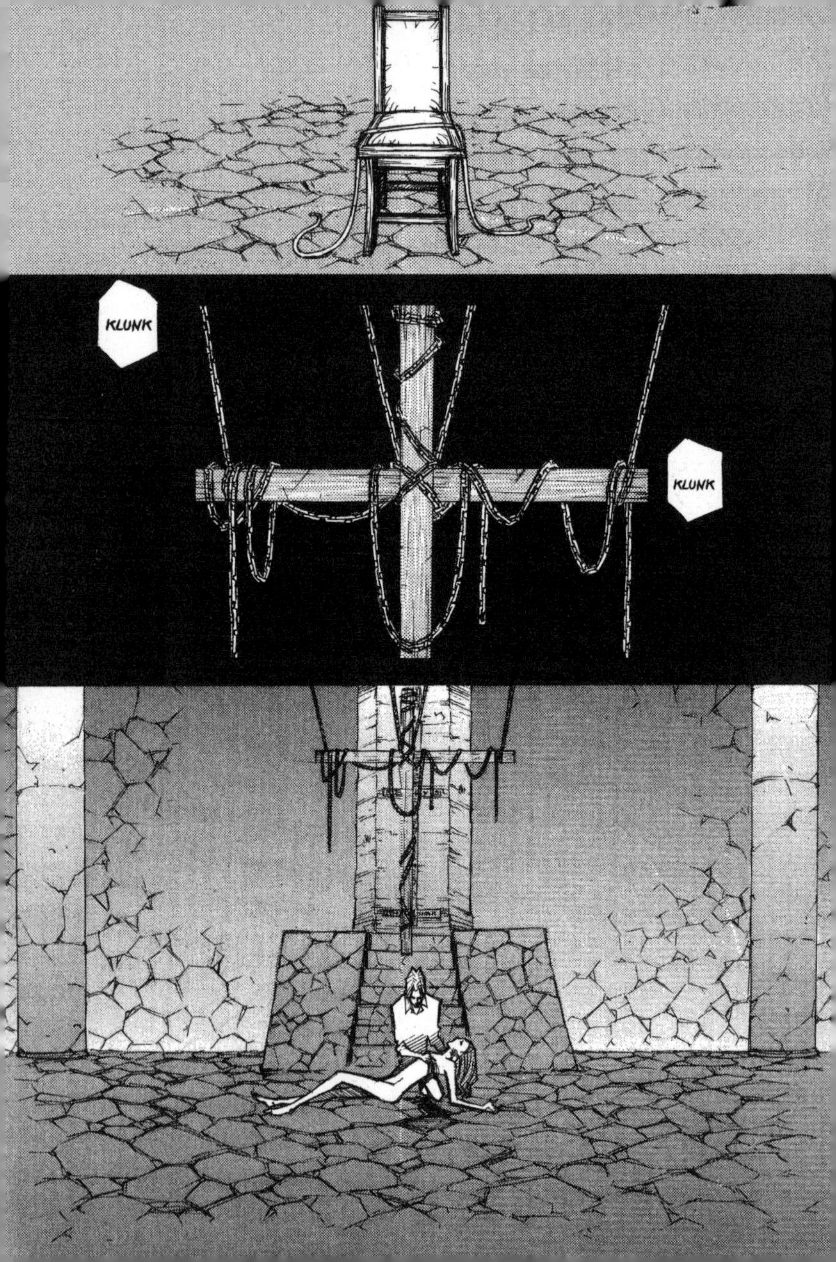
KLUNK
KLUNK

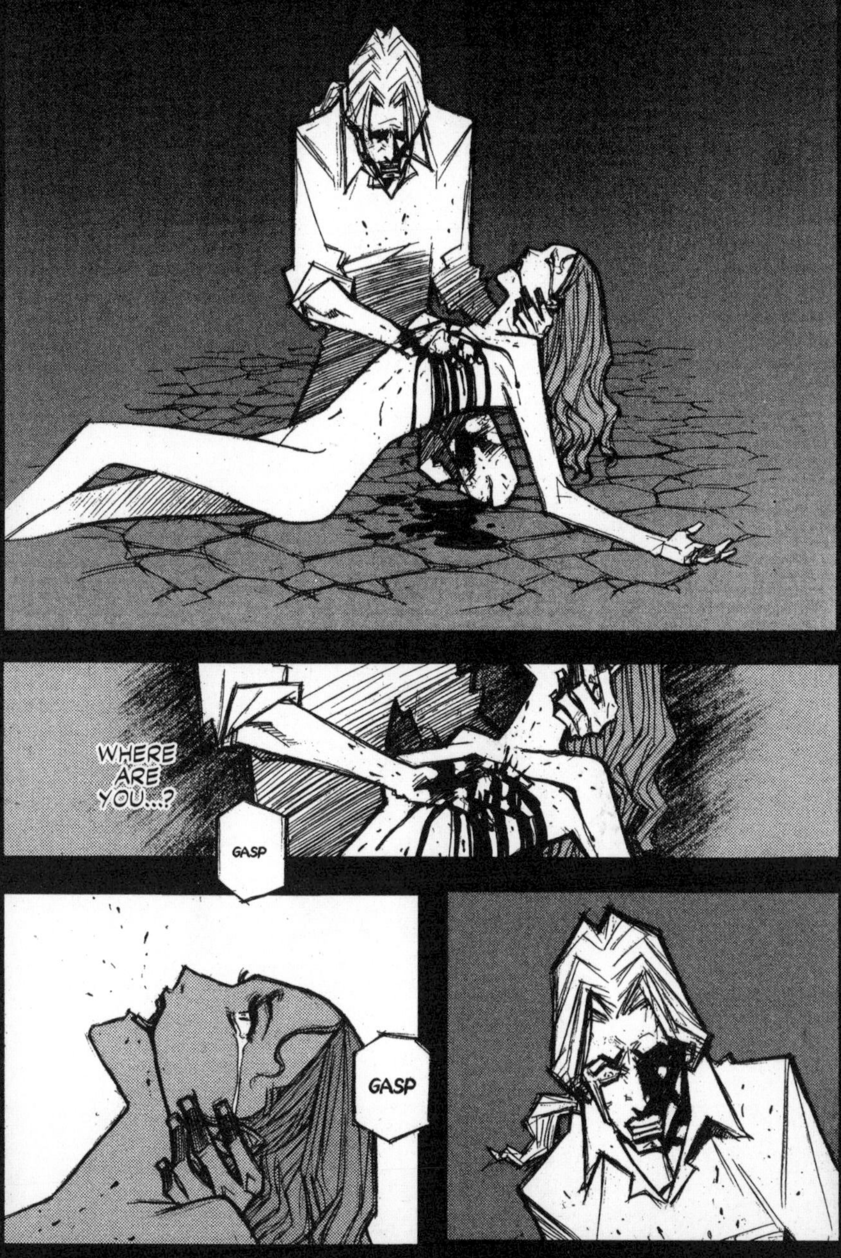
WHERE ARE YOU...?
GASP
GASP

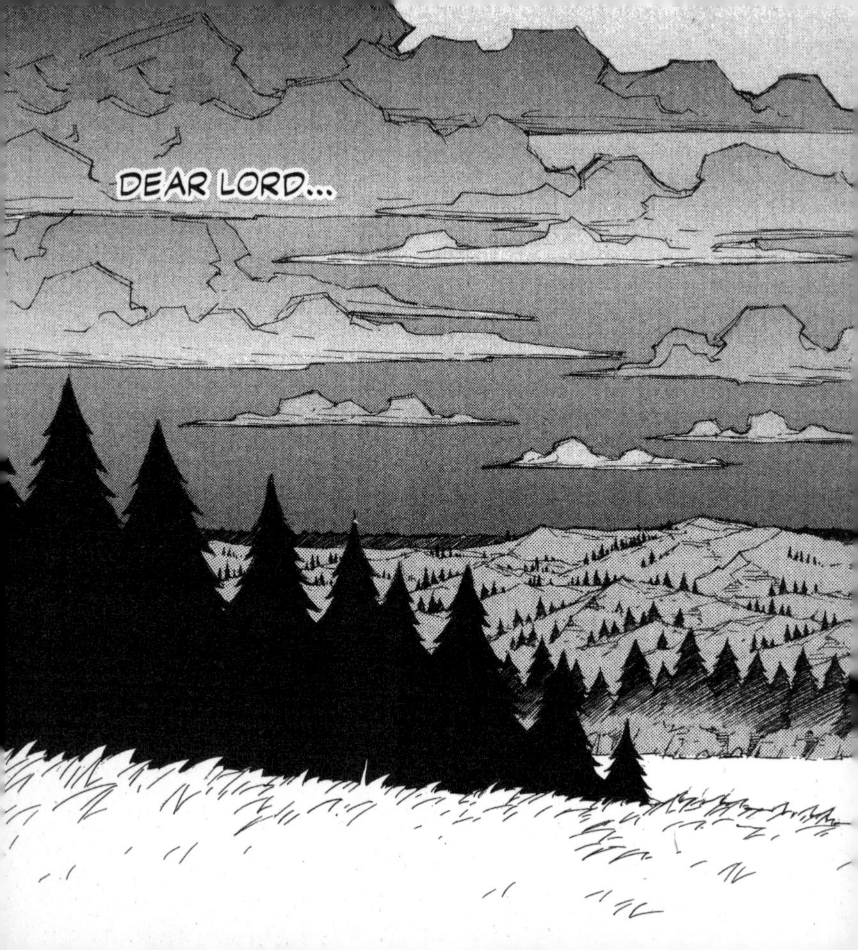
DEAR LORD...

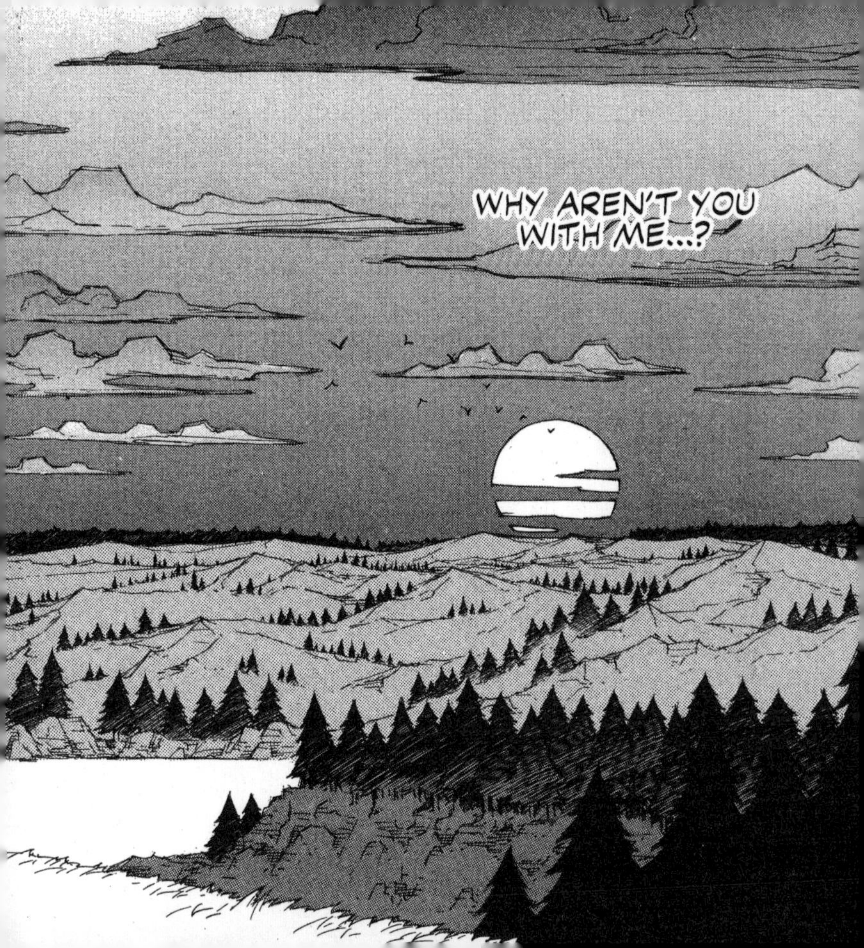
WHY AREN'T YOU WITH ME...?

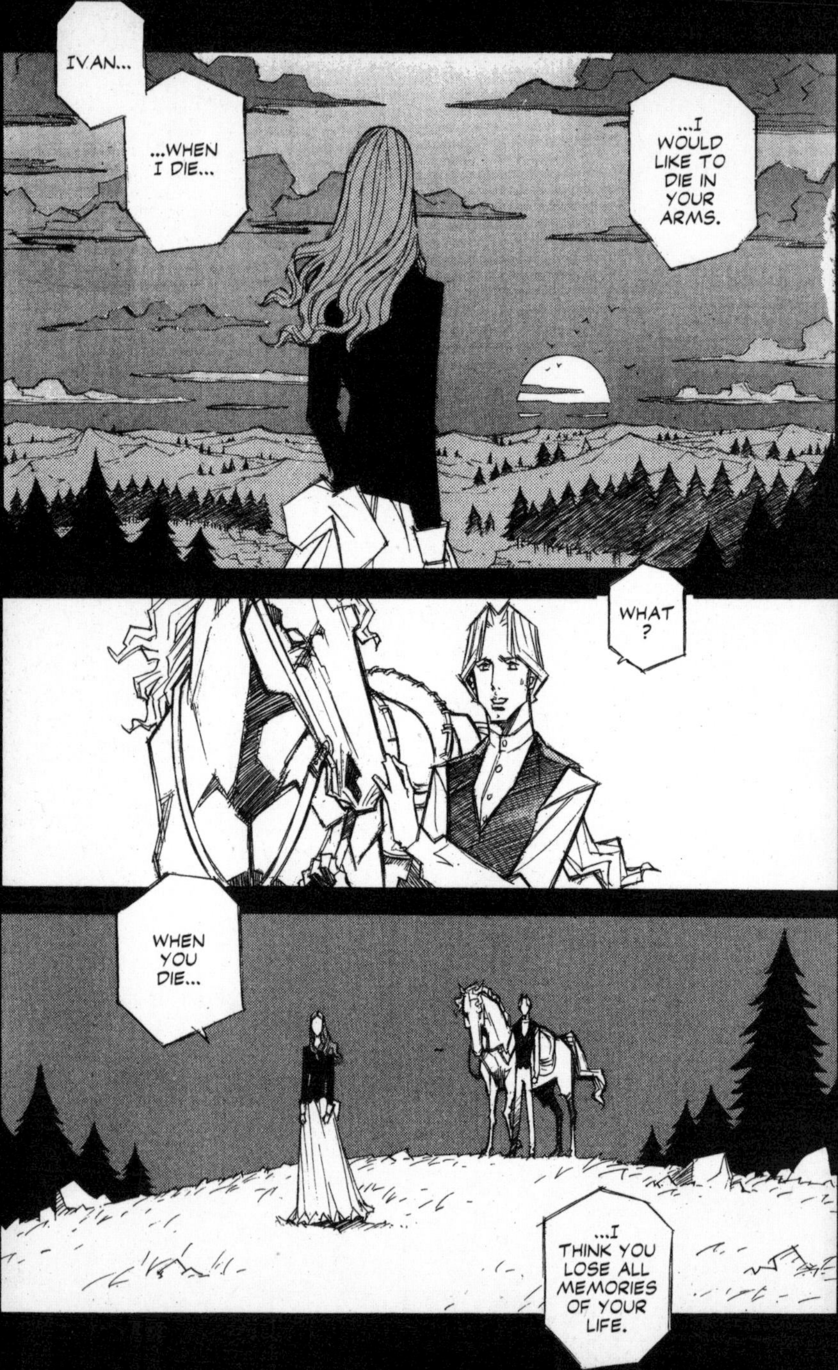
IVAN...
...WHEN I DIE...
...I WOULD LIKE TO DIE IN YOUR ARMS.
WHAT?
WHEN YOU DIE...
...I THINK YOU LOSE ALL MEMORIES OF YOUR LIFE.

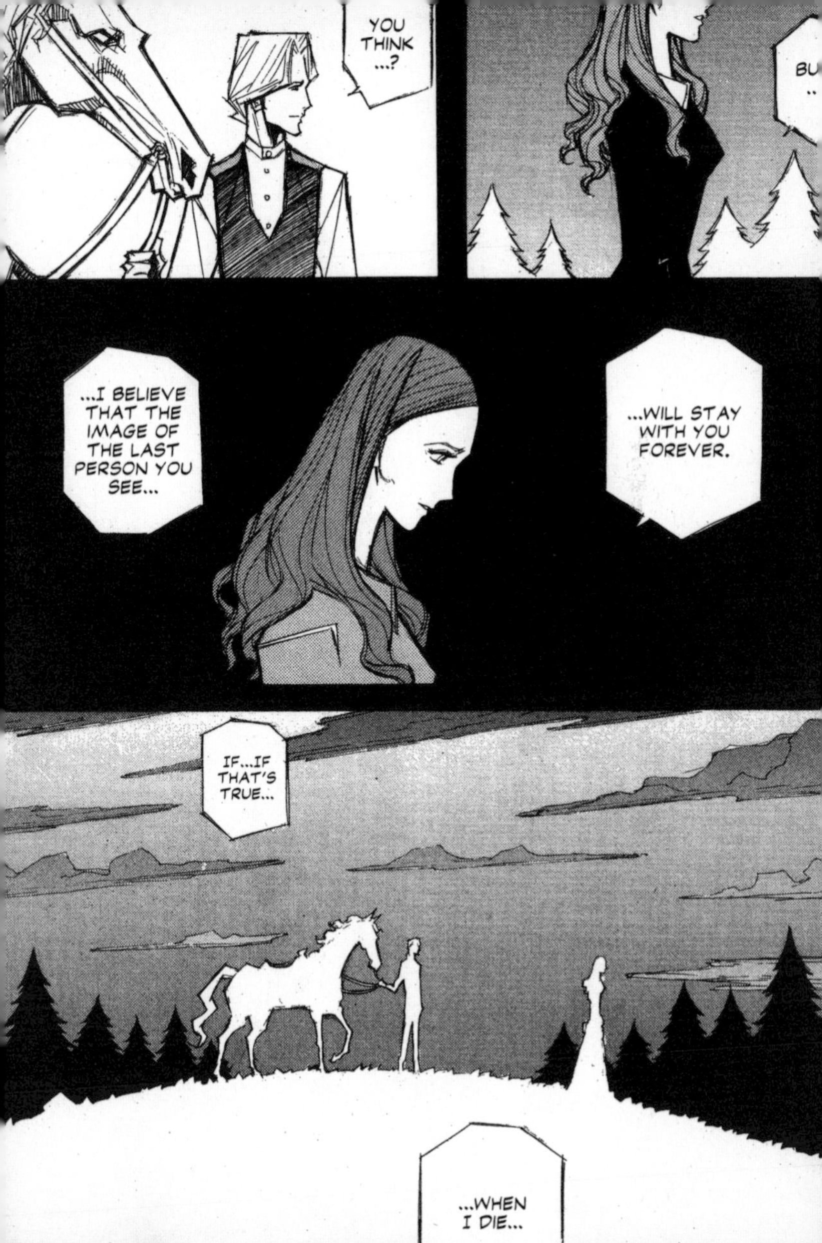
YOU THINK ...?
...I BELIEVE THAT THE IMAGE OF THE LAST PERSON YOU SEE...
...WILL STAY WITH YOU FOREVER.
IF...IF THAT'S TRUE...
...WHEN I DIE...

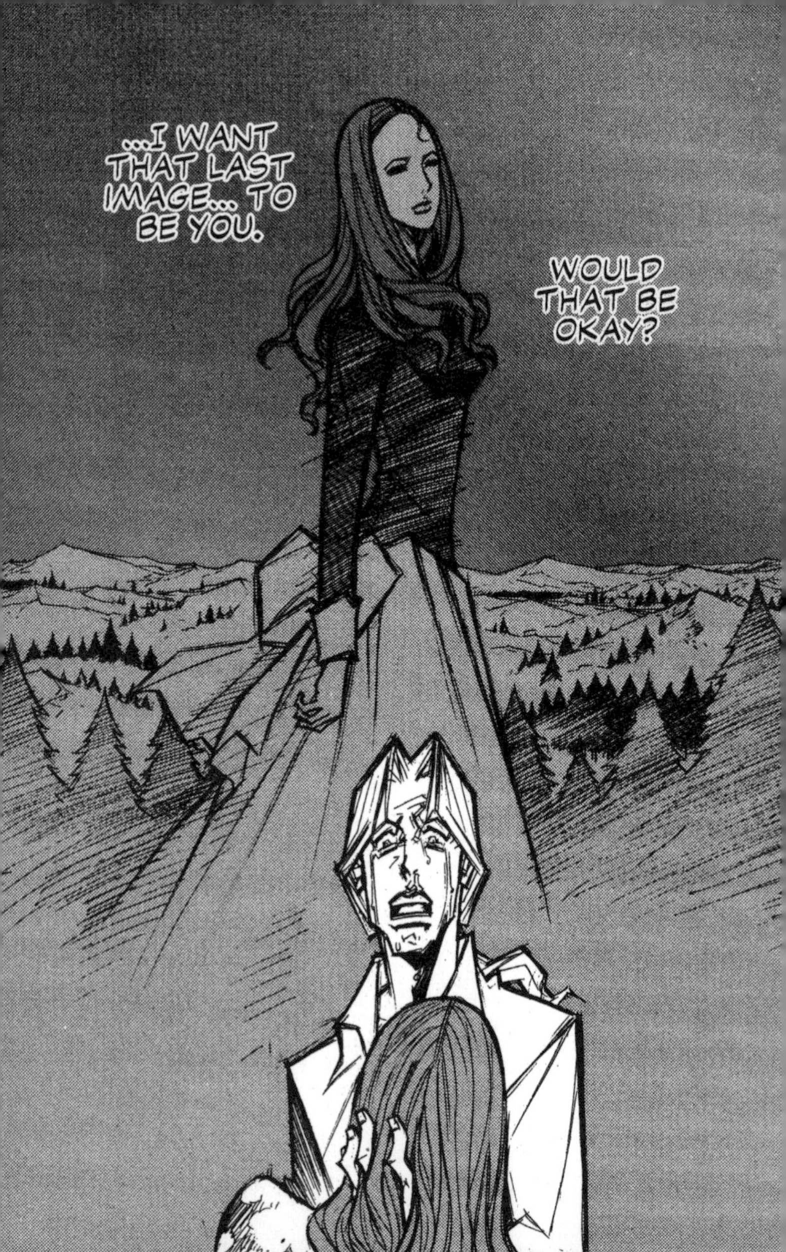
...I WANT THAT LAST IMAGE... TO BE YOU.
WOULD THAT BE OKAY?

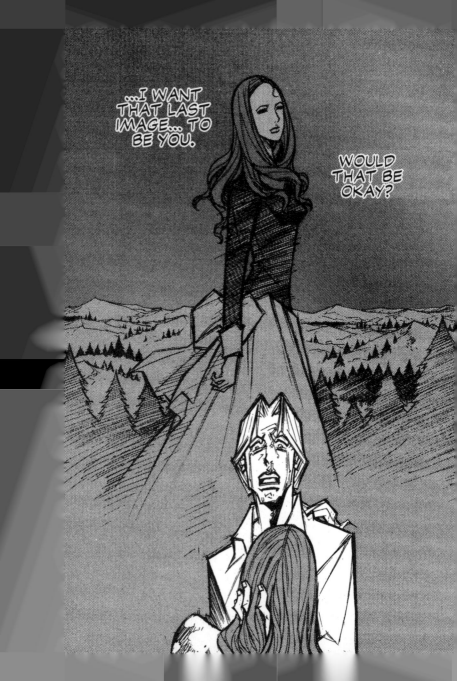

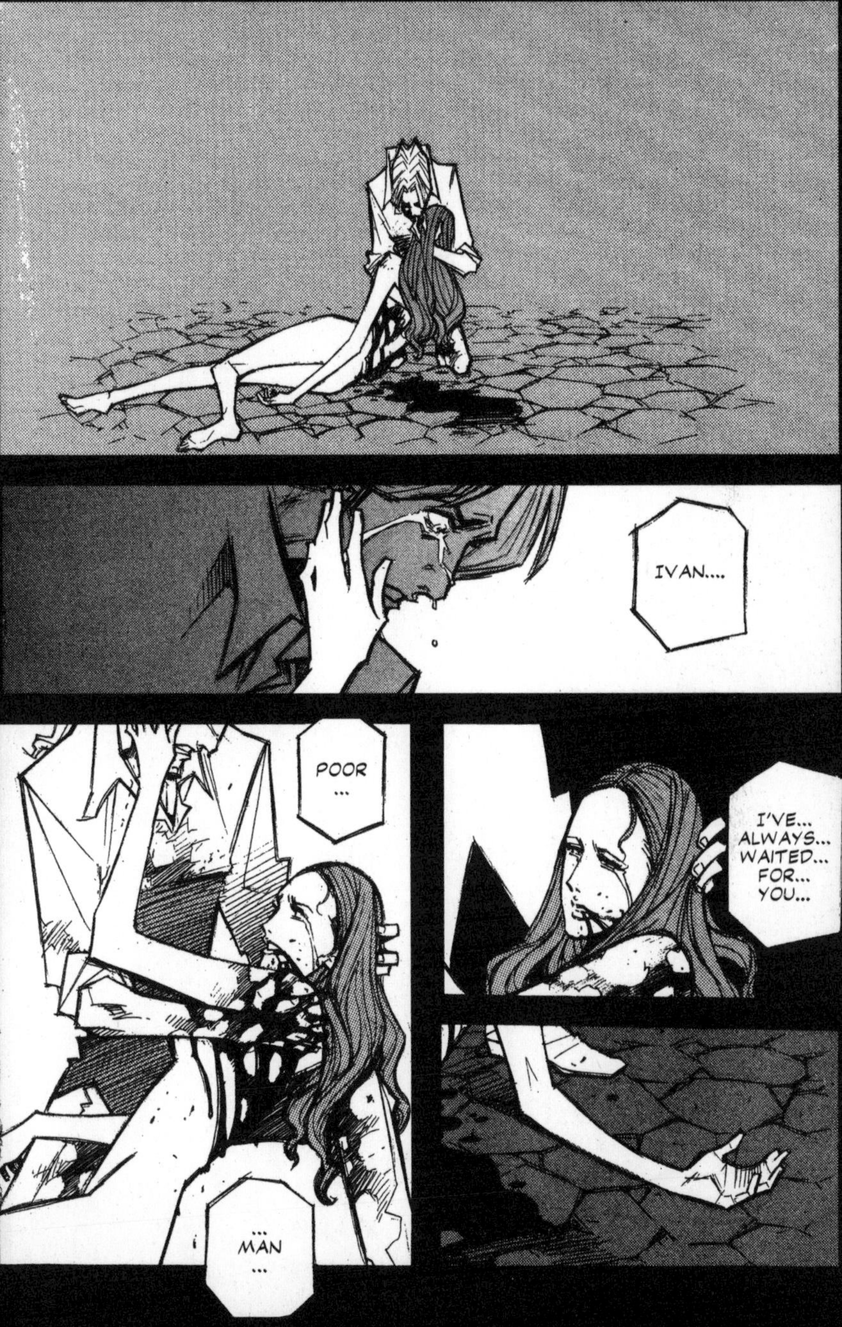
IVAN....
I'VE... ALWAYS... WAITED... FOR... YOU...
POOR ...
... MAN ...

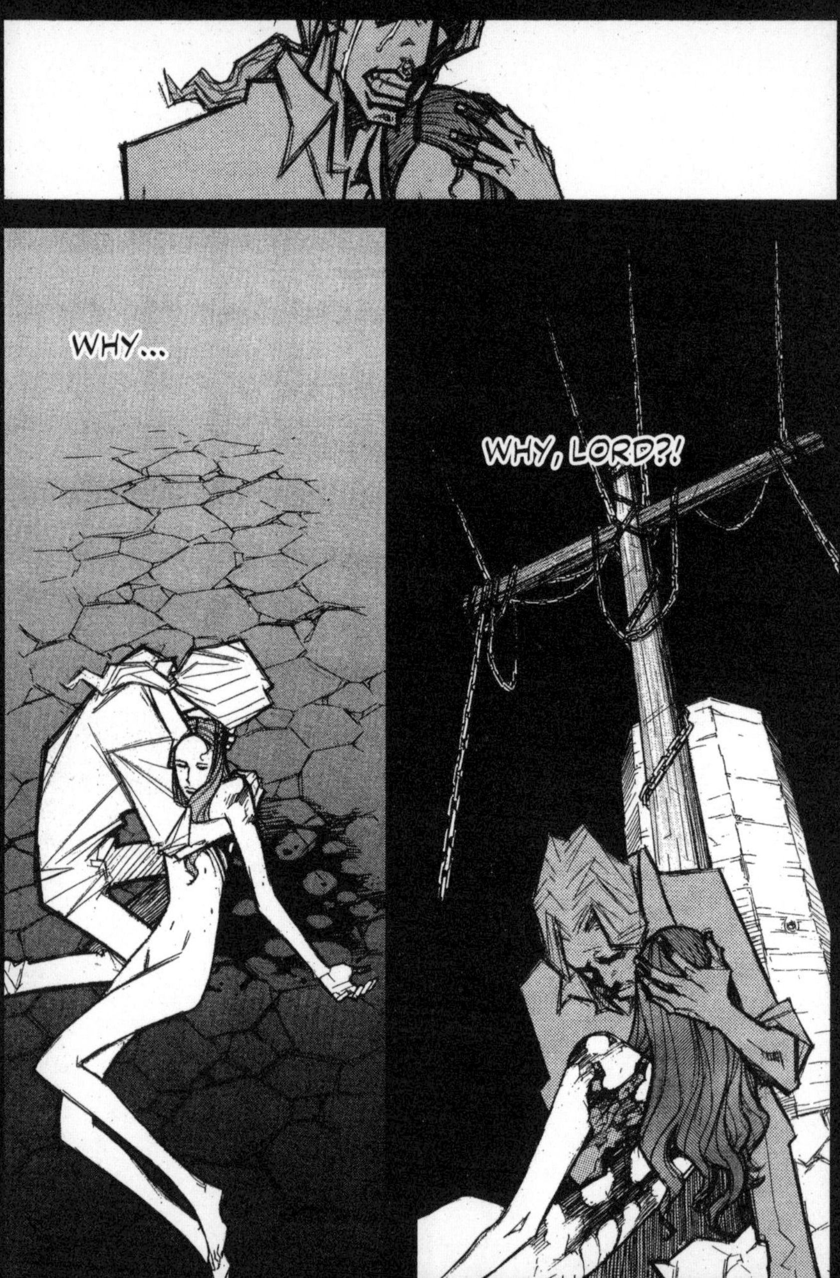
WHY...
WHY, LORD?!

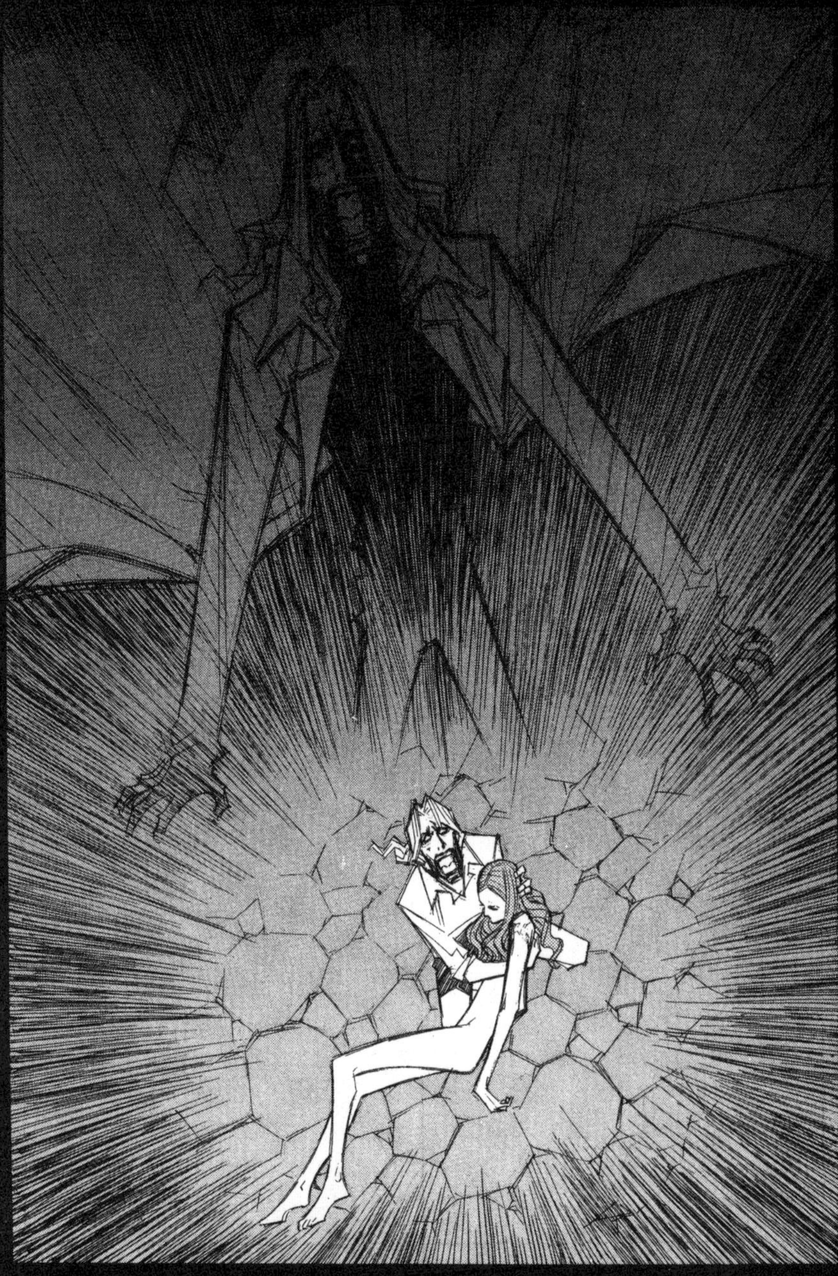

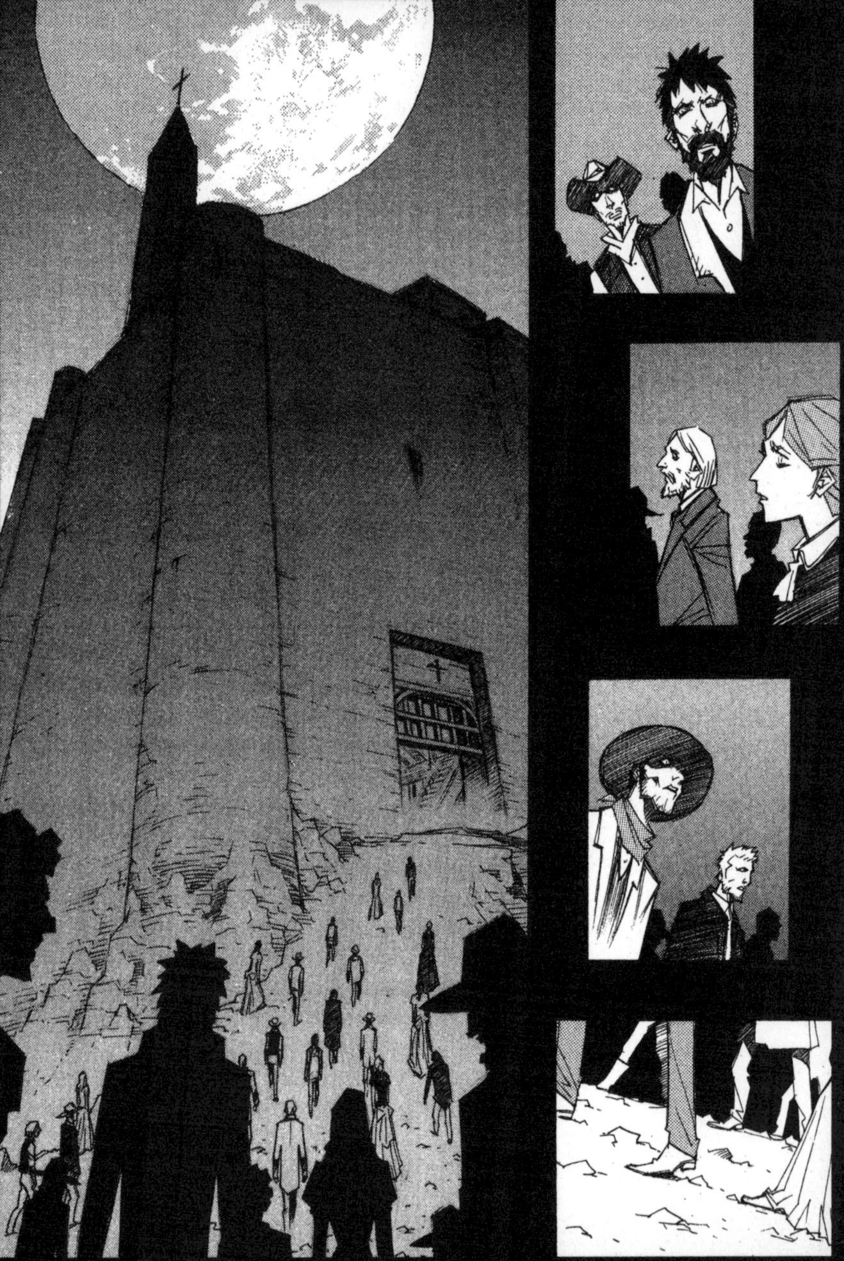

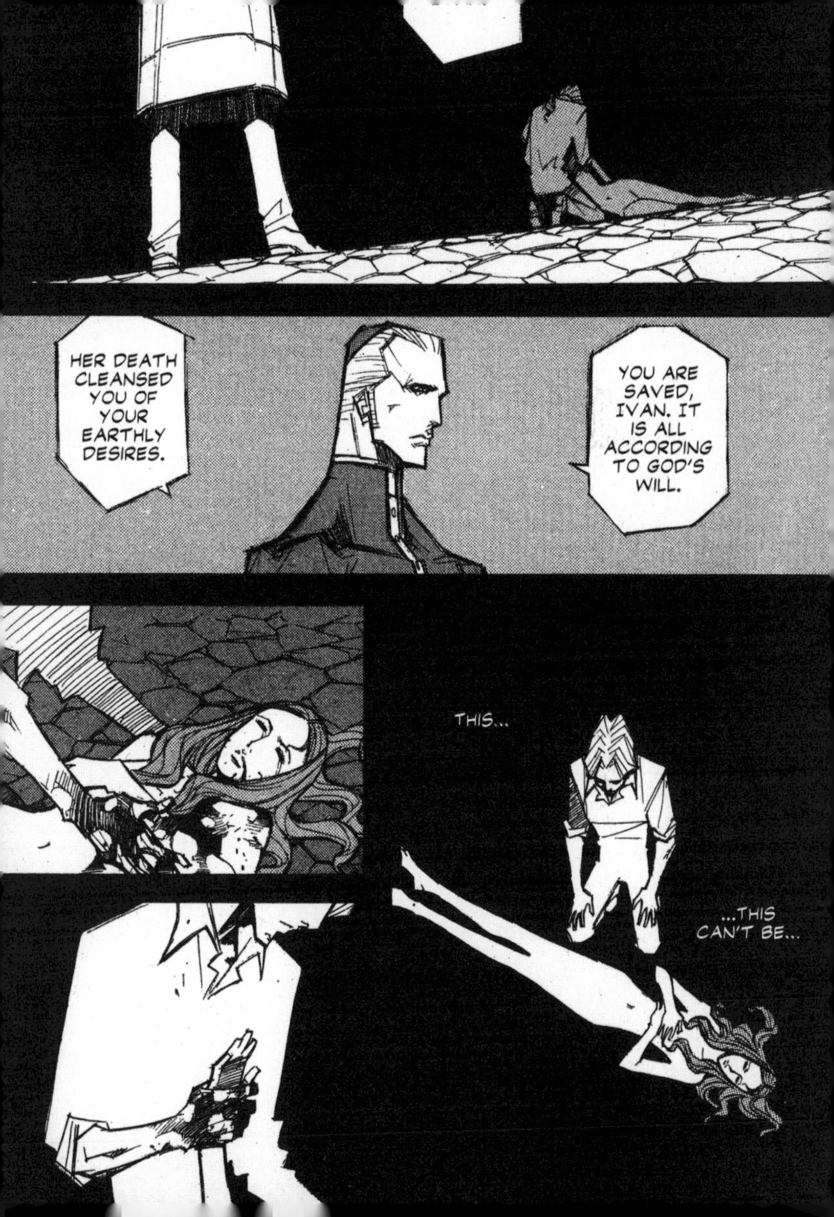
HER DEATH CLEANSED YOU OF YOUR EARTHLY DESIRES.
YOU ARE SAVED, IVAN. IT IS ALL ACCORDING TO GOD'S WILL.
THIS...
...THIS CAN'T BE...

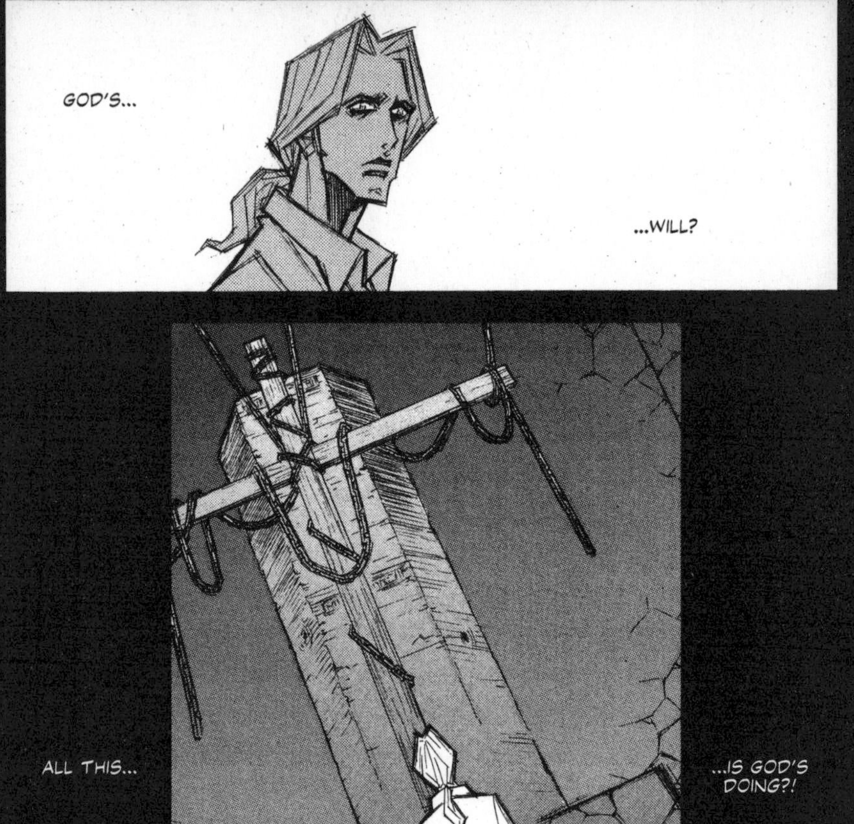
GOD'S...
...WILL?
ALL THIS...
...IS GOD'S DOING?!

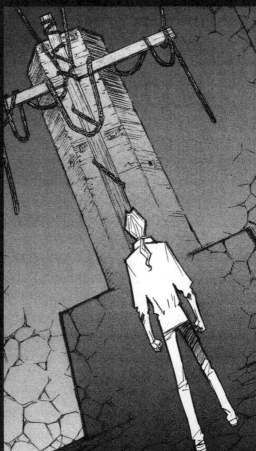

M∙d∙ſ

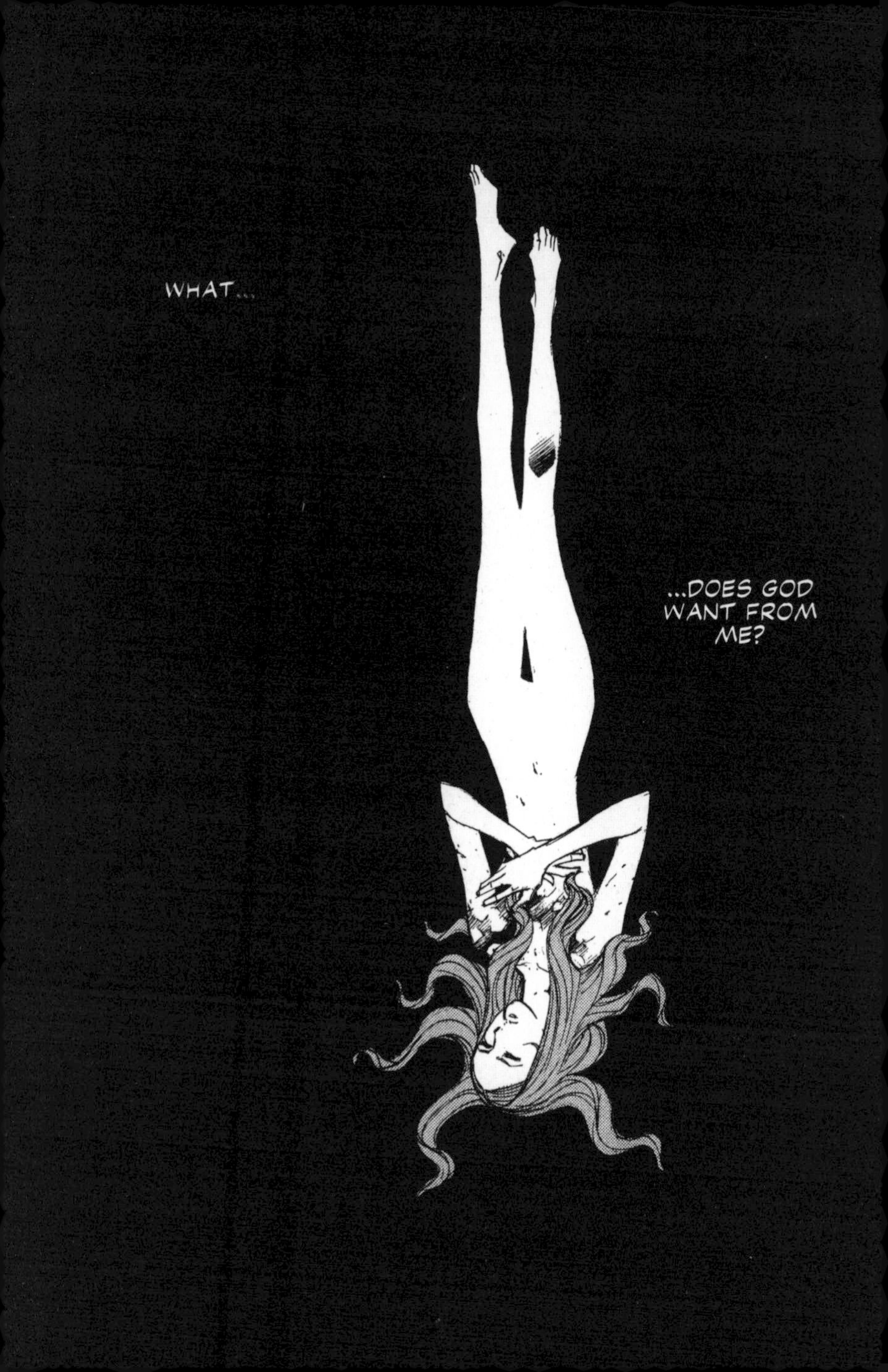
WHAT...
...DOES GOD WANT FROM ME?

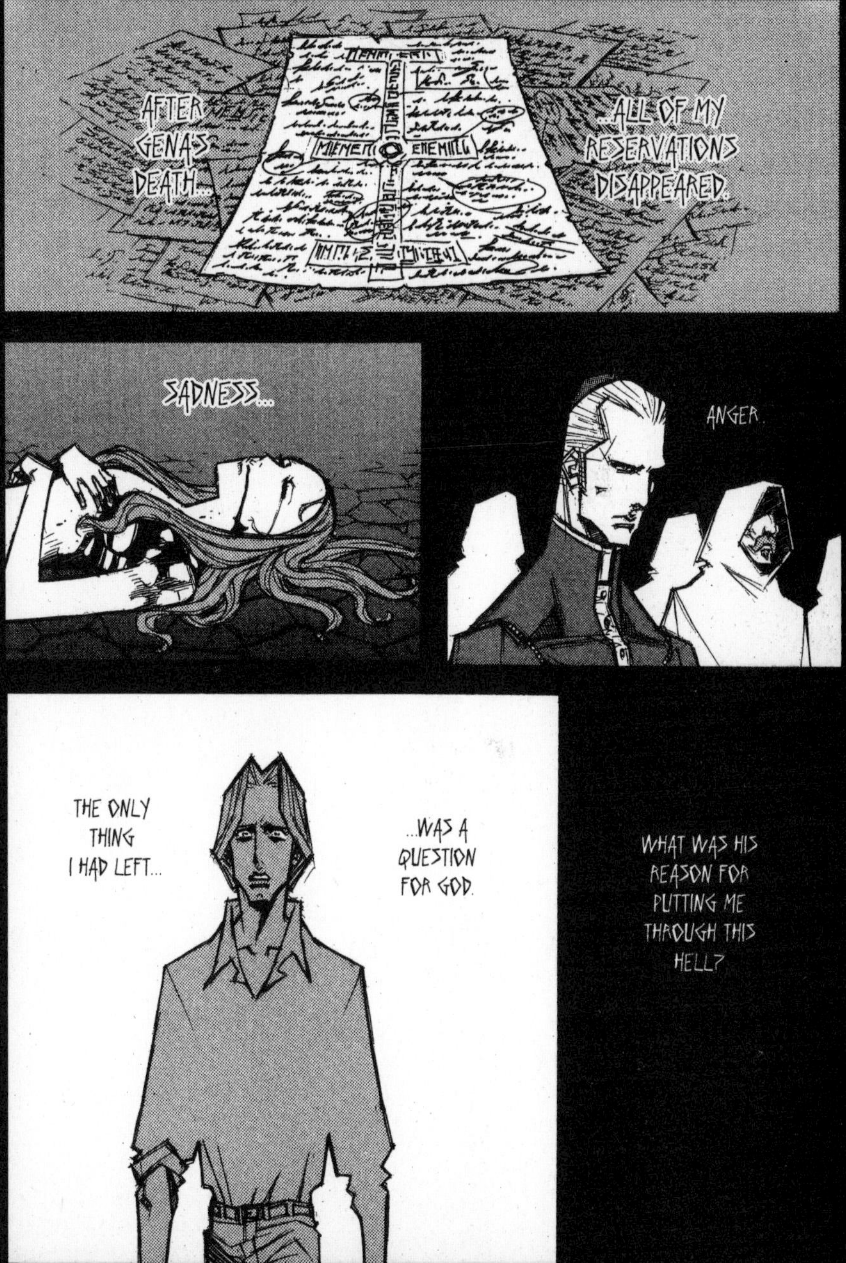
AFTER GENA'S DEATH...
...ALL OF MY RESERVATIONS DISAPPEARED.
SADNESS...
ANGER.
THE ONLY THING I HAD LEFT...
...WAS A QUESTION FOR GOD.
WHAT WAS HIS REASON FOR PUTTING ME THROUGH THIS HELL?

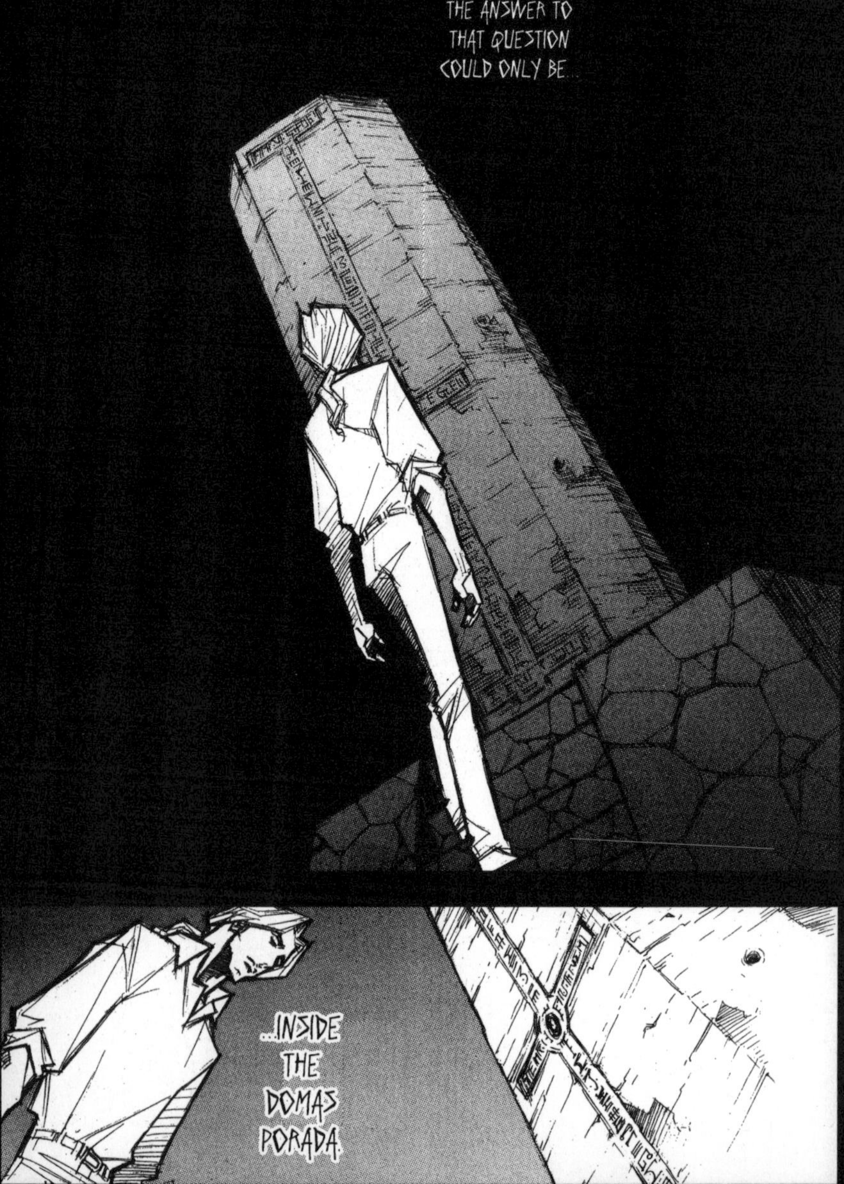
THE ANSWER TO THAT QUESTION COULD ONLY BE...
...INSIDE THE DOMAS PORADA.

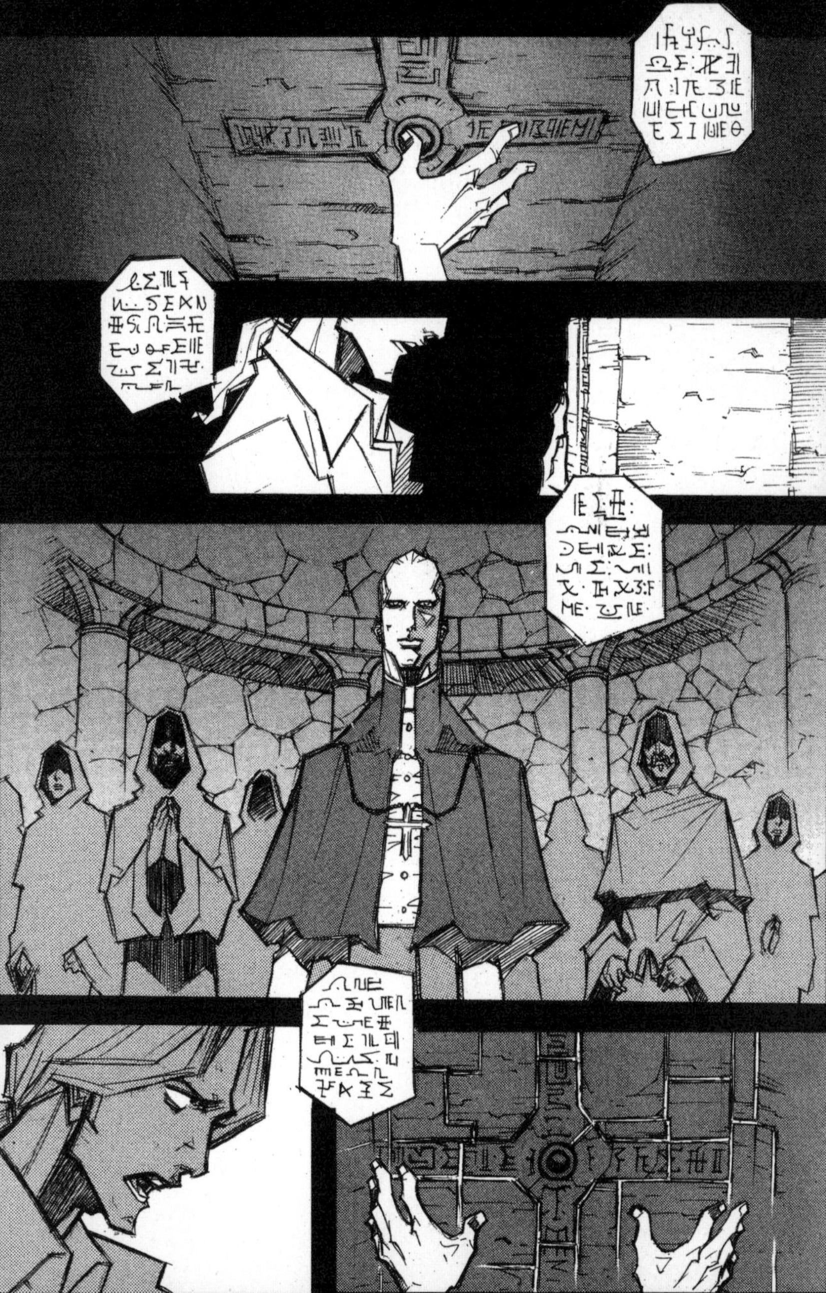

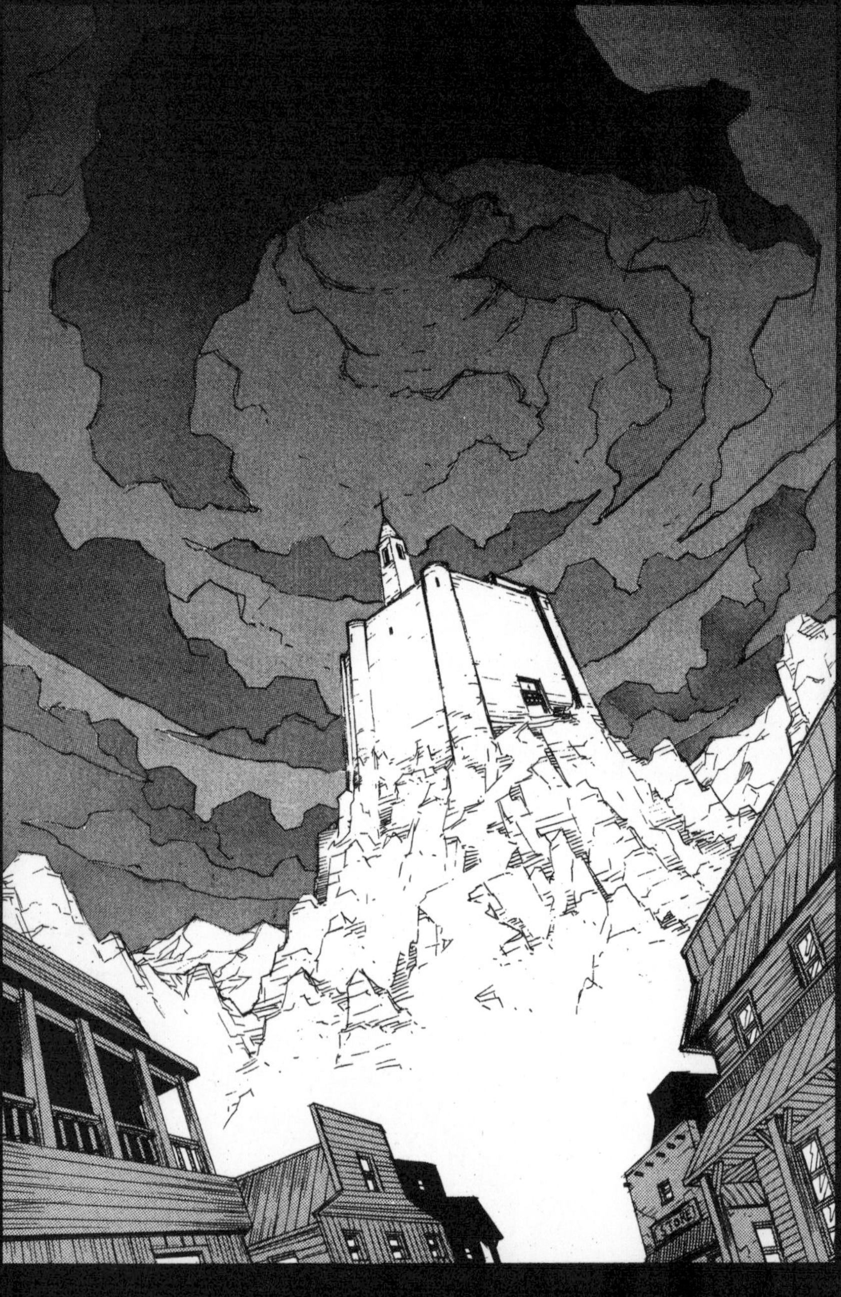
STORE

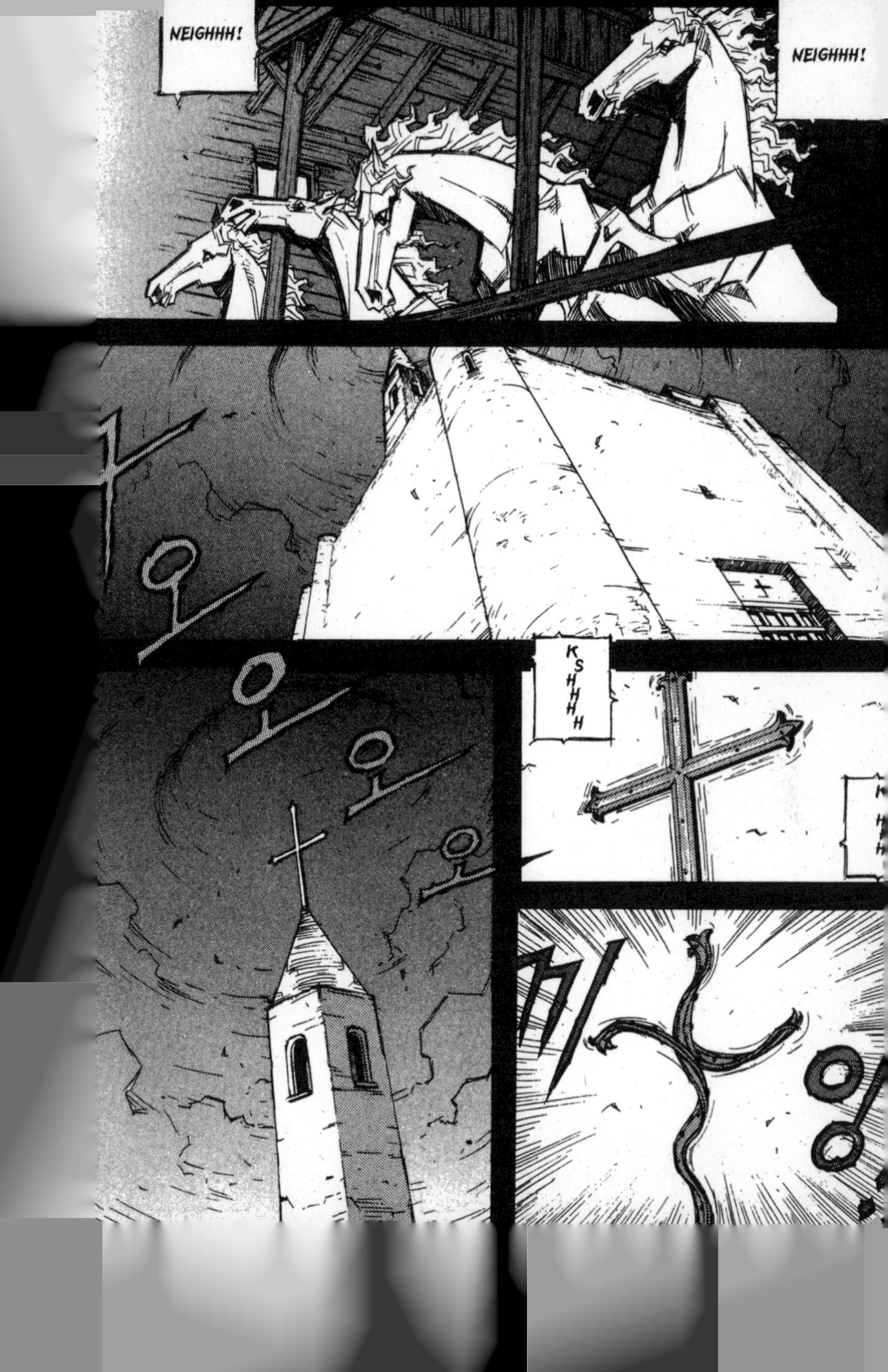
NEIGHHH!
NEIGHHH!
KSHHHH

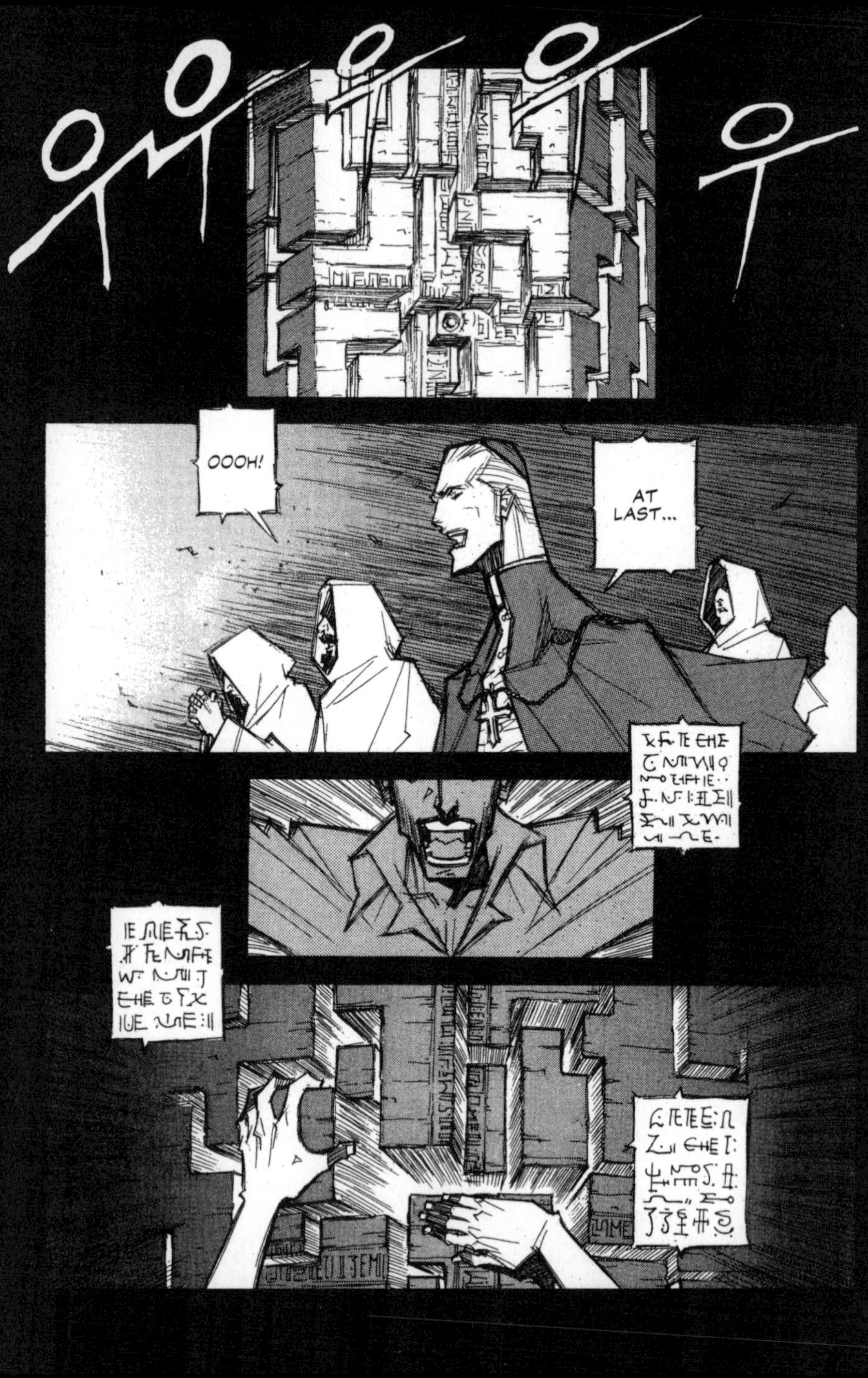
OOOH!
AT LAST...

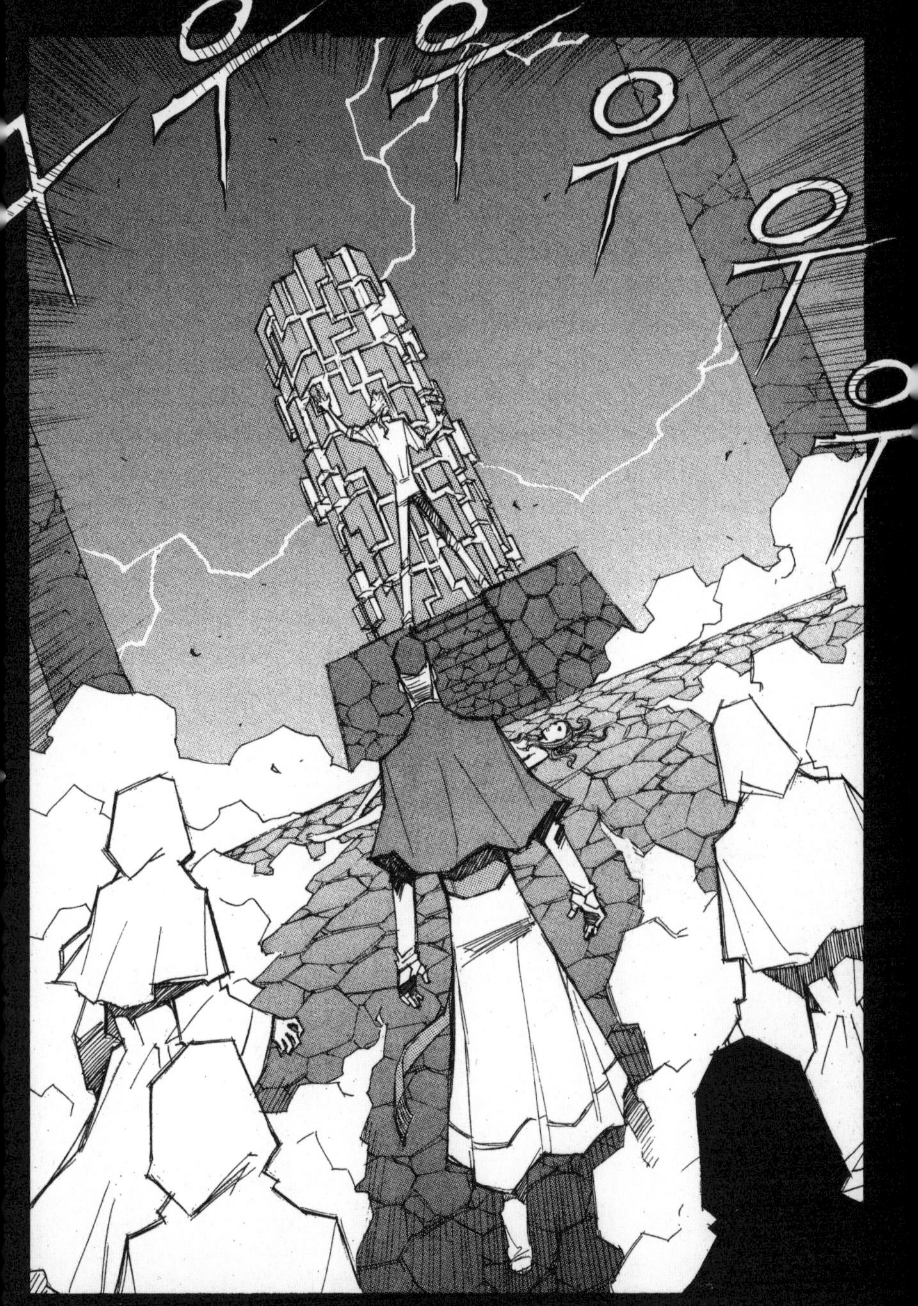

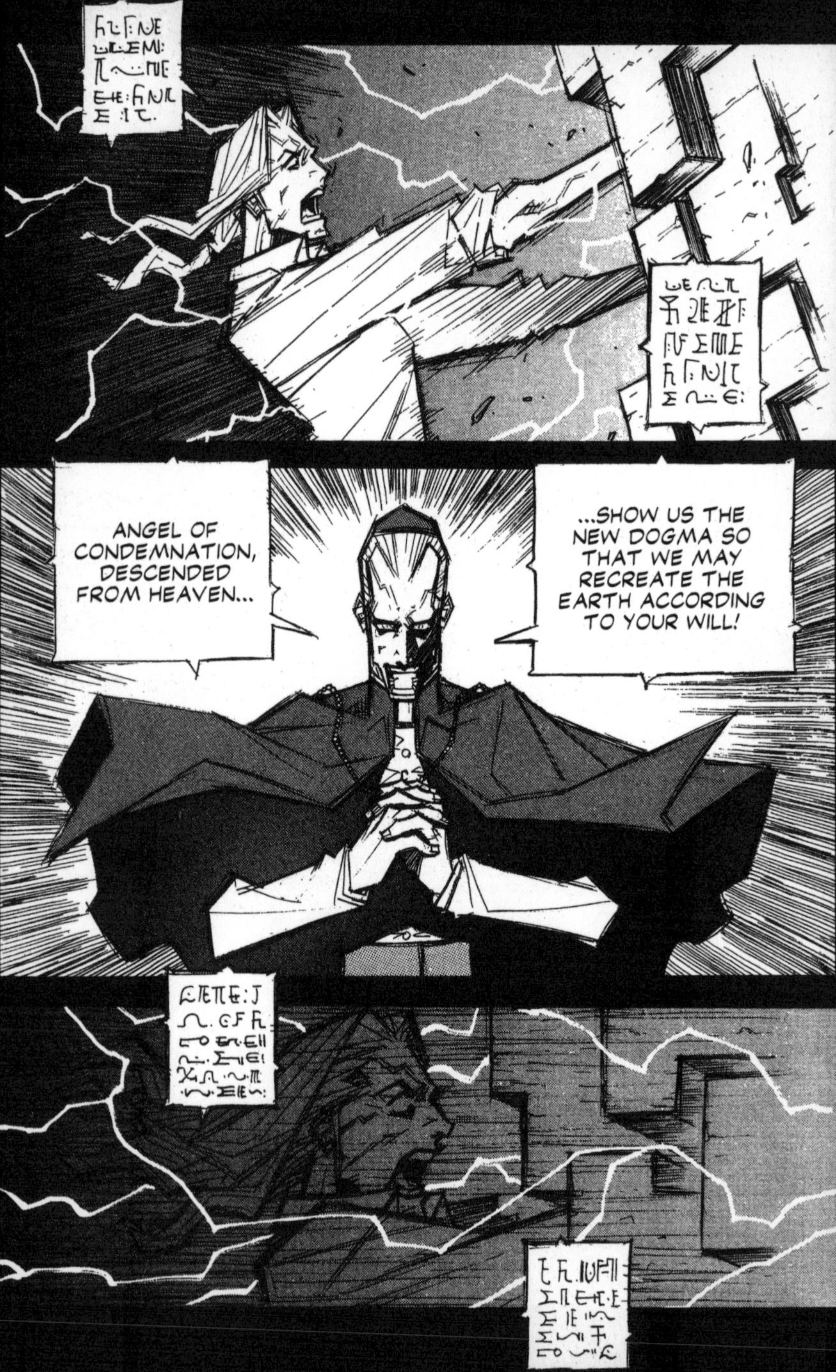
ANGEL OF CONDEMNATION, DESCENDED FROM HEAVEN...
...SHOW US THE NEW DOGMA SO THAT WE MAY RECREATE THE EARTH ACCORDING TO YOUR WILL!

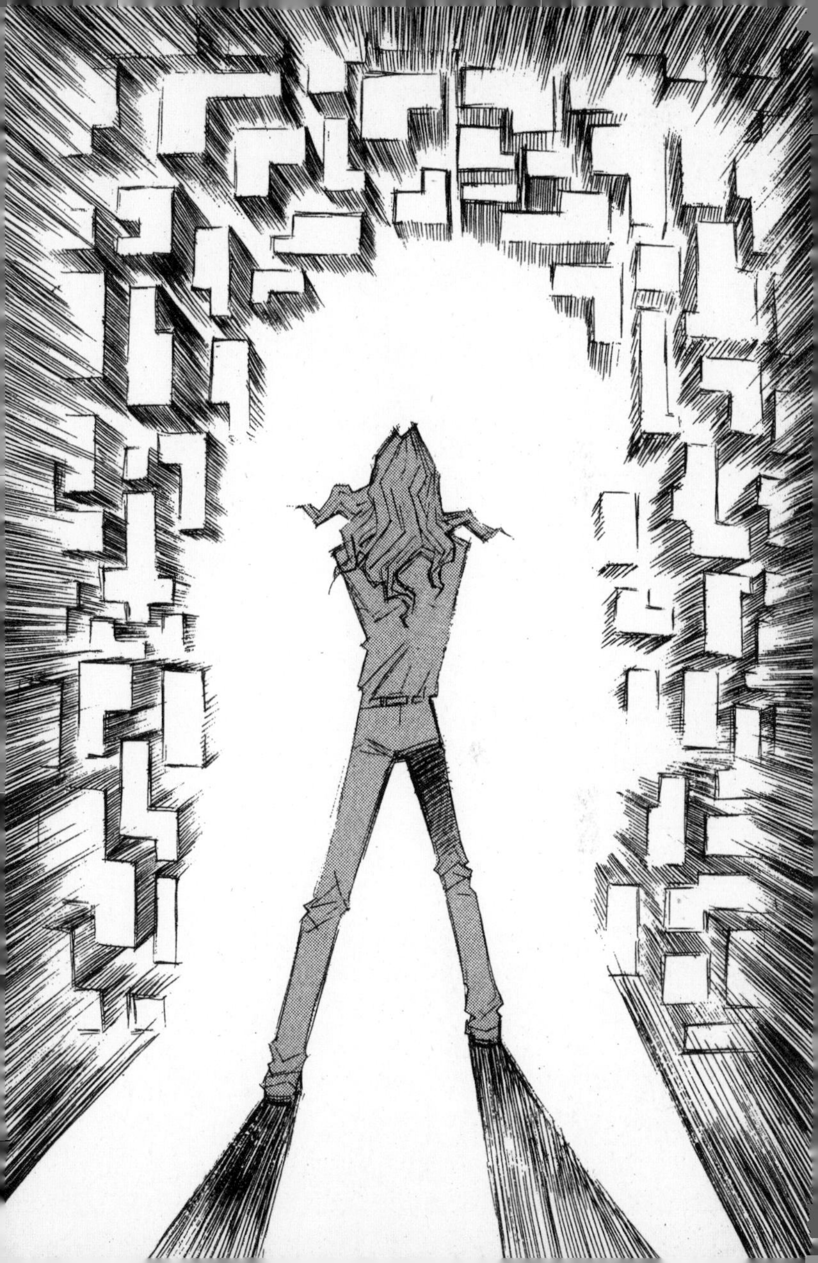

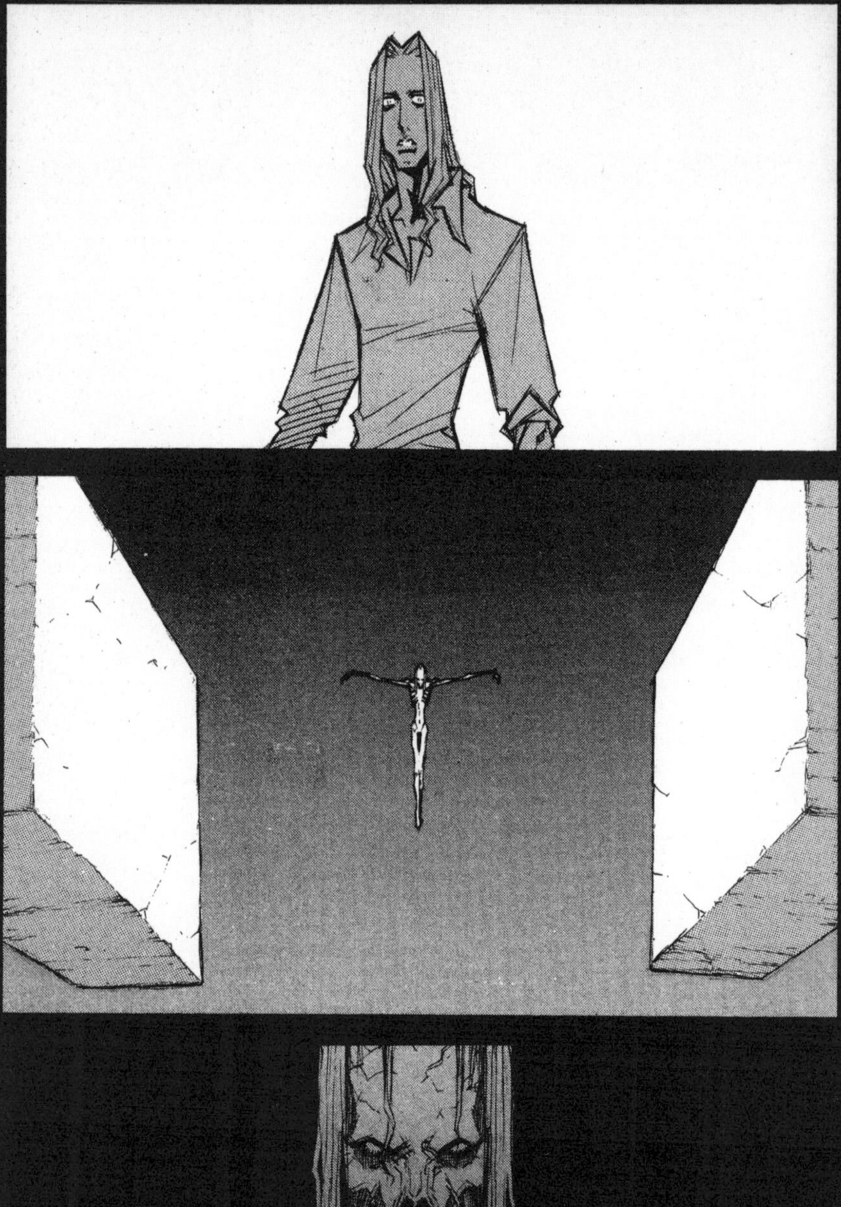

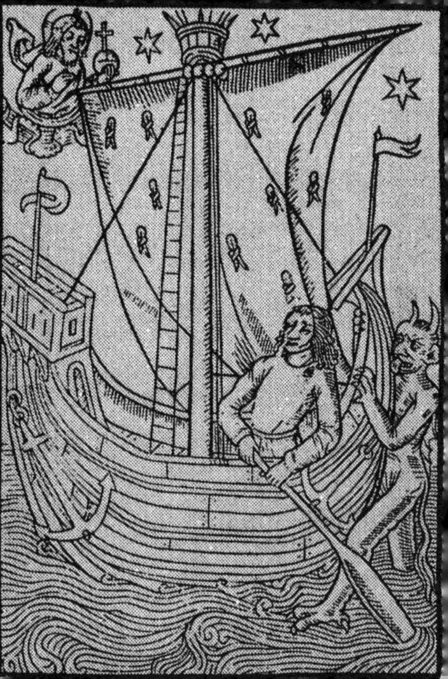

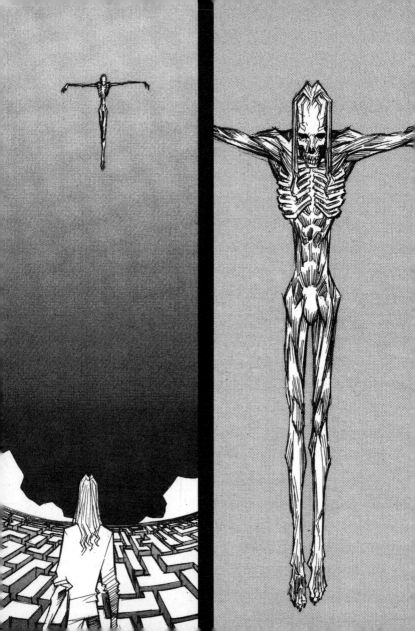

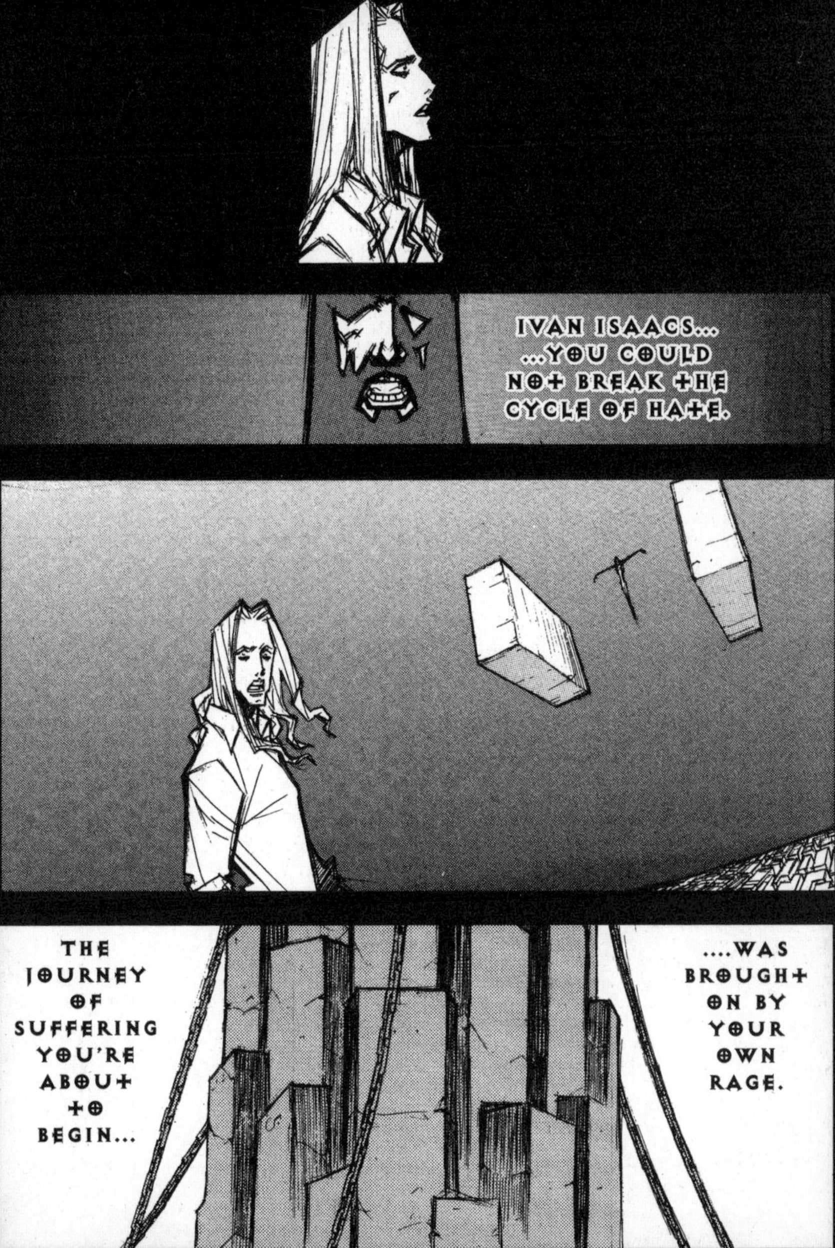

IVAN ISAACS...
...YOU COULD
NOT BREAK THE
CYCLE OF HATE.

THE
JOURNEY
OF
SUFFERING
YOU'RE
ABOUT
TO
BEGIN...

....WAS
BROUGHT
ON BY
YOUR
OWN
RAGE.

YOU ARE NOW PART...
...OF THE BATTLE BETWEEN THOSE WHO HAVE REJECTED GOD.

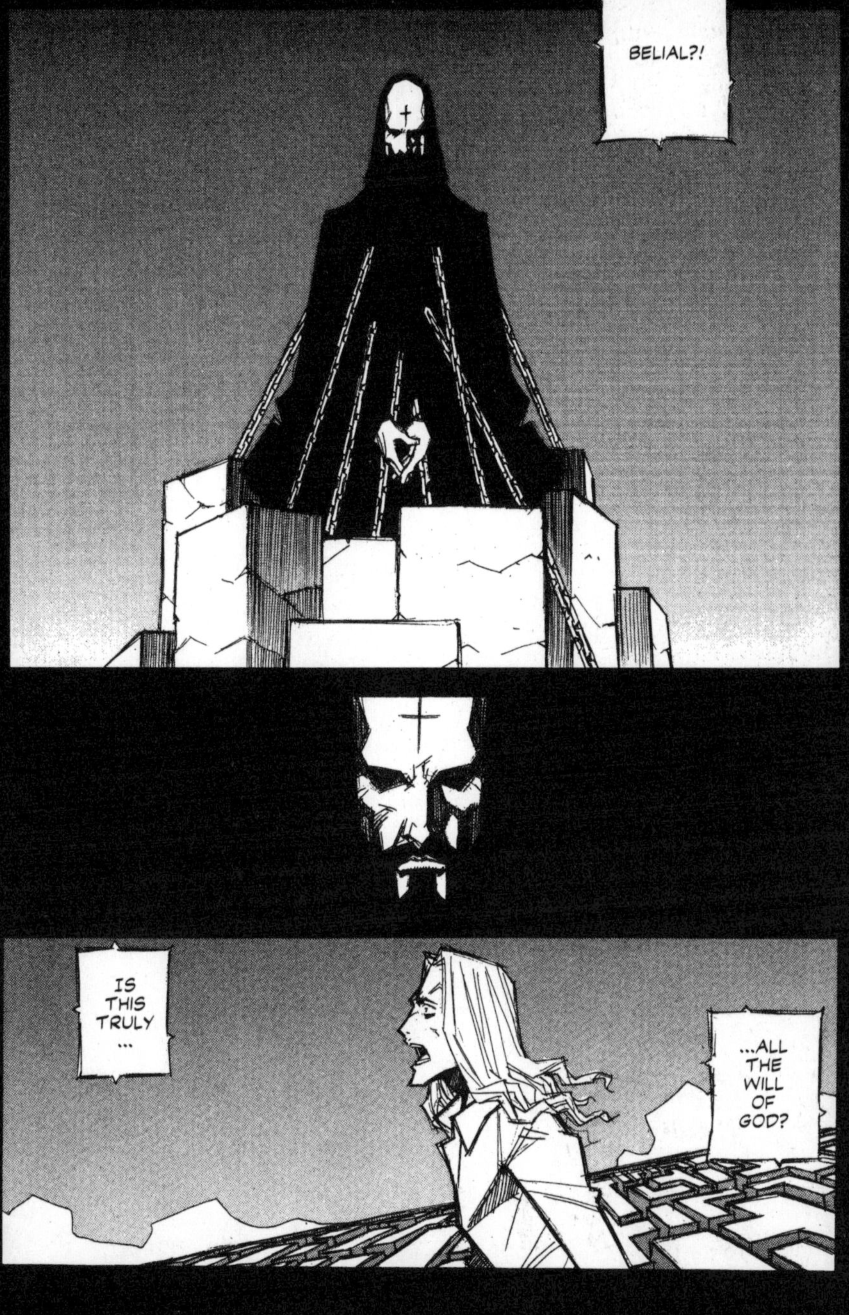
BELIAL?!
IS THIS TRULY ...
...ALL THE WILL OF GOD?

FORGE+
ABOU+
GOD!

HE'LL
ALWAYS
REMAIN A
BYS+ANDER!

HE DID
NO+
ABANDON
US.

HE WAS
NEVER
WI+H US
+O BEGIN
WI+H!

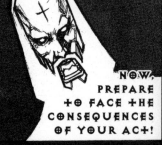

NOW,
PREPARE
+O FACE +HE
CONSEQUENCES
OF YOUR AC+!

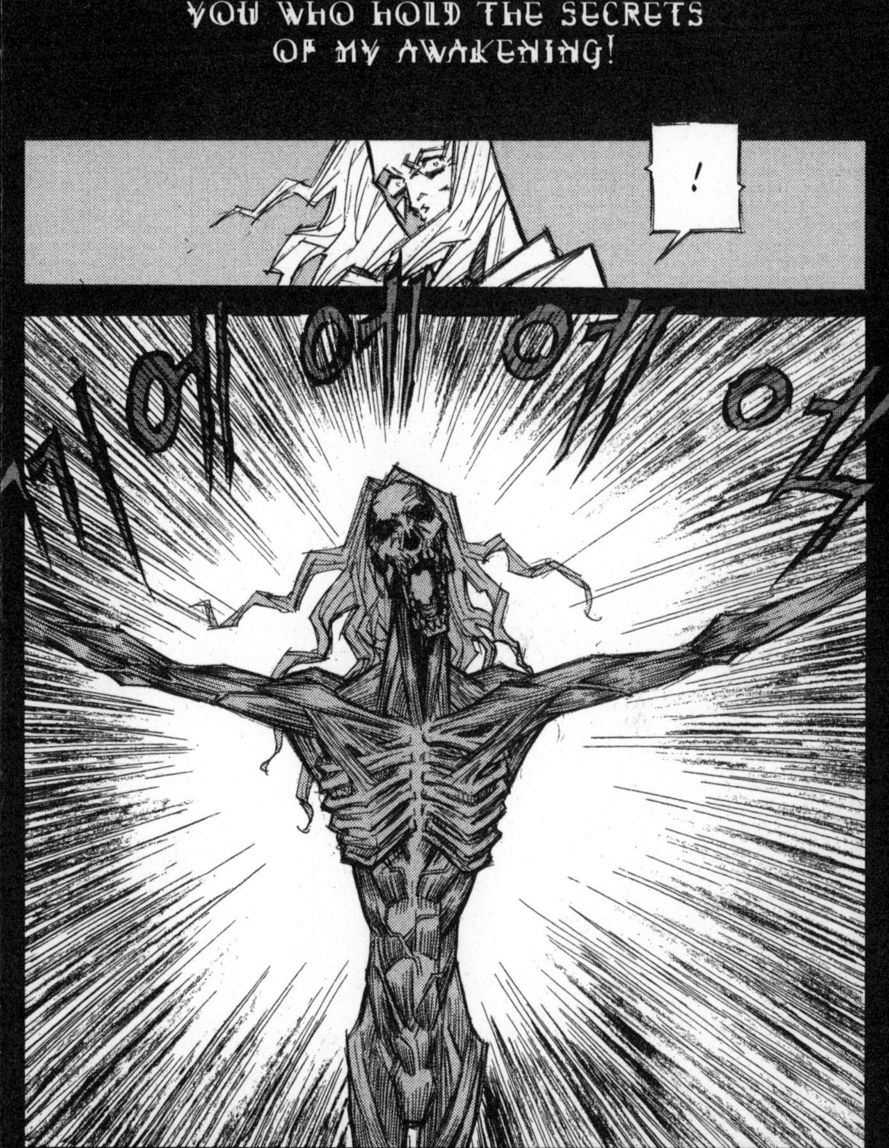
YOU WHO HOLD THE SECRETS OF MY AWAKENING!
!

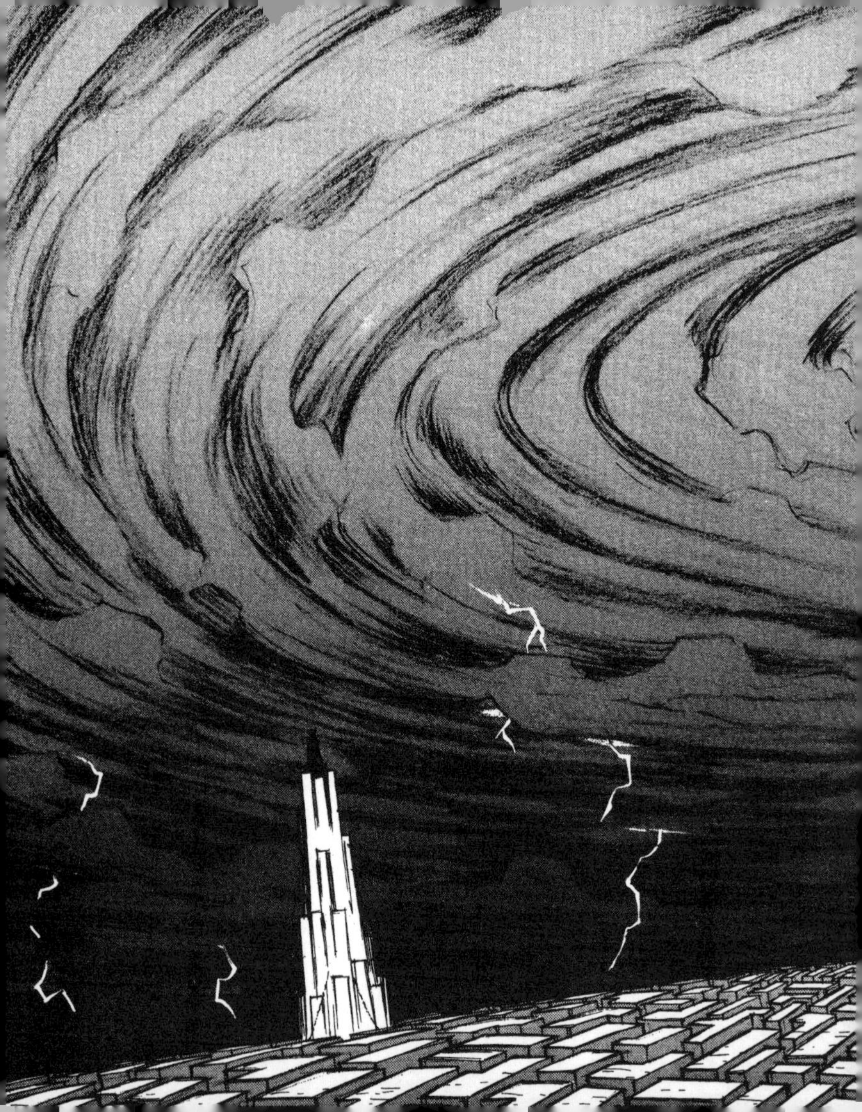

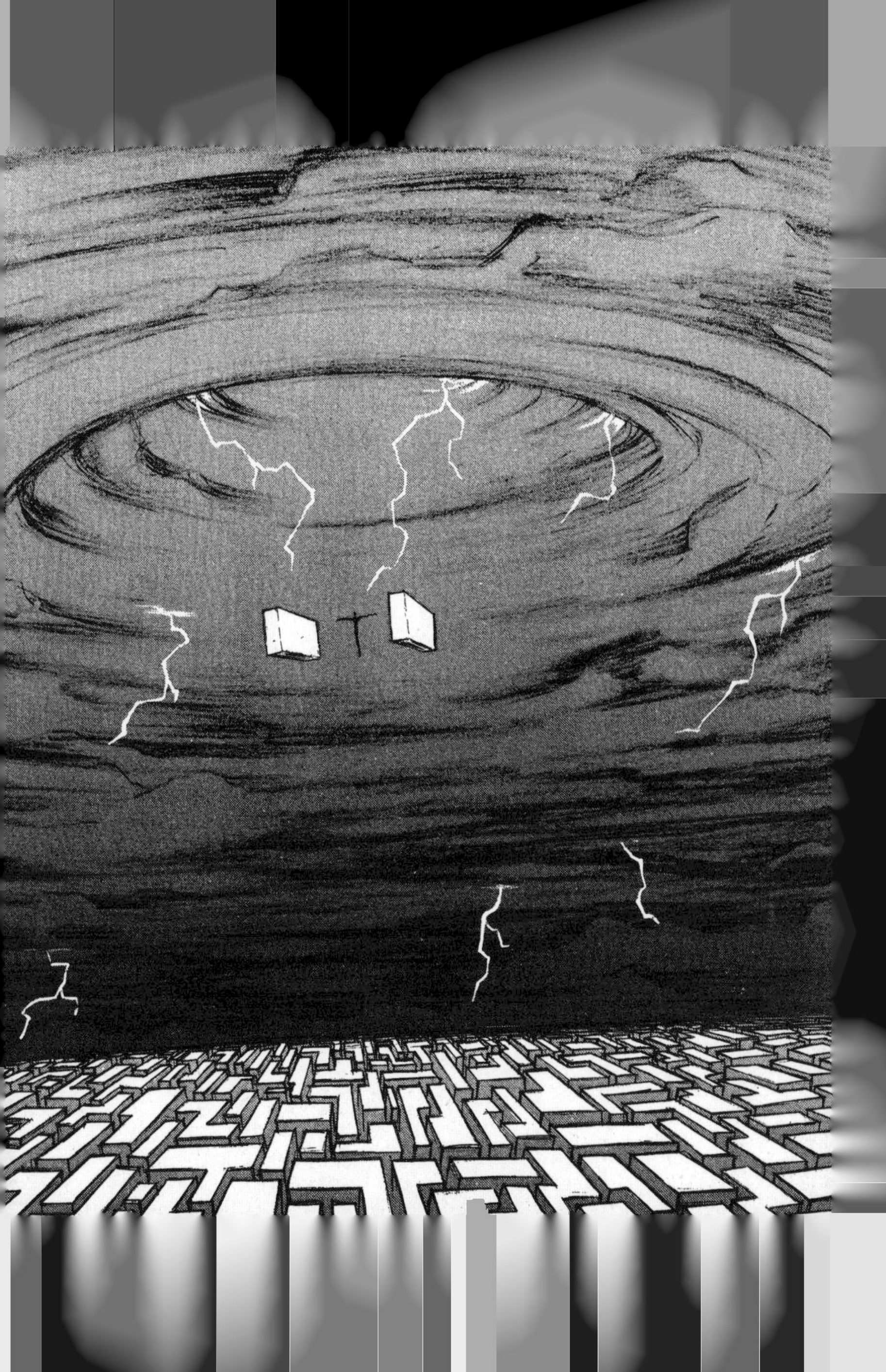

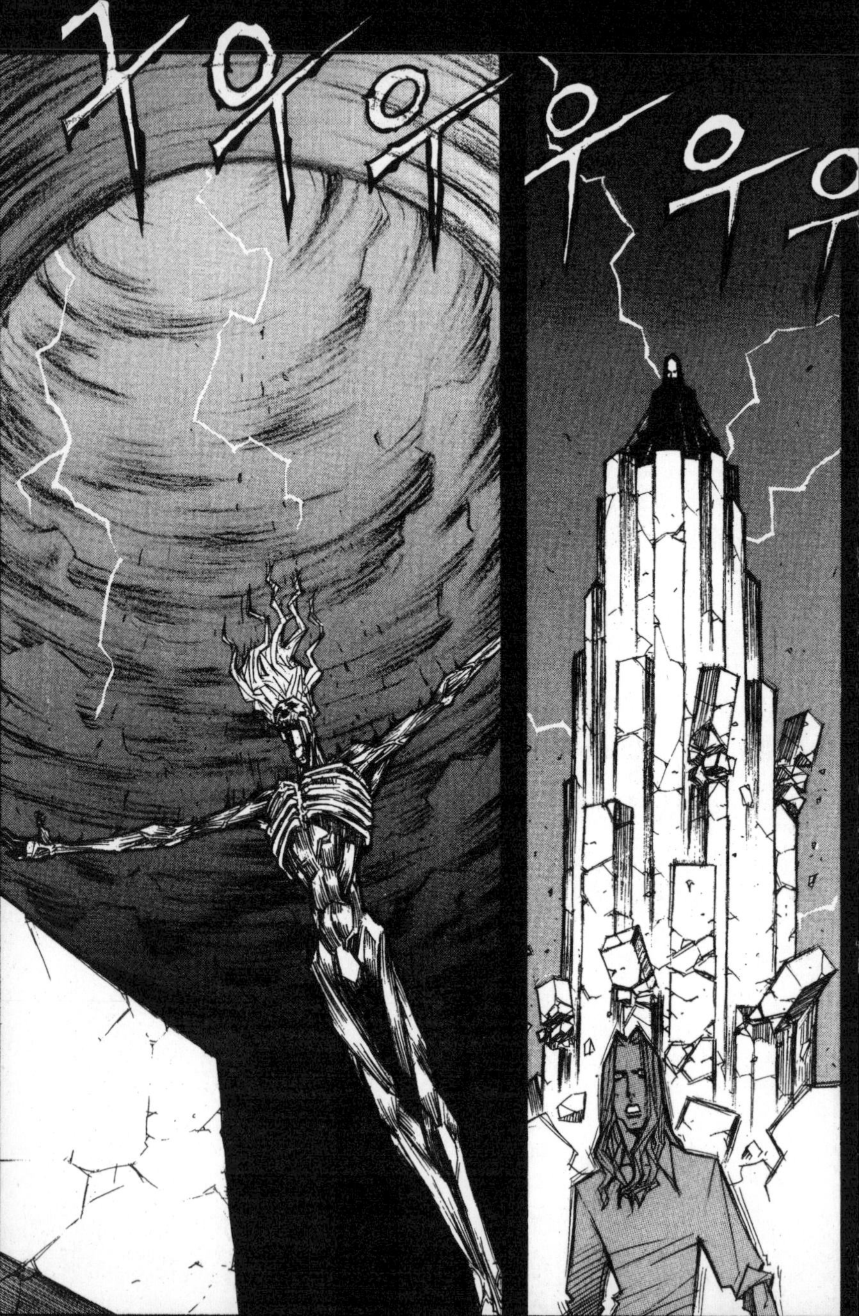
구우우우우우

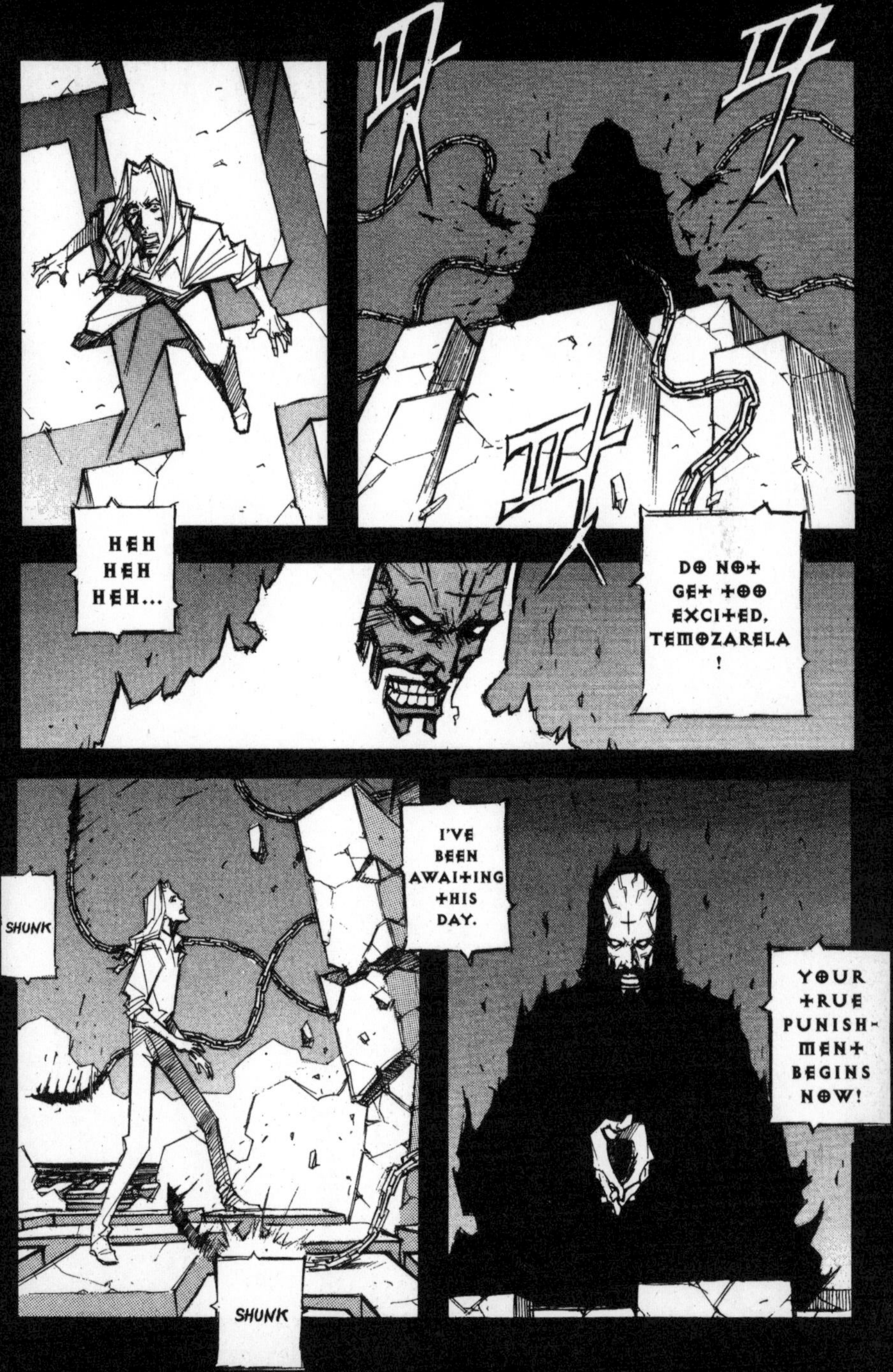
HEH HEH HEH...
DO NOT GET TOO EXCITED, TEMOZARELA!
SHUNK
I'VE BEEN AWAITING THIS DAY.
SHUNK
YOUR TRUE PUNISHMENT BEGINS NOW!

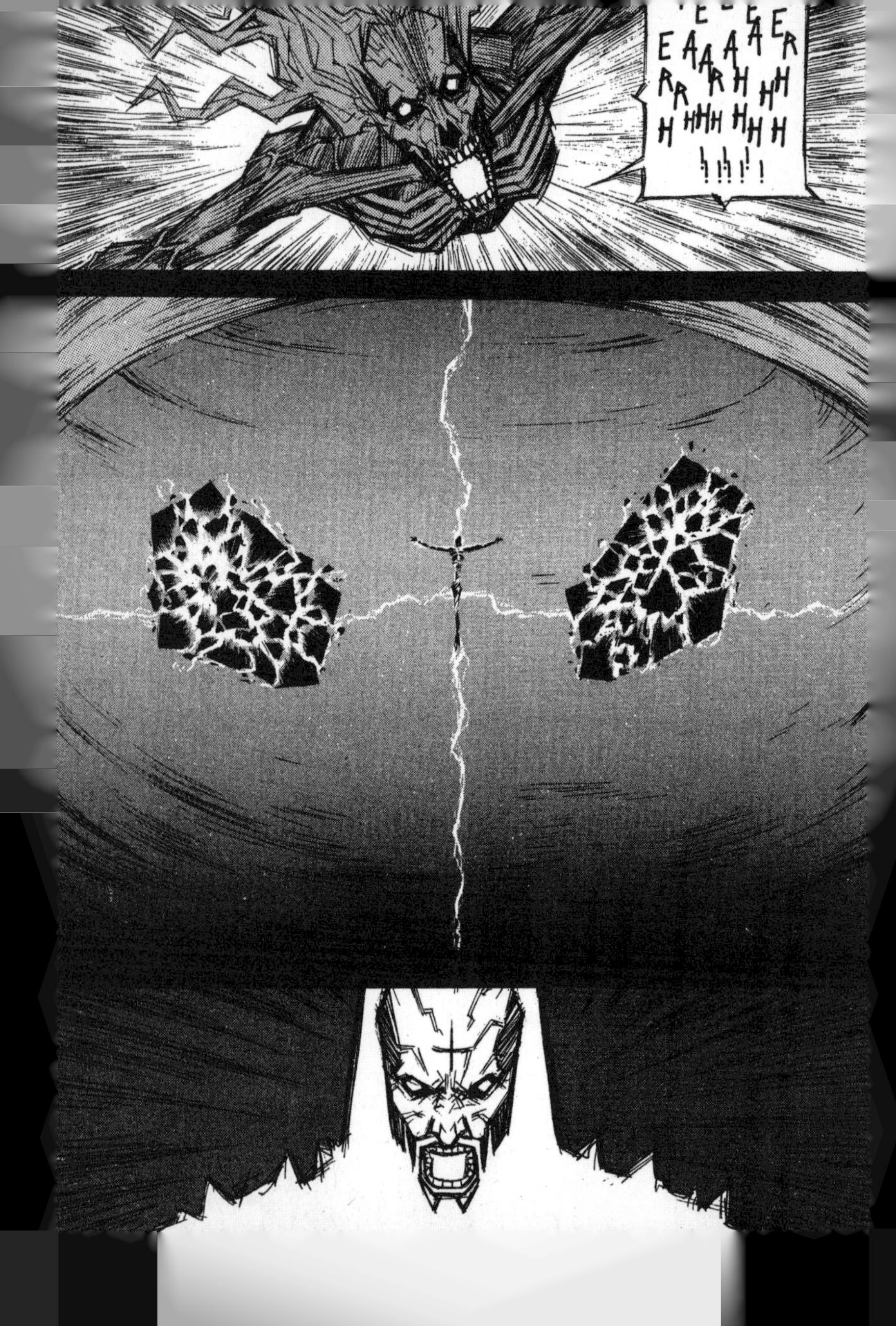
EAAAAER
RRRHHH
HHHHHHHH
!!!!!

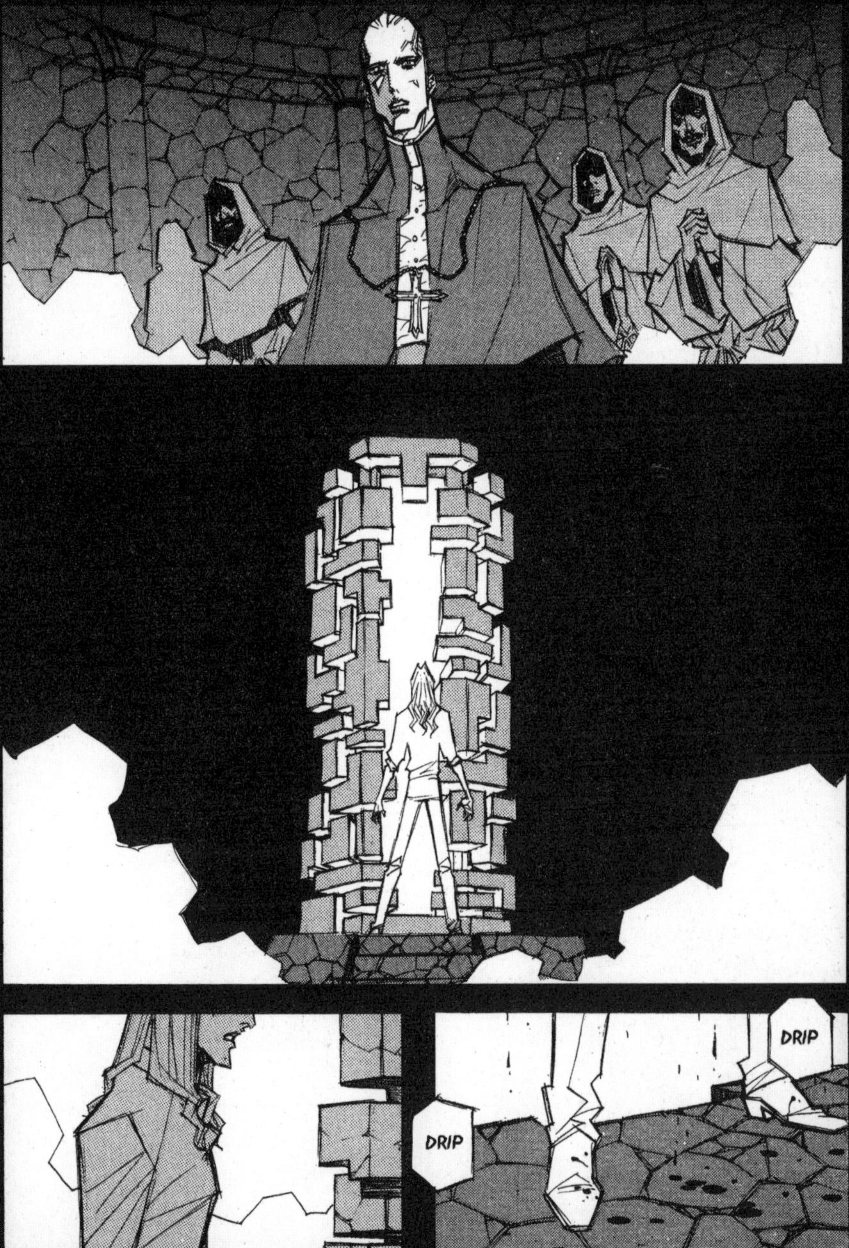
DRIP
DRIP

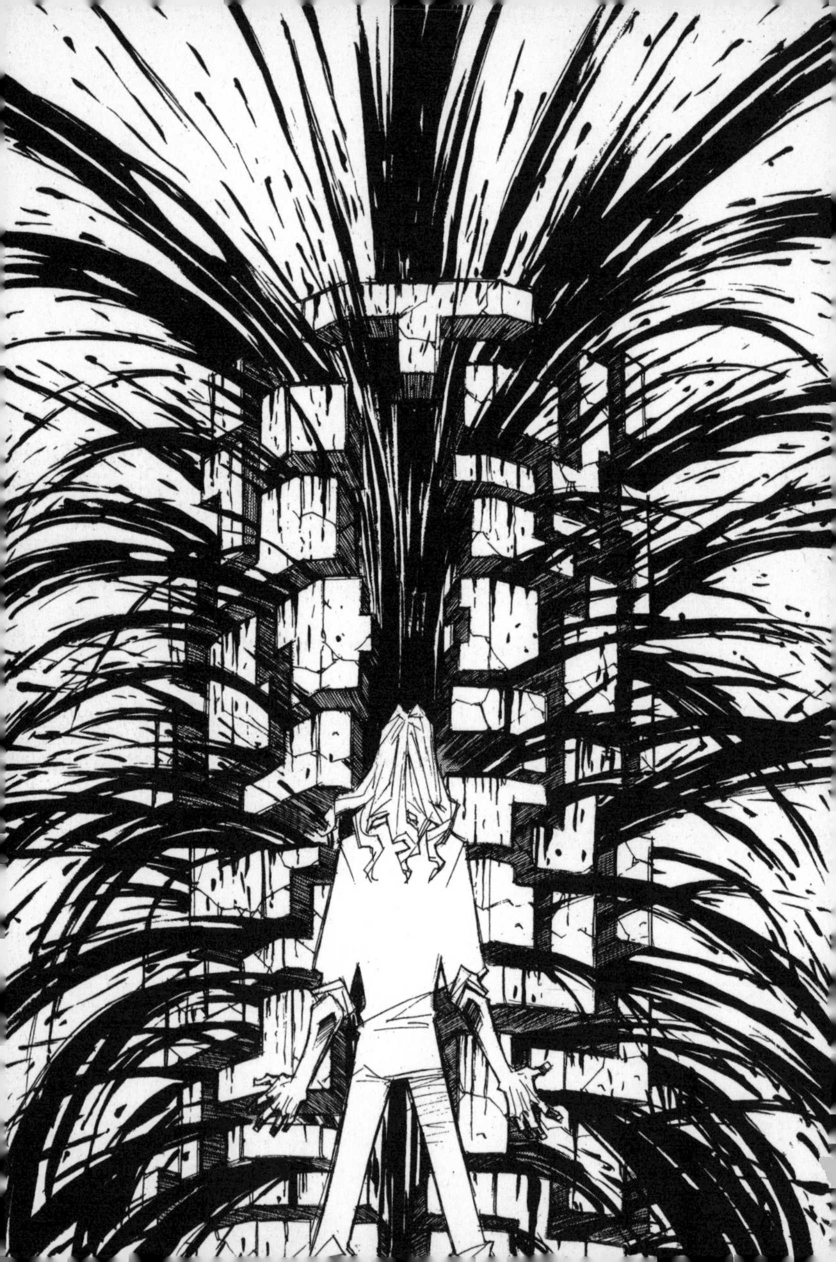

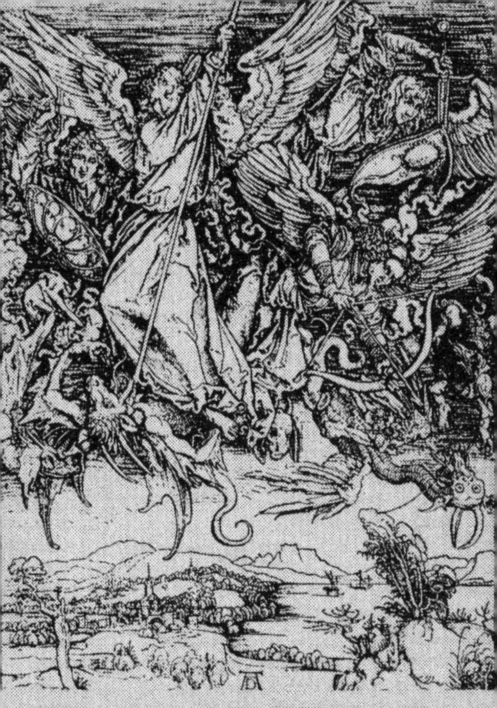

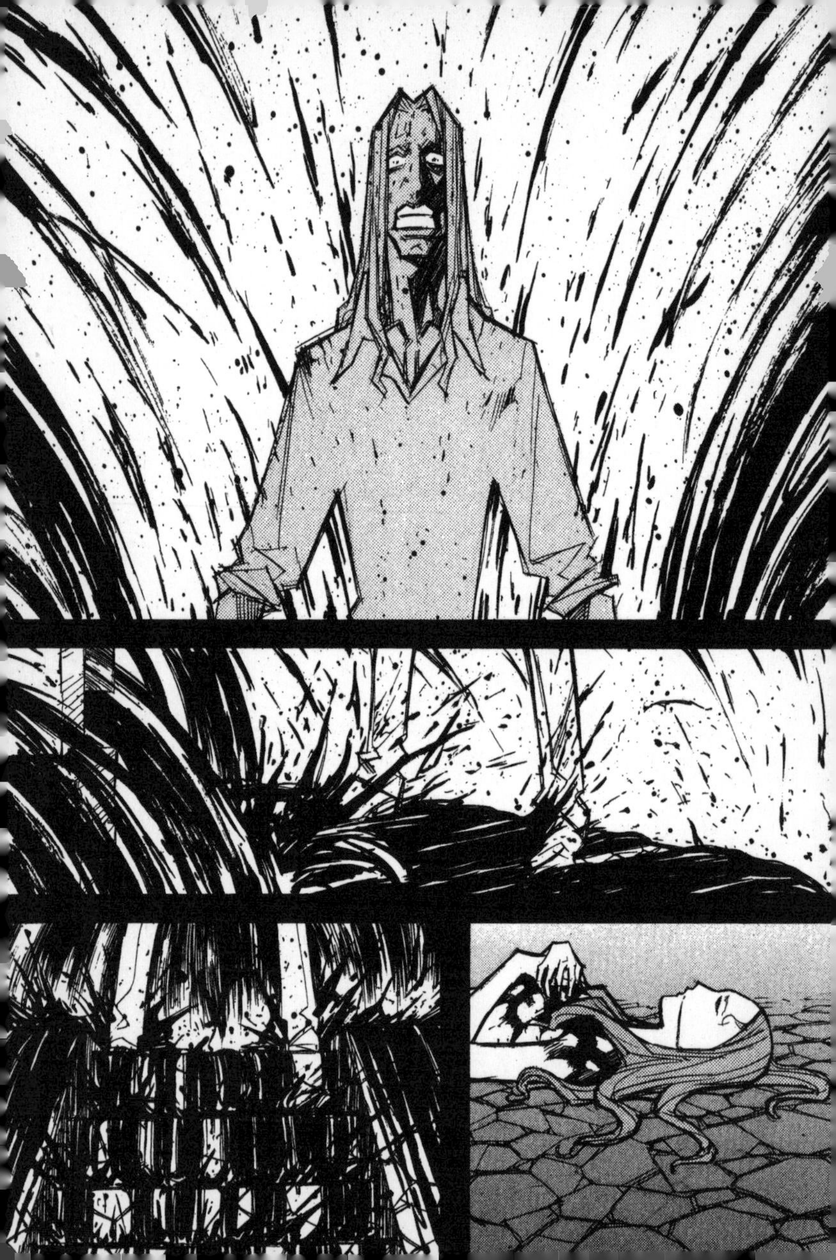

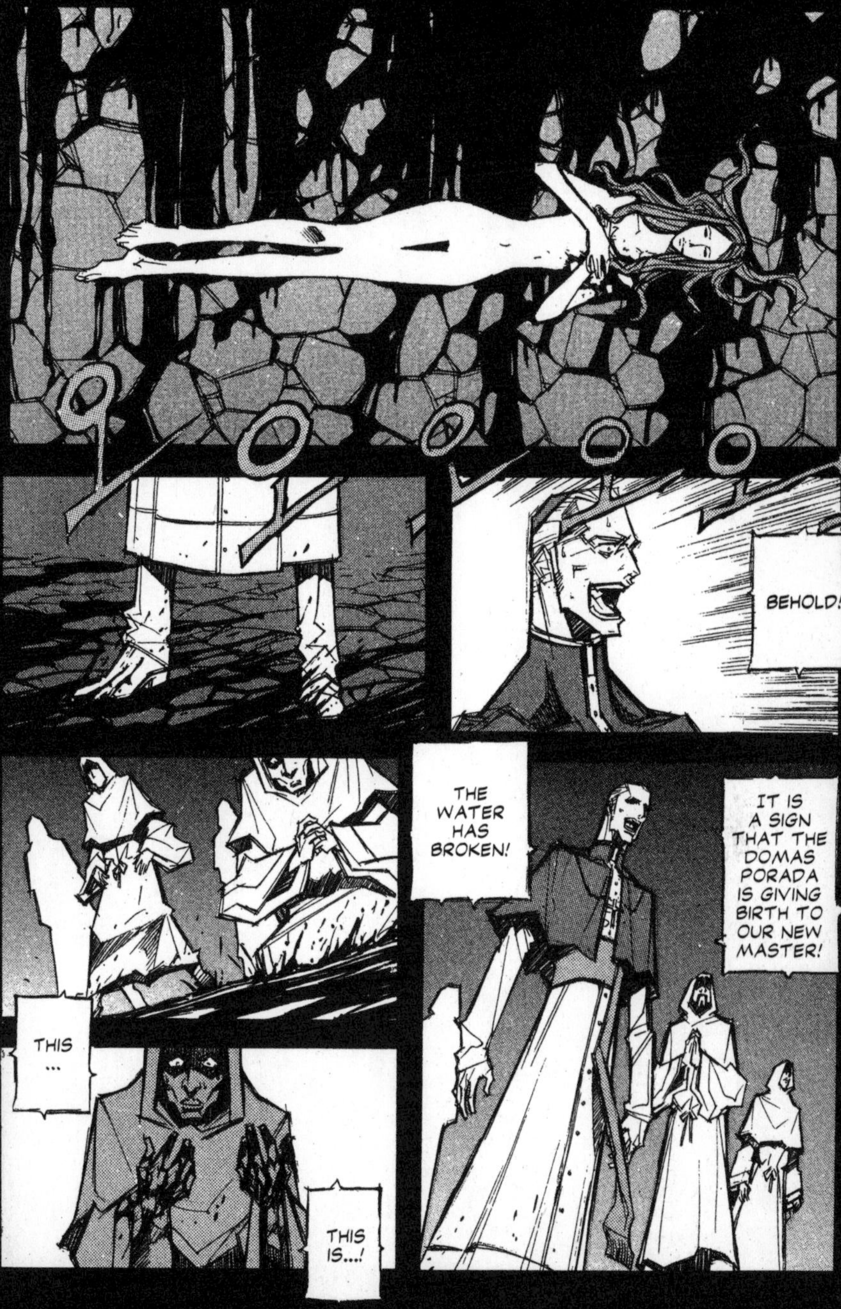
BEHOLD!
THIS ...
THE WATER HAS BROKEN!
IT IS A SIGN THAT THE DOMAS PORADA IS GIVING BIRTH TO OUR NEW MASTER!
THIS IS...!

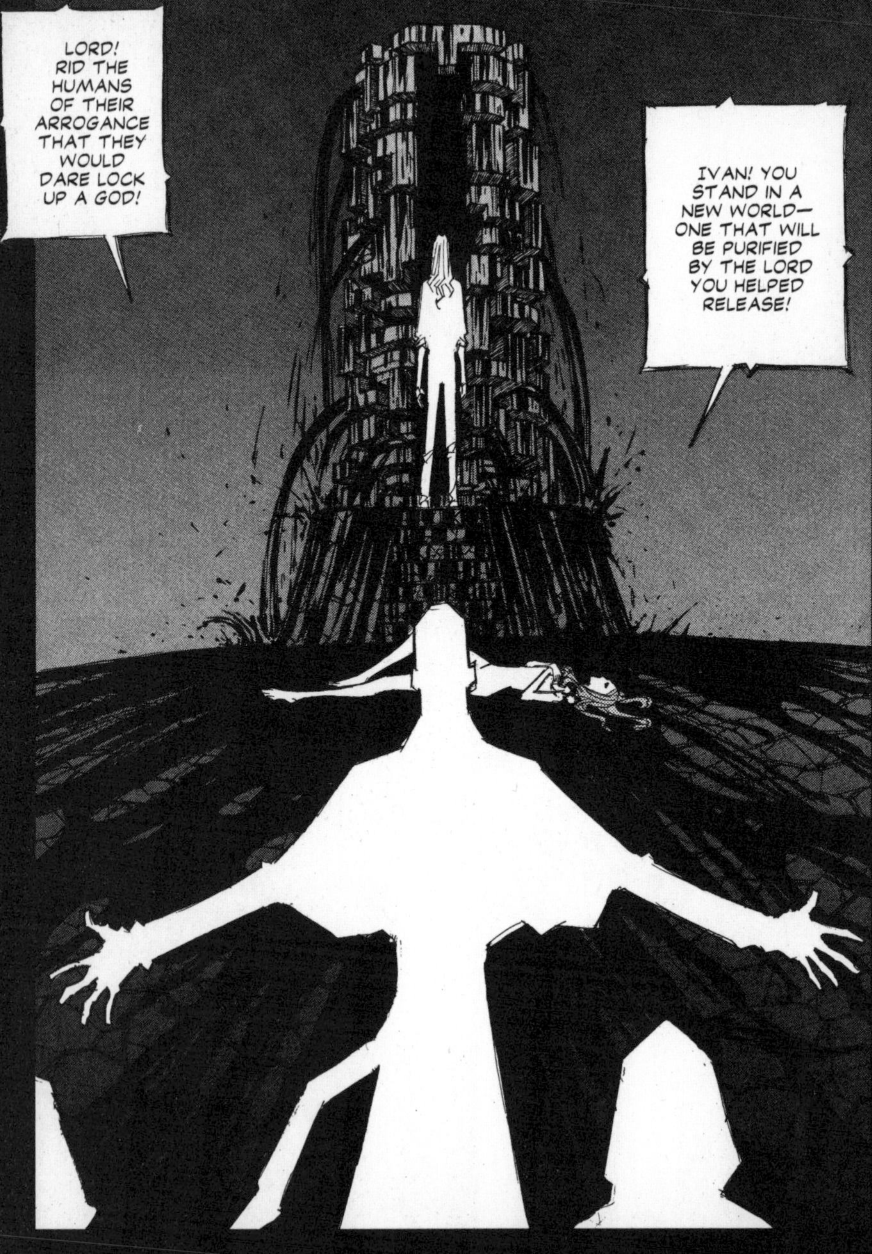
LORD! RID THE HUMANS OF THEIR ARROGANCE THAT THEY WOULD DARE LOCK UP A GOD!
IVAN! YOU STAND IN A NEW WORLD— ONE THAT WILL BE PURIFIED BY THE LORD YOU HELPED RELEASE!

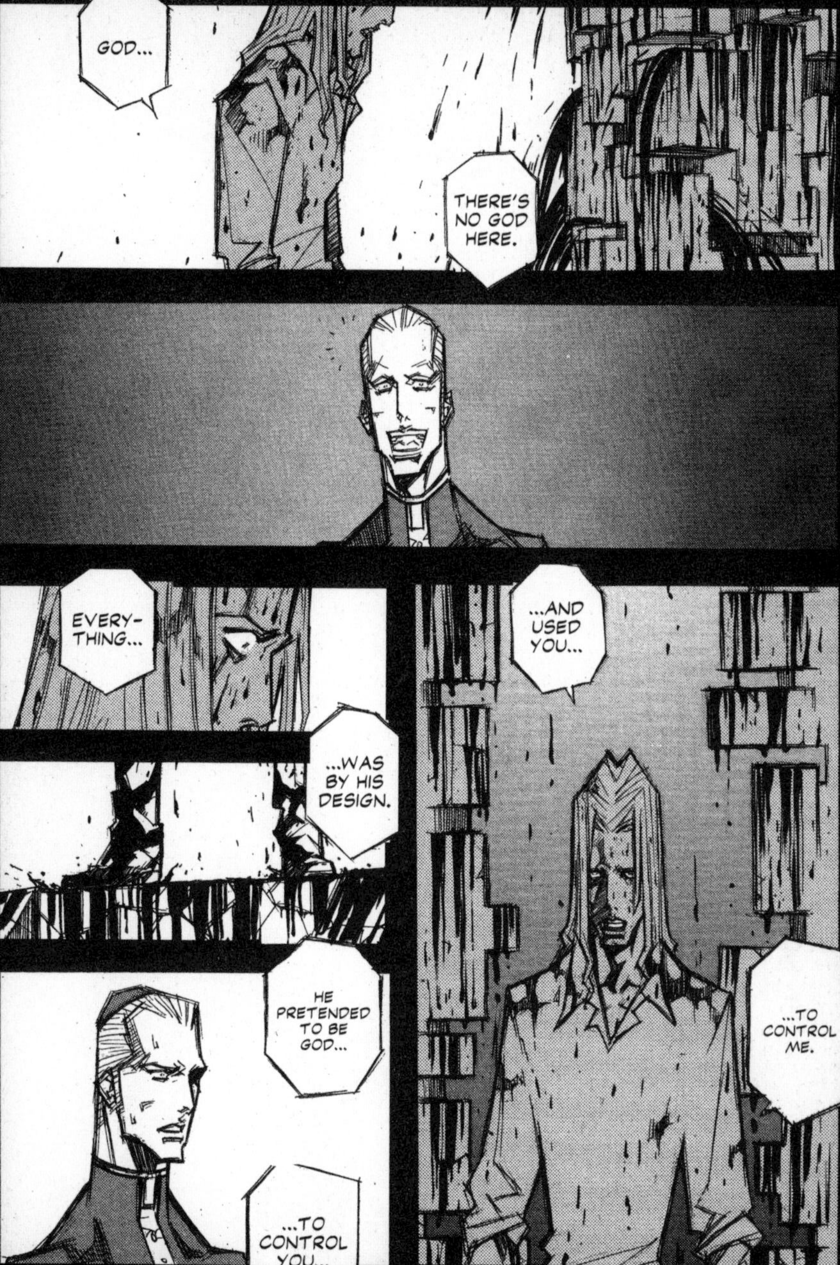
GOD...
THERE'S NO GOD HERE.
EVERY-THING...
...WAS BY HIS DESIGN.
HE PRETENDED TO BE GOD...
...TO CONTROL YOU...
...AND USED YOU...
...TO CONTROL ME.

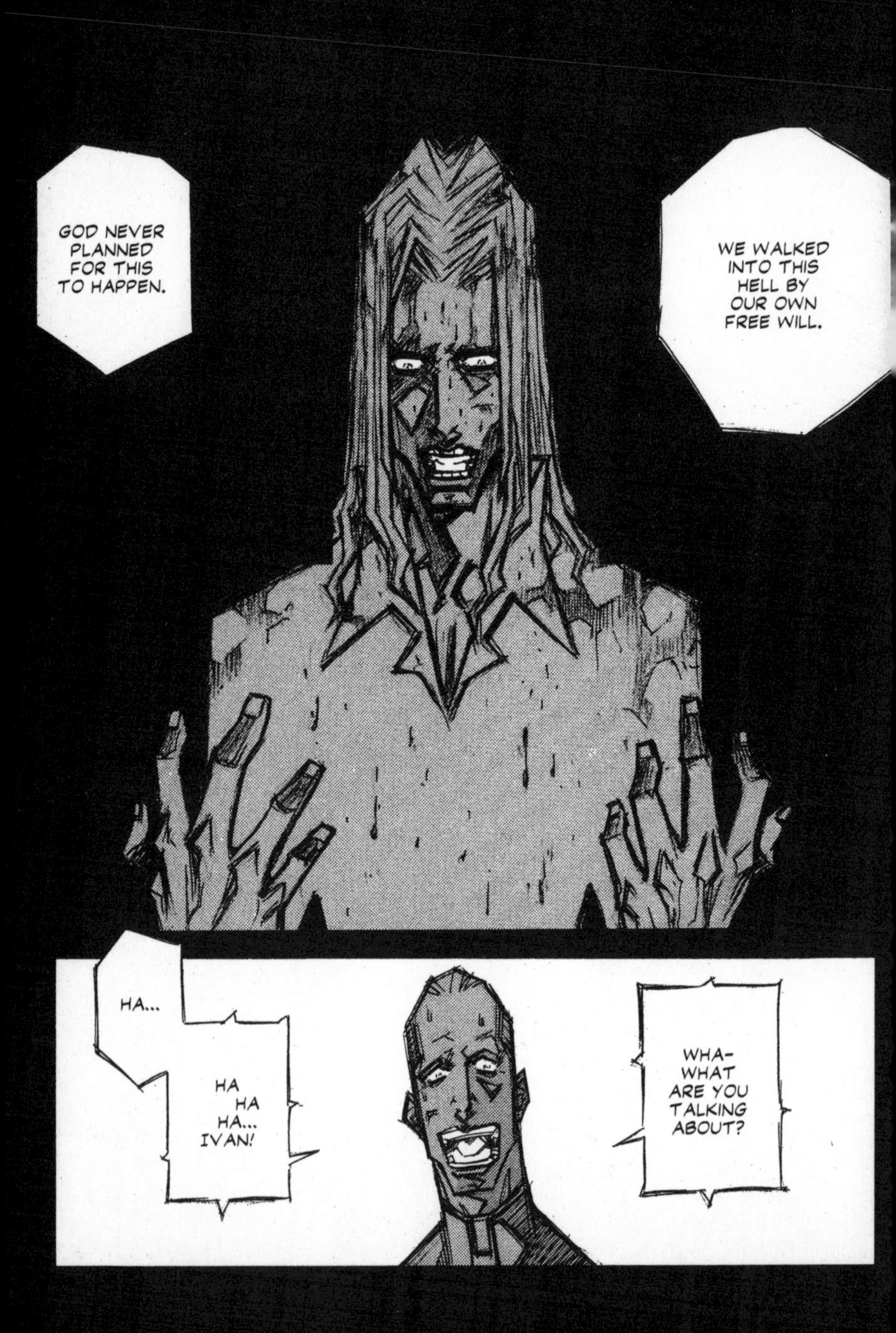
GOD NEVER PLANNED FOR THIS TO HAPPEN.
WE WALKED INTO THIS HELL BY OUR OWN FREE WILL.
HA...
HA HA HA... IVAN!
WHA-WHAT ARE YOU TALKING ABOUT?

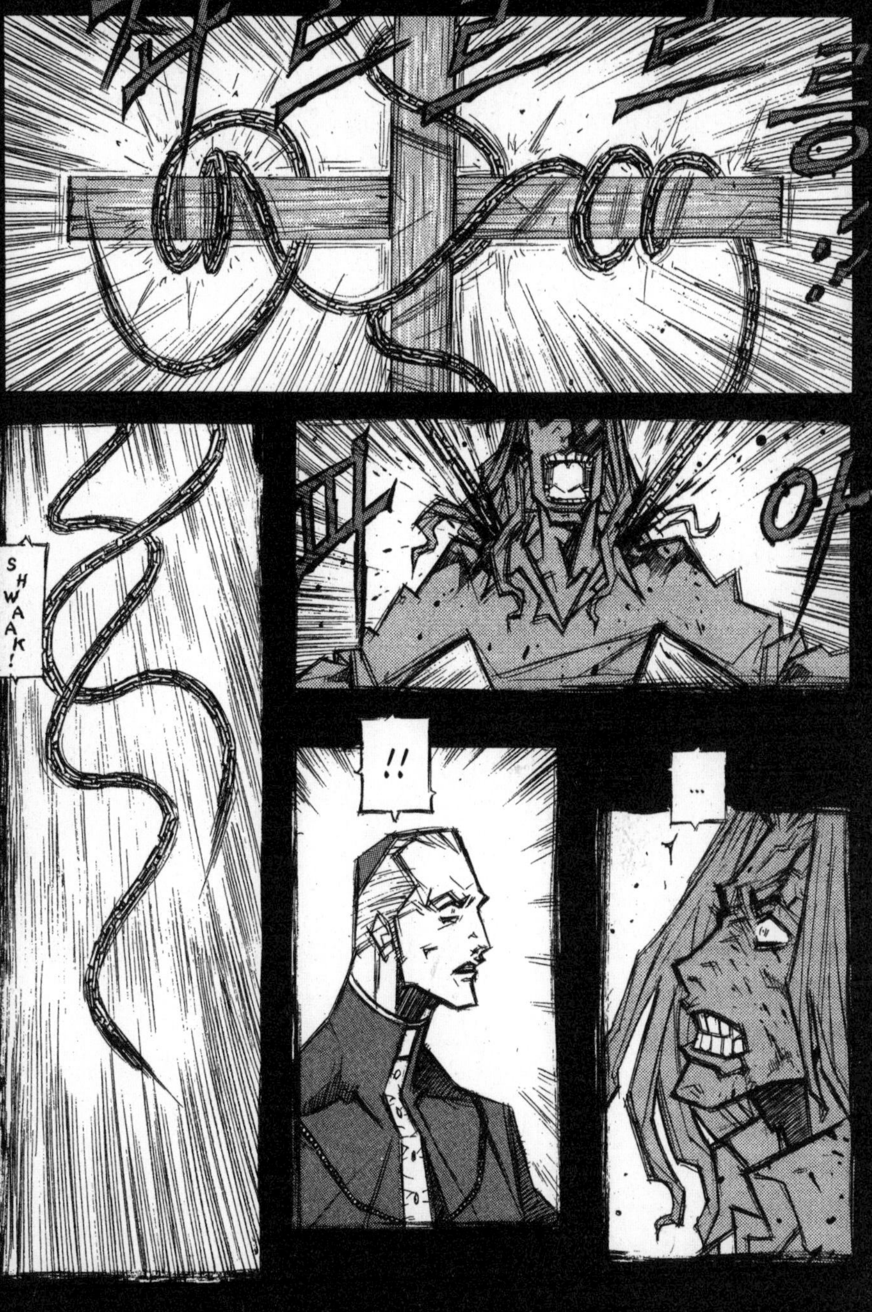

촤르르르릉!!
SHWAK!
파아
!!
...

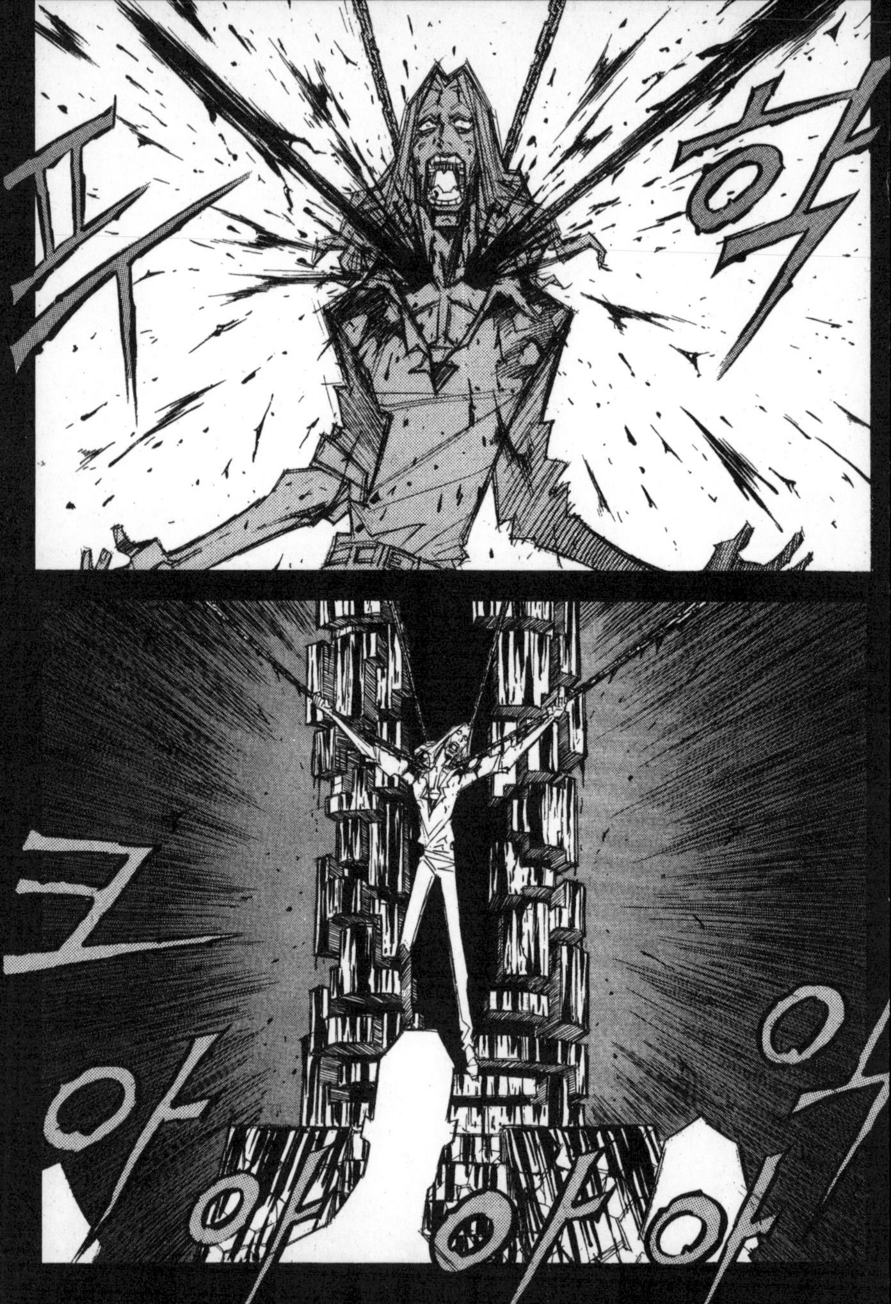
푸학
크아아아아아

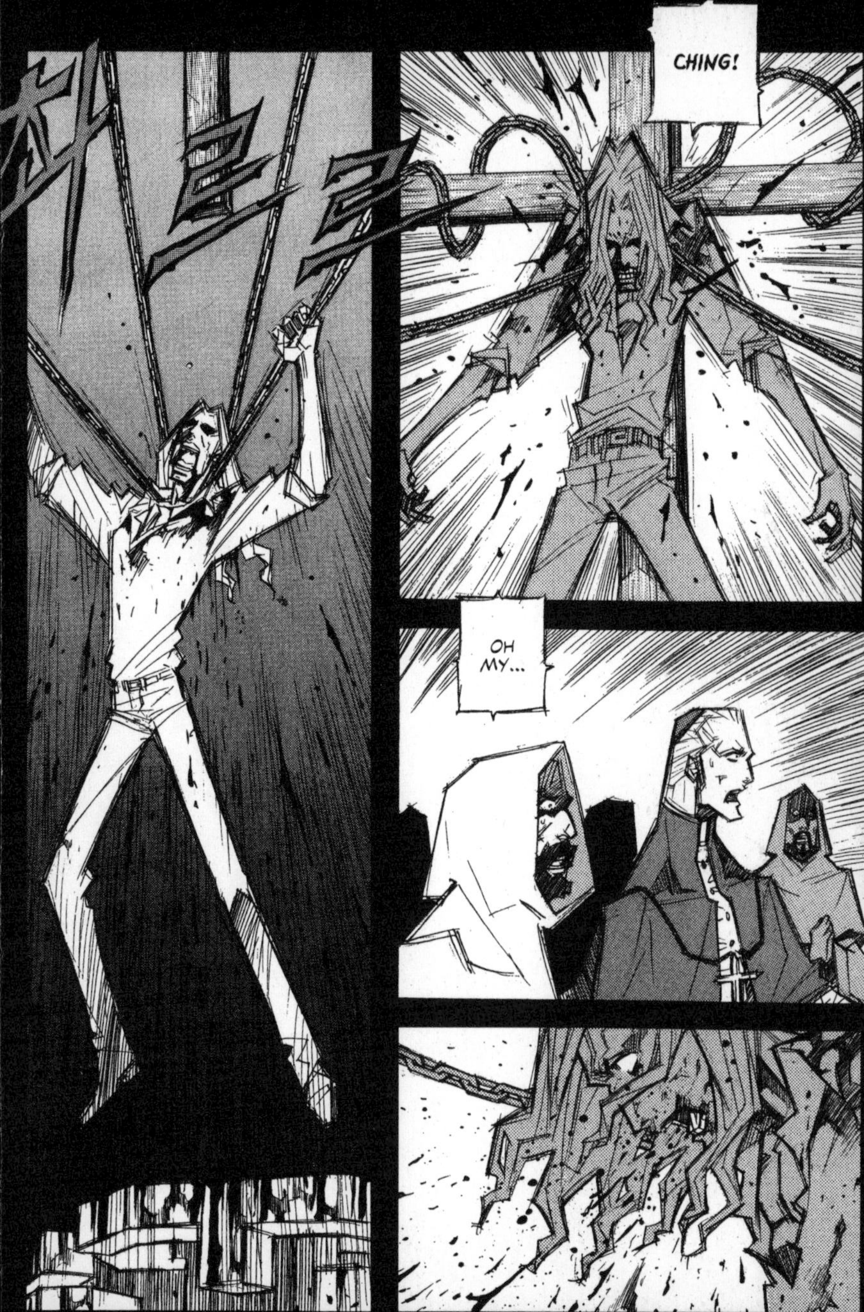
CHING!
OH MY...

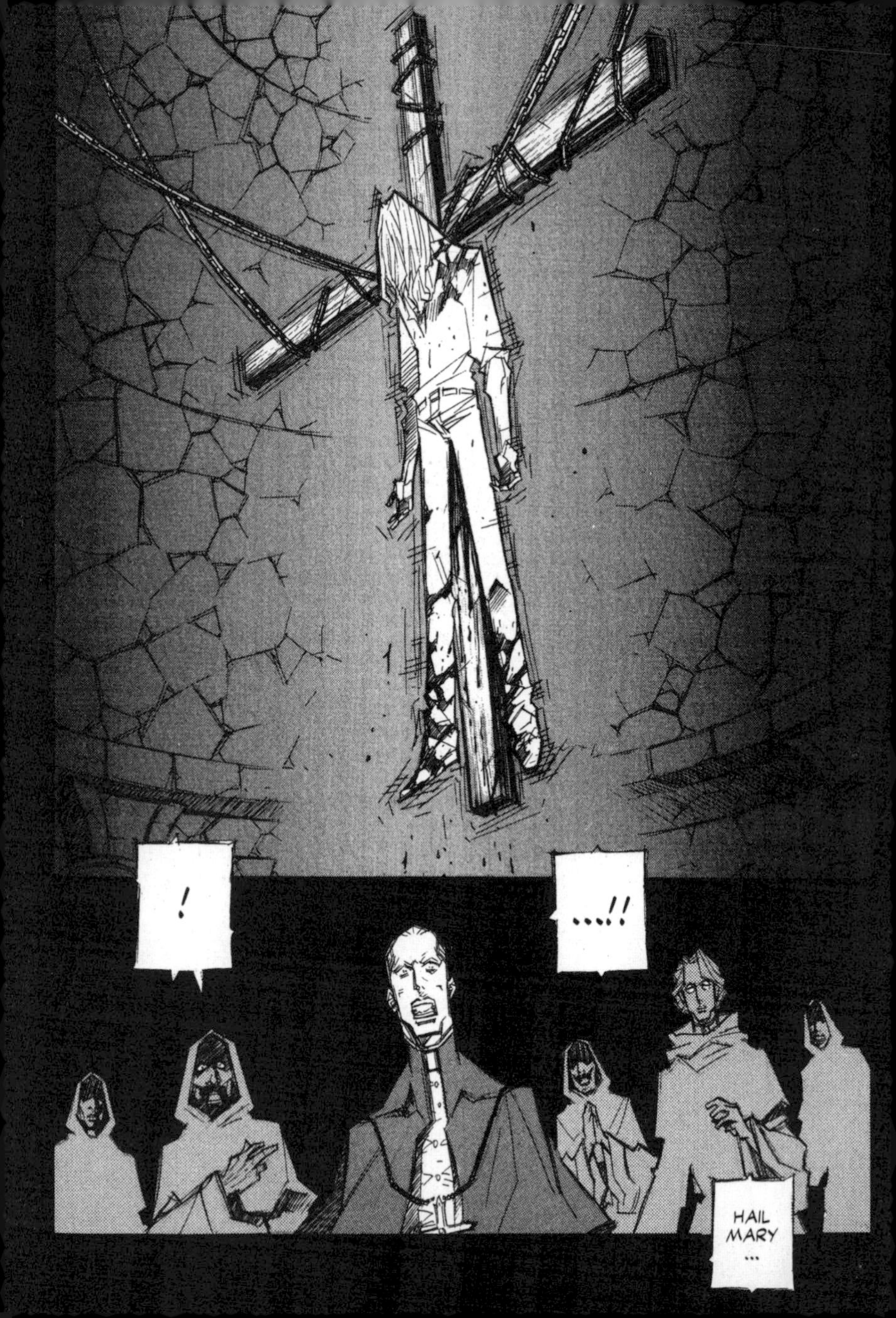
!
...!!
HAIL MARY ...

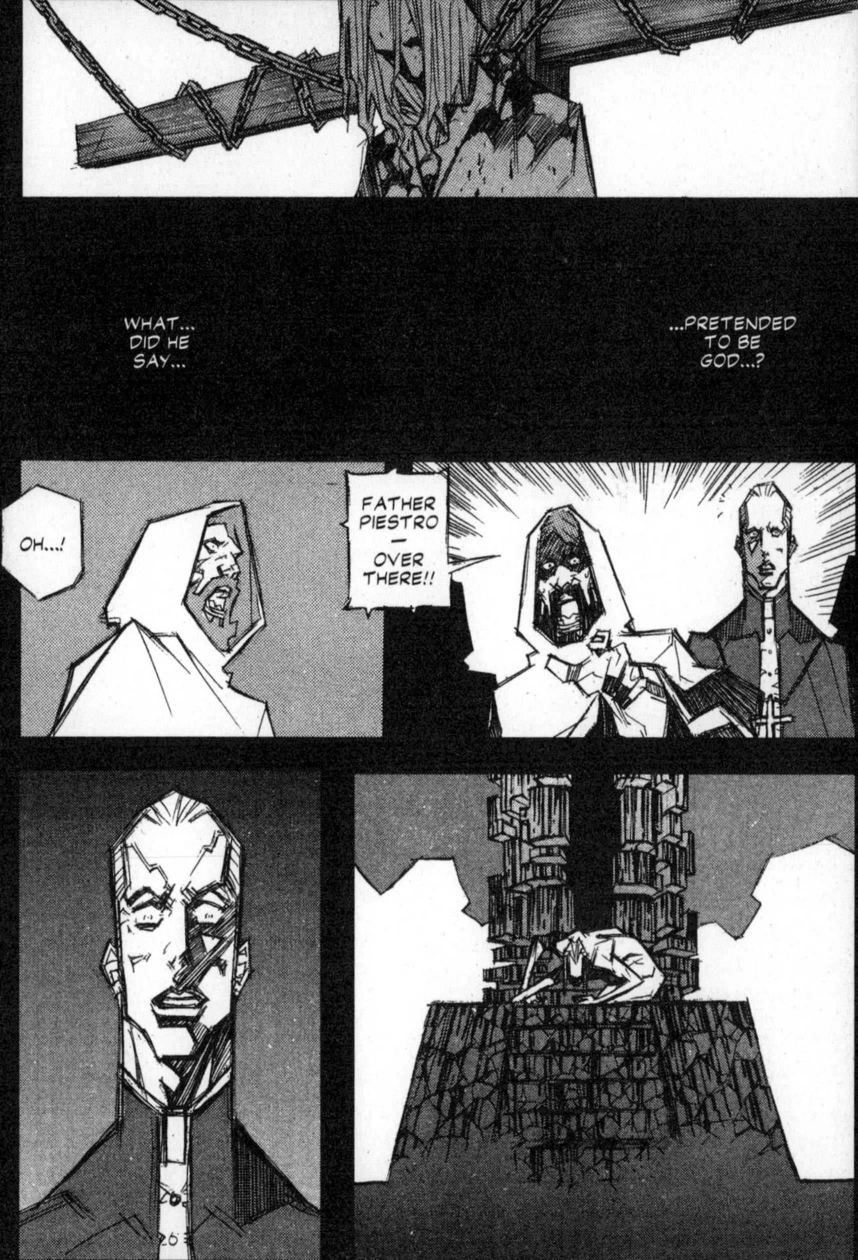
WHAT... DID HE SAY...
...PRETENDED TO BE GOD...?
OH...!
FATHER PIESTRO — OVER THERE!!

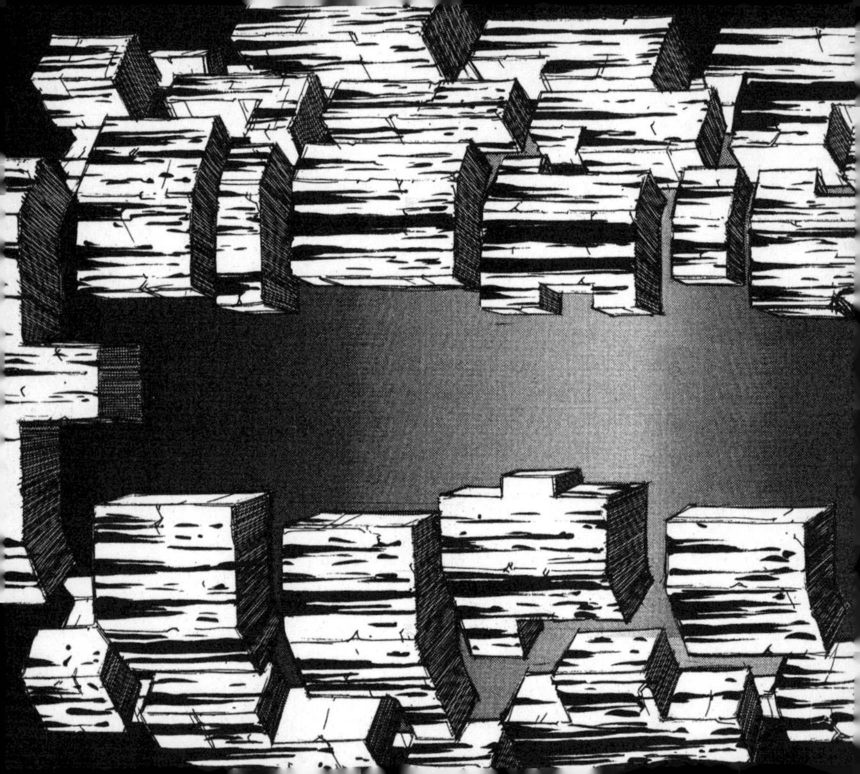

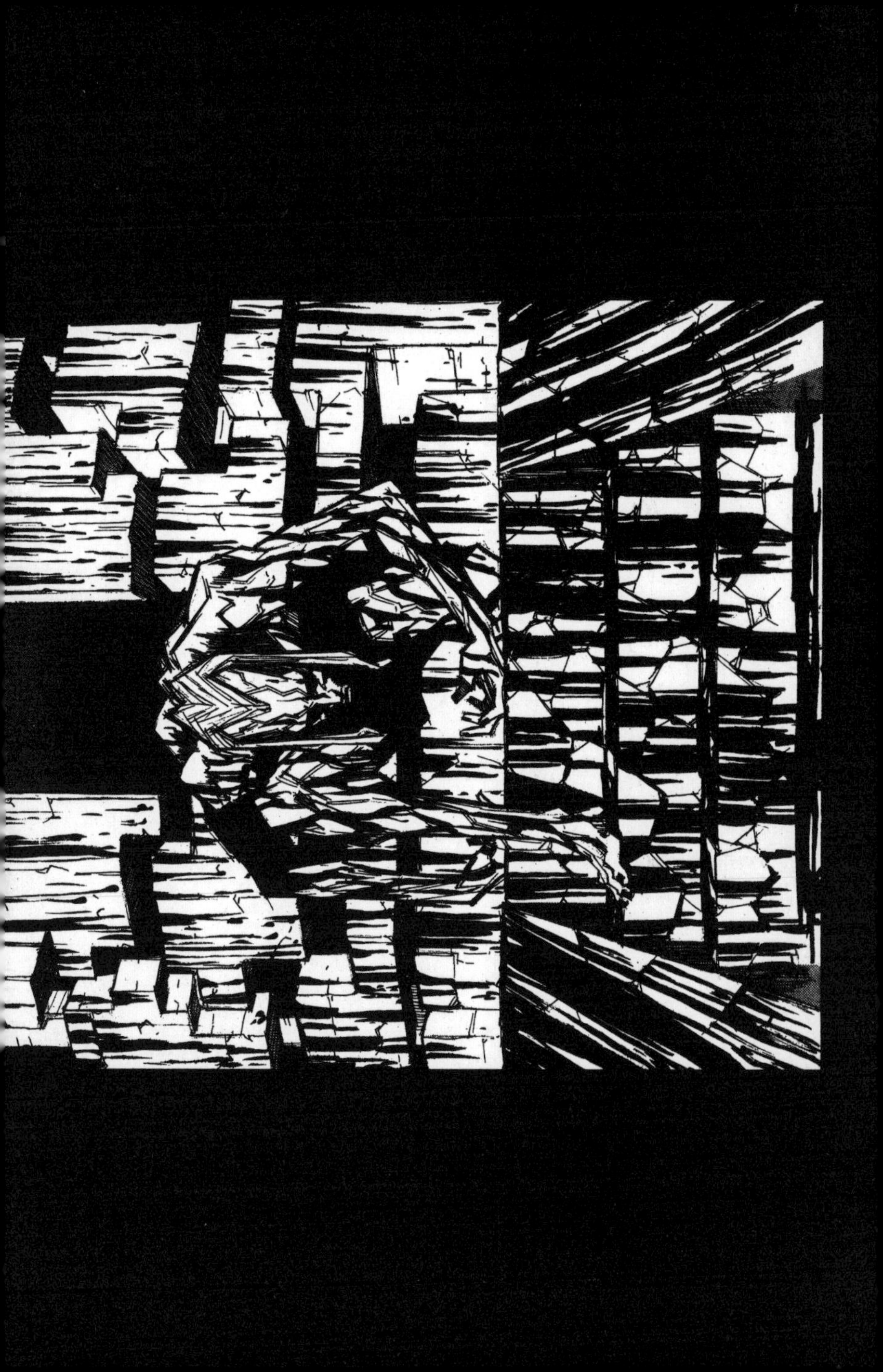

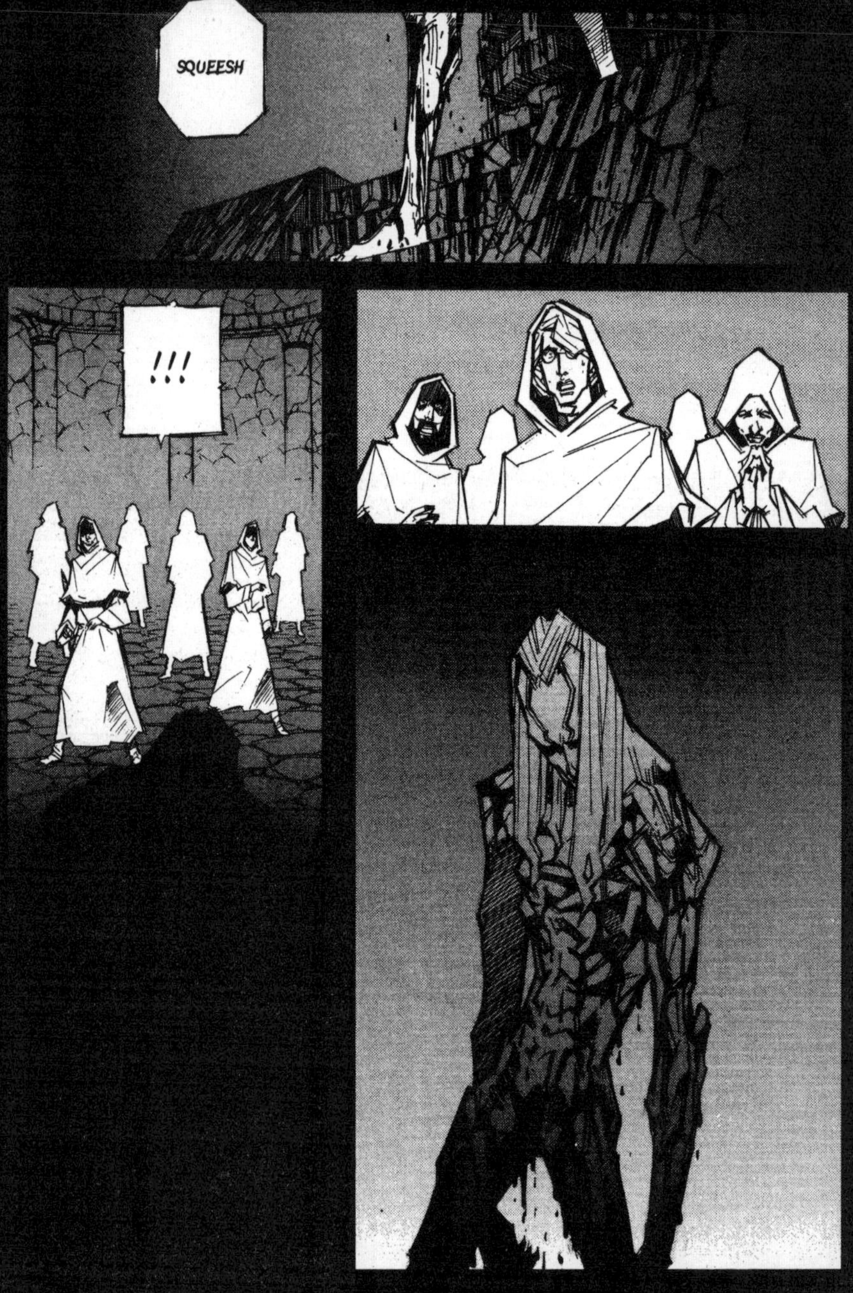
SQUEESH
!!!

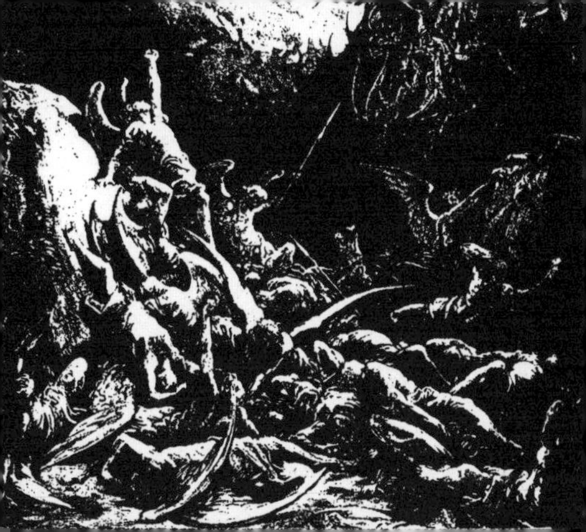

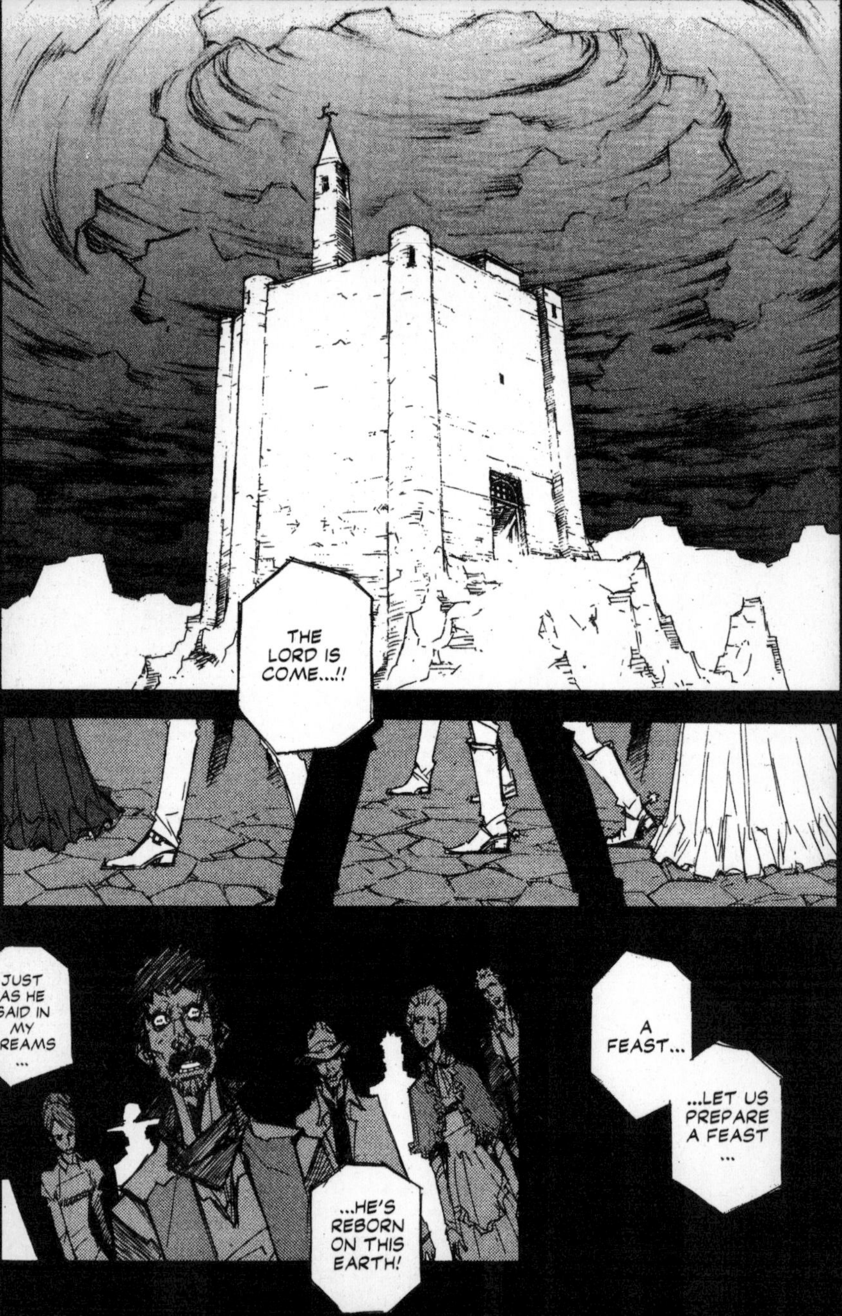

THE LORD IS COME...!!
JUST AS HE SAID IN MY DREAMS ...
...HE'S REBORN ON THIS EARTH!
A FEAST...
...LET US PREPARE A FEAST ...

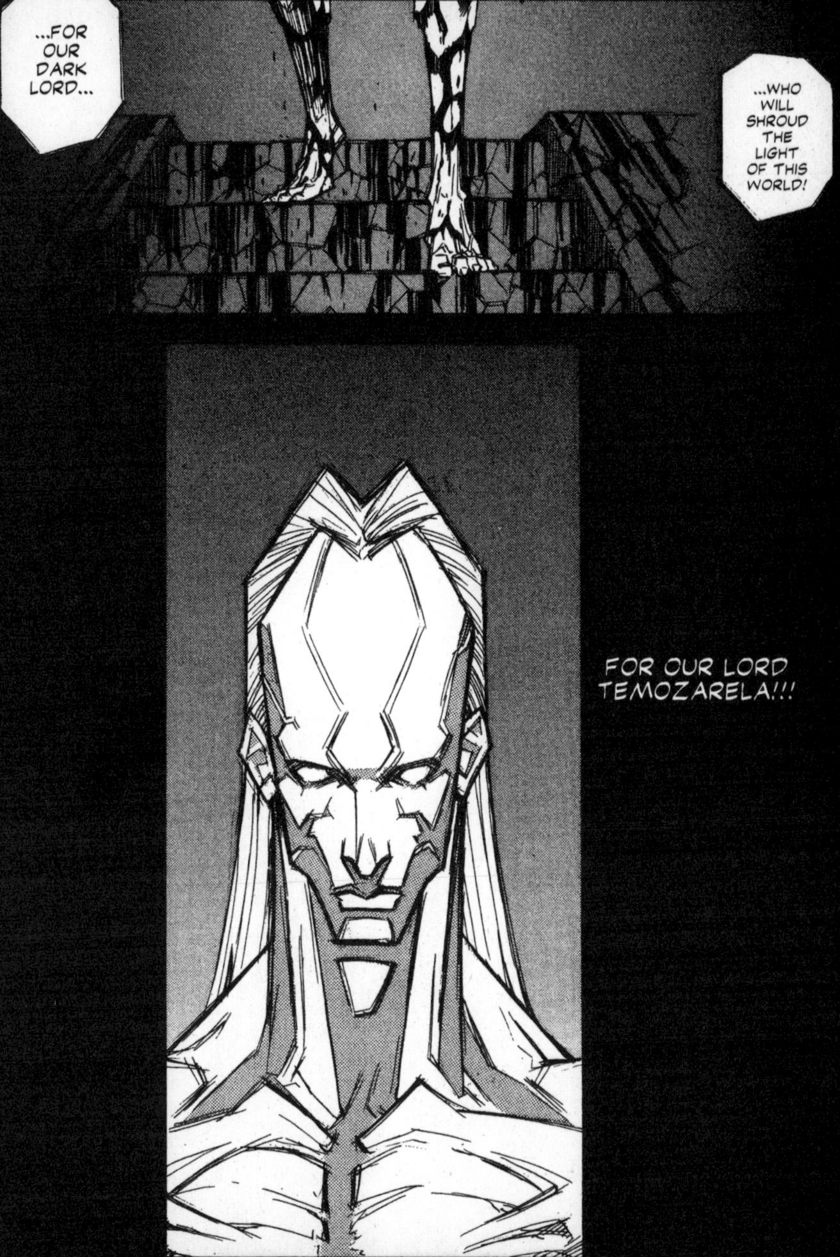
...FOR OUR DARK LORD...
...WHO WILL SHROUD THE LIGHT OF THIS WORLD!
FOR OUR LORD TEMOZARELA!!!

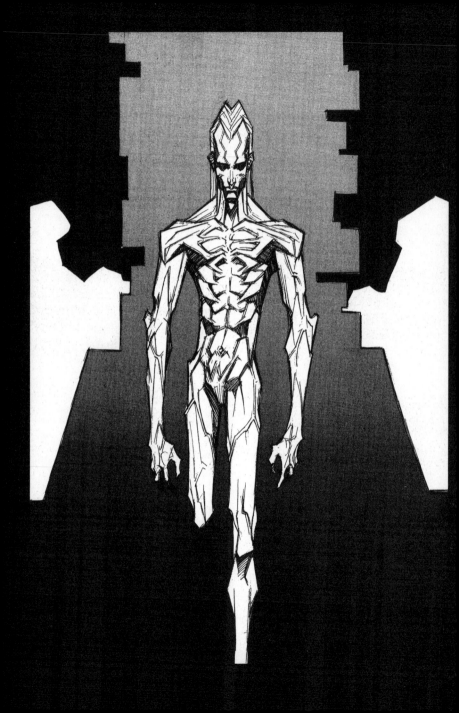

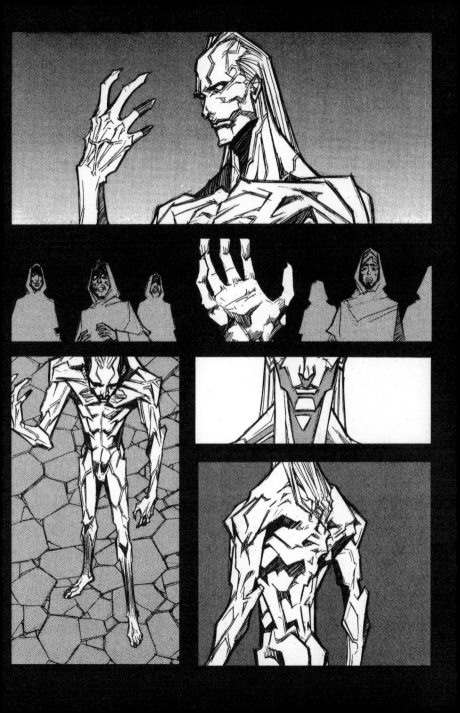

THAT...
THAT
IS...

TE...MO...Z
A...RE...LA
???

...

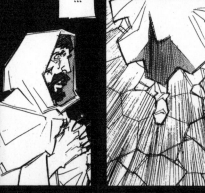

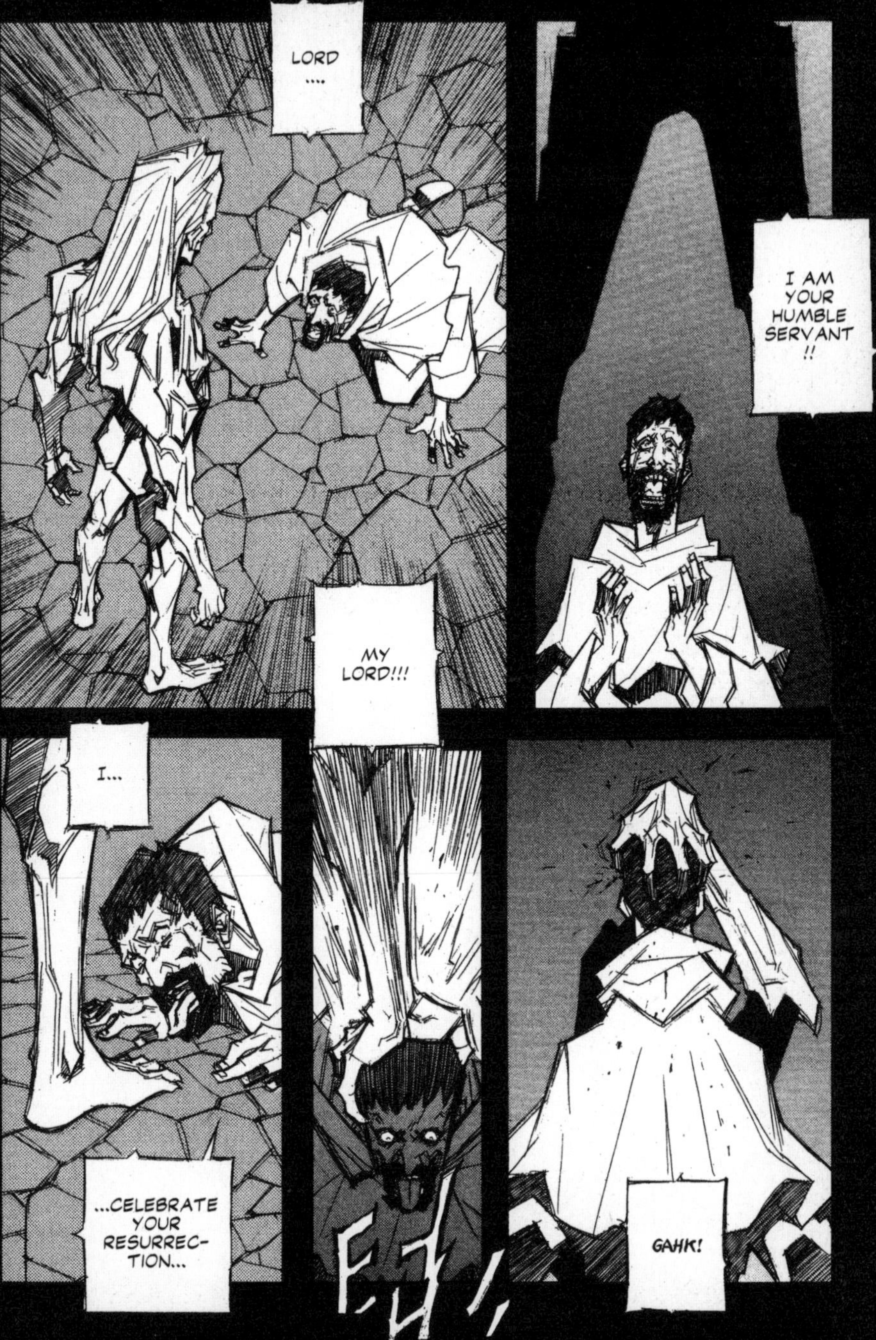
LORD ....
MY LORD!!!
I AM YOUR HUMBLE SERVANT !!
I...
...CELEBRATE YOUR RESURREC- TION...
GAHK!

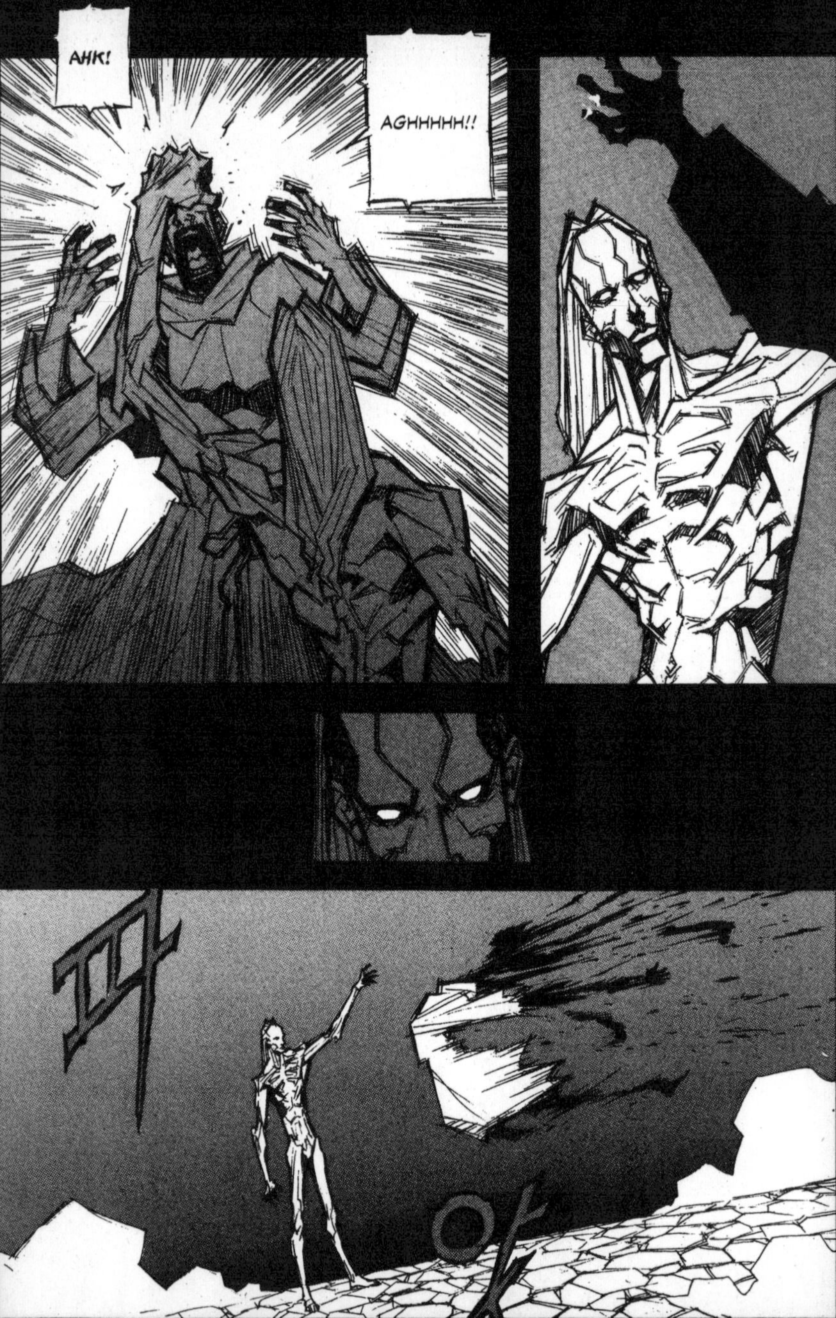
AHK!
AGHHHHH!!

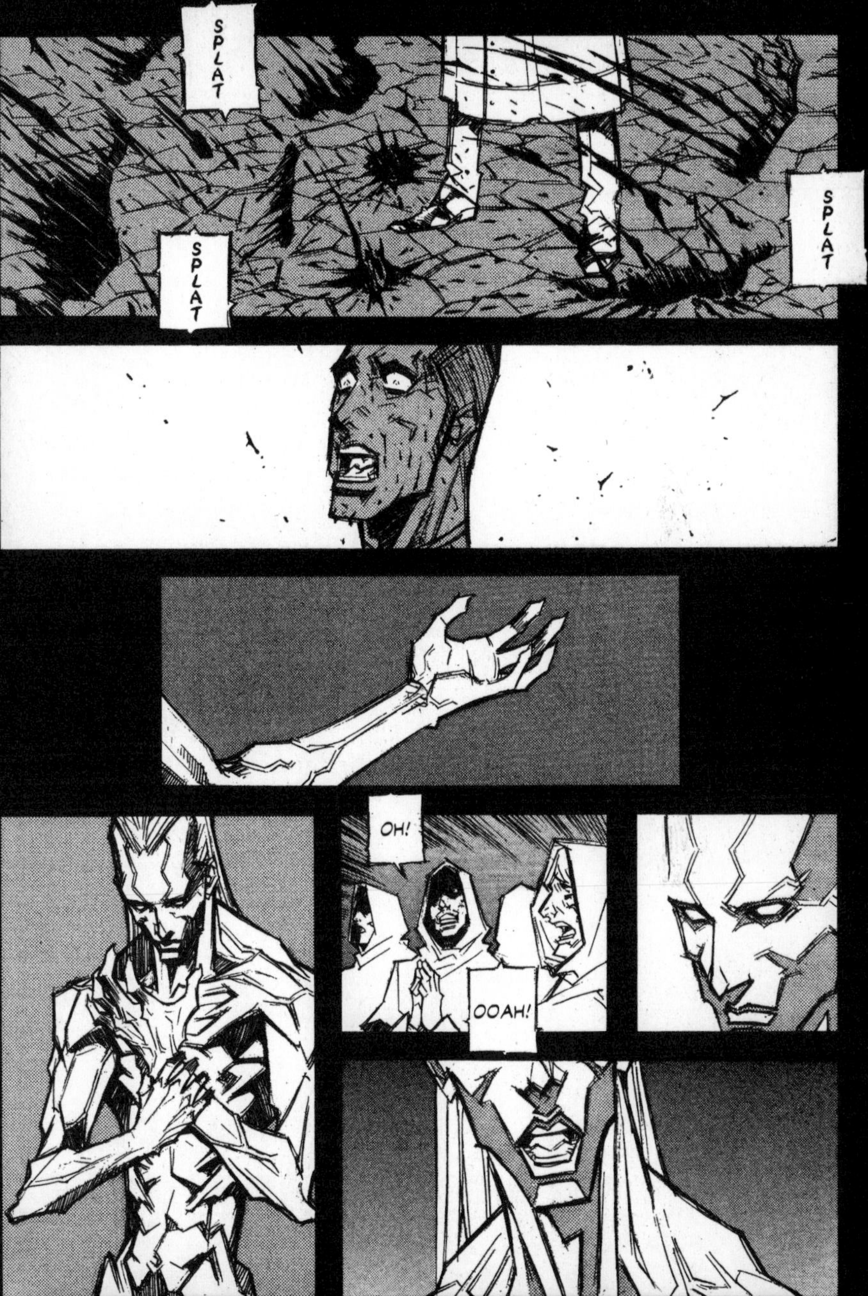
SPLAT
SPLAT
SPLAT
OH!
OOAH!

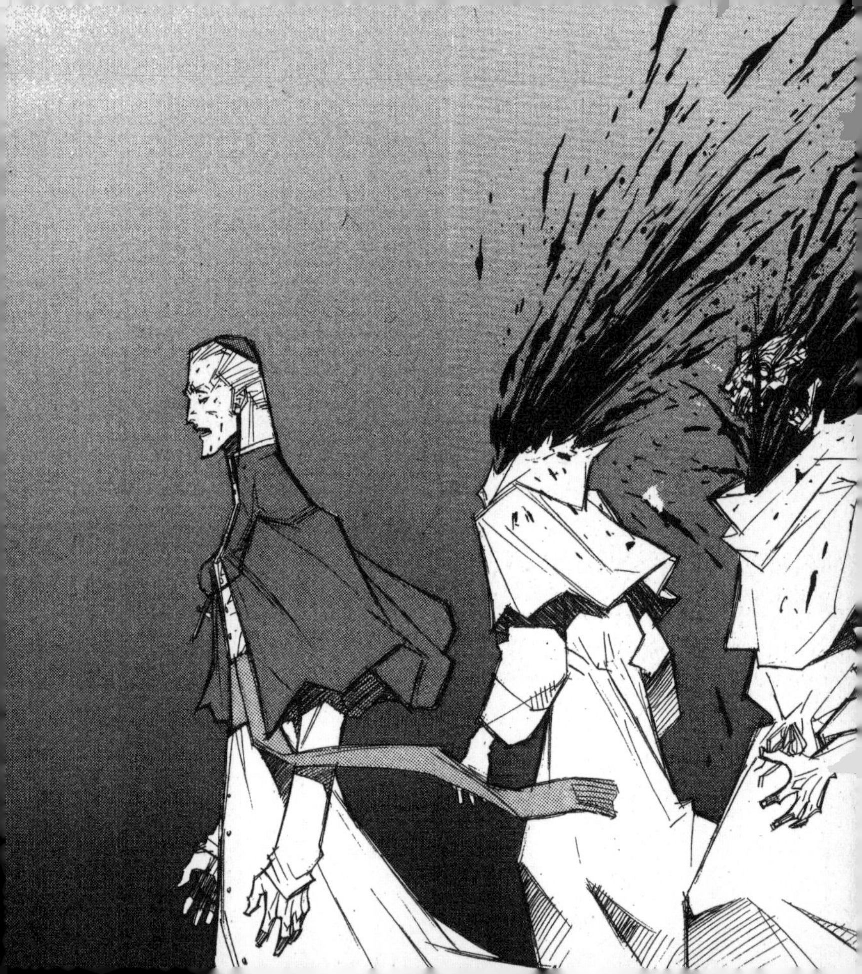

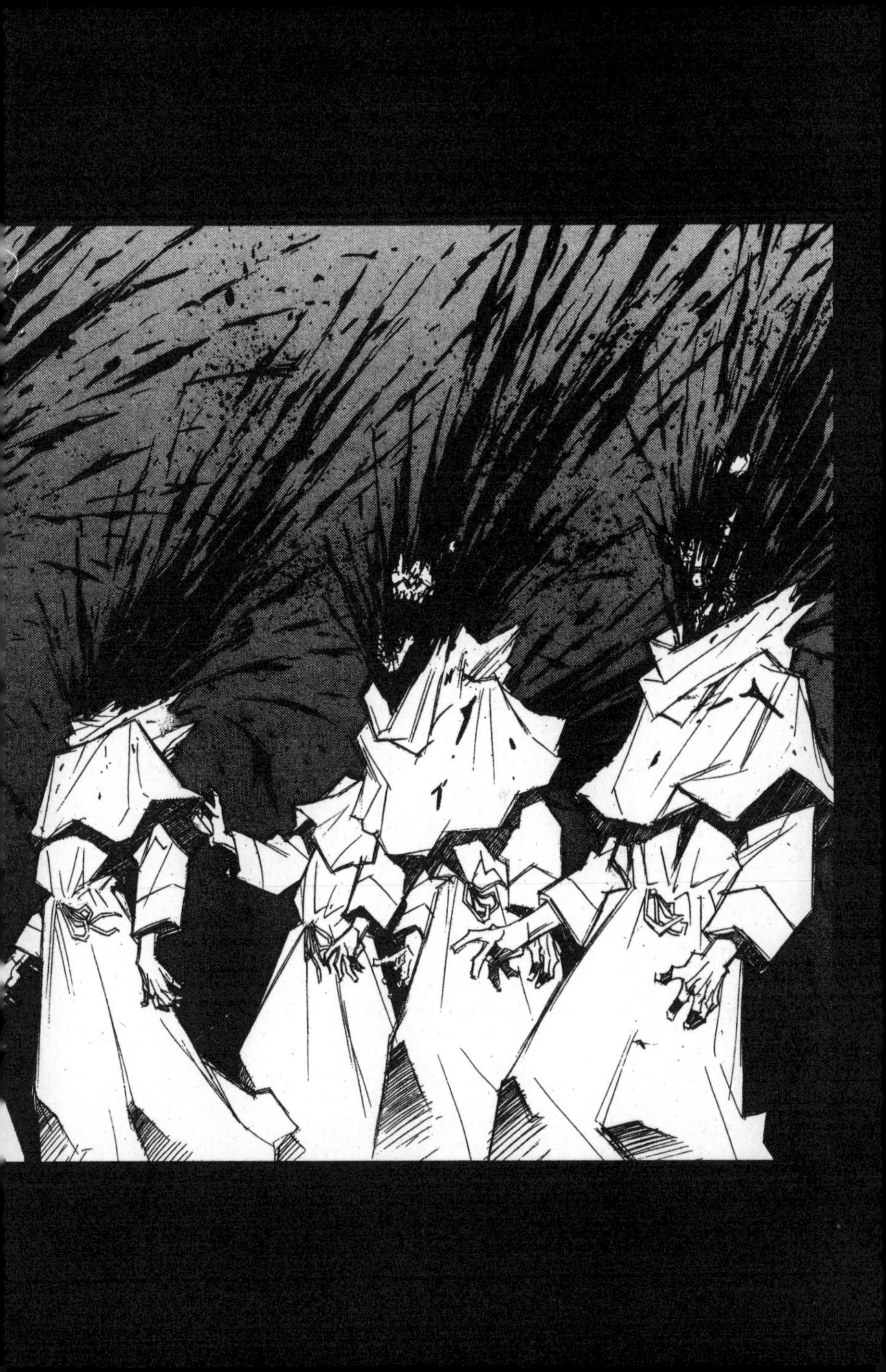

KING OF HELL

IN-SOO NA - WRITER
JAE-KWAN KIM - ARTIST

THERE'S A RIFT BETWEEN HELL AND THE MORTAL WORLD AND LOST SOULS HAVE BEEN ESCAPING TO TORMENT THE LIVING.

TO DEAL WITH THE PROBLEM, THE KING OF HELL HAS RELEASED MAJEH, THE GREATEST SWORDSMAN IN THE UNDERWORLD, TO STOP THE MISCHEIVOUS SOULS.

STEEPED IN EASTERN AND WESTERN MYTHOLOGY AND FEATURING STRIKING ARTWORK, KING OF HELL IS NOW ONE OF THE HOTTEST NEW SERIES FROM KOREA.

Coming soon from
TOKYOPOP.

W**PREVIEW**PREVIEW**PREVIEW**PR

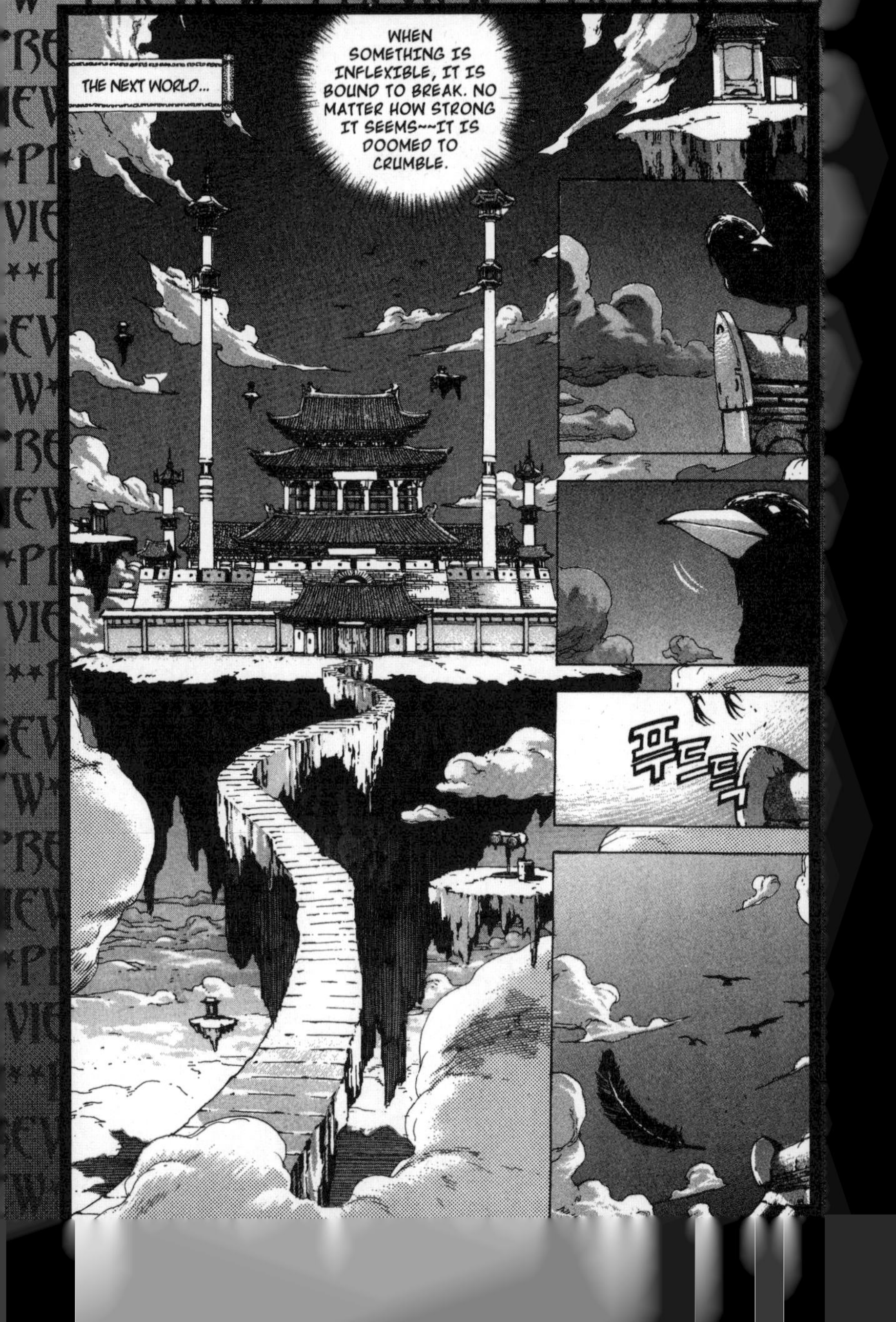
THE NEXT WORLD...
WHEN SOMETHING IS INFLEXIBLE, IT IS BOUND TO BREAK. NO MATTER HOW STRONG IT SEEMS~~IT IS DOOMED TO CRUMBLE.
푸드득

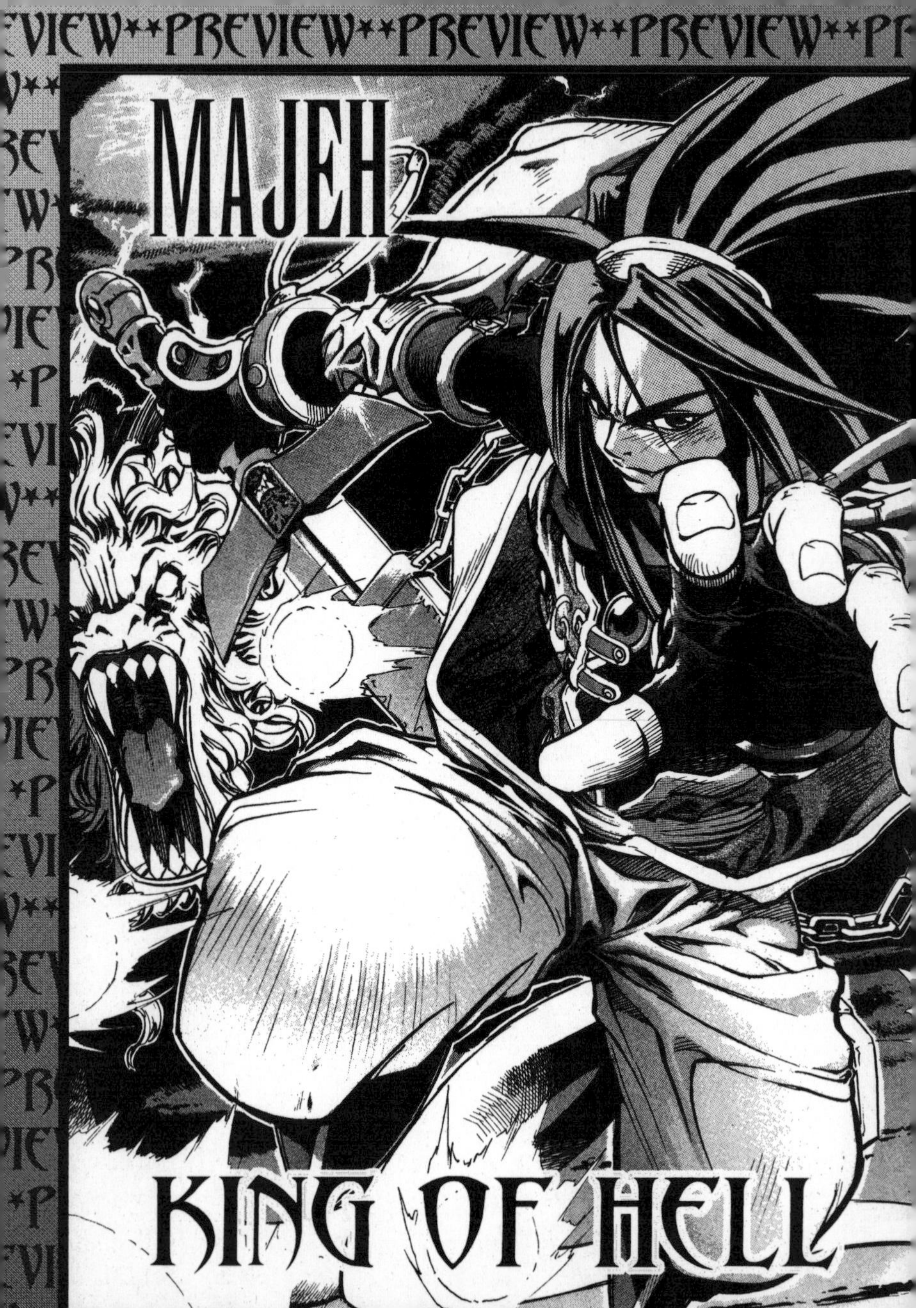
PREVIEW**PREVIEW**PREVIEW**PREVIEW
MAJEH
KING OF HELL

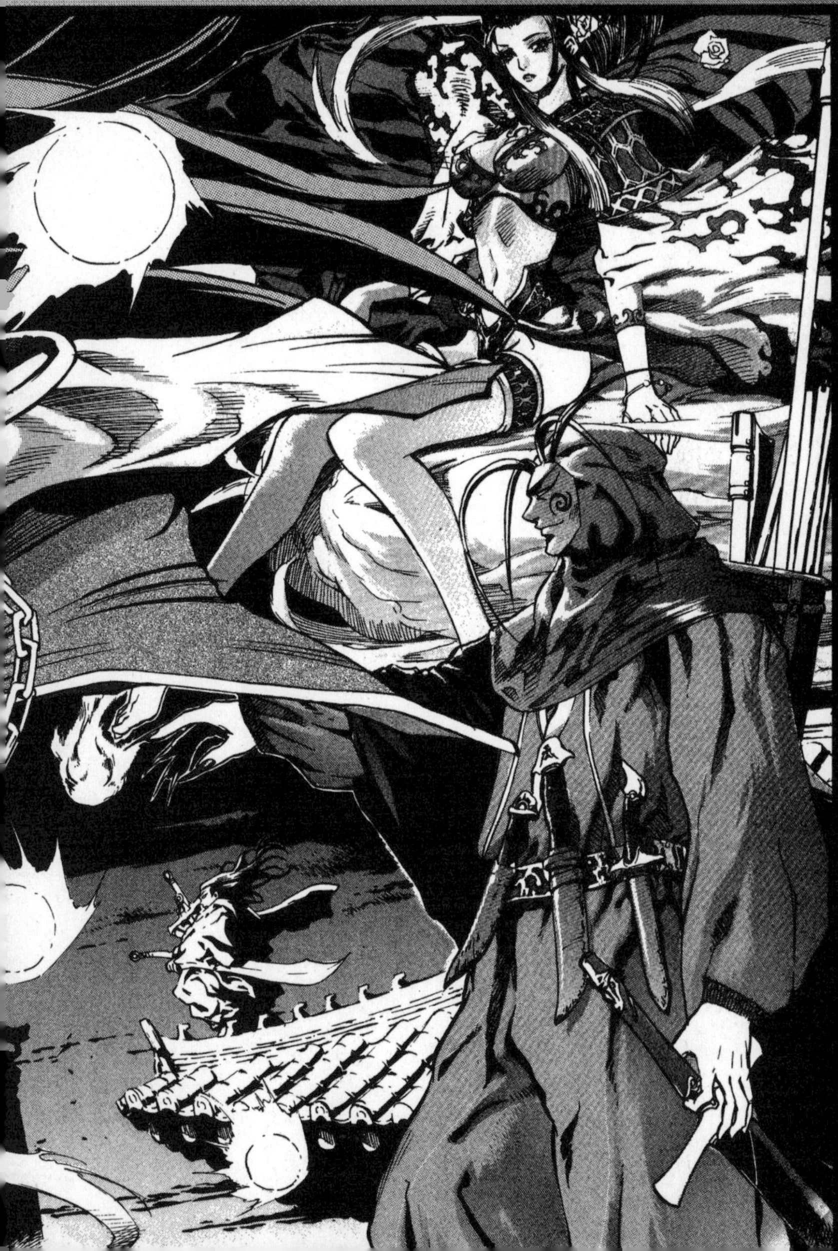

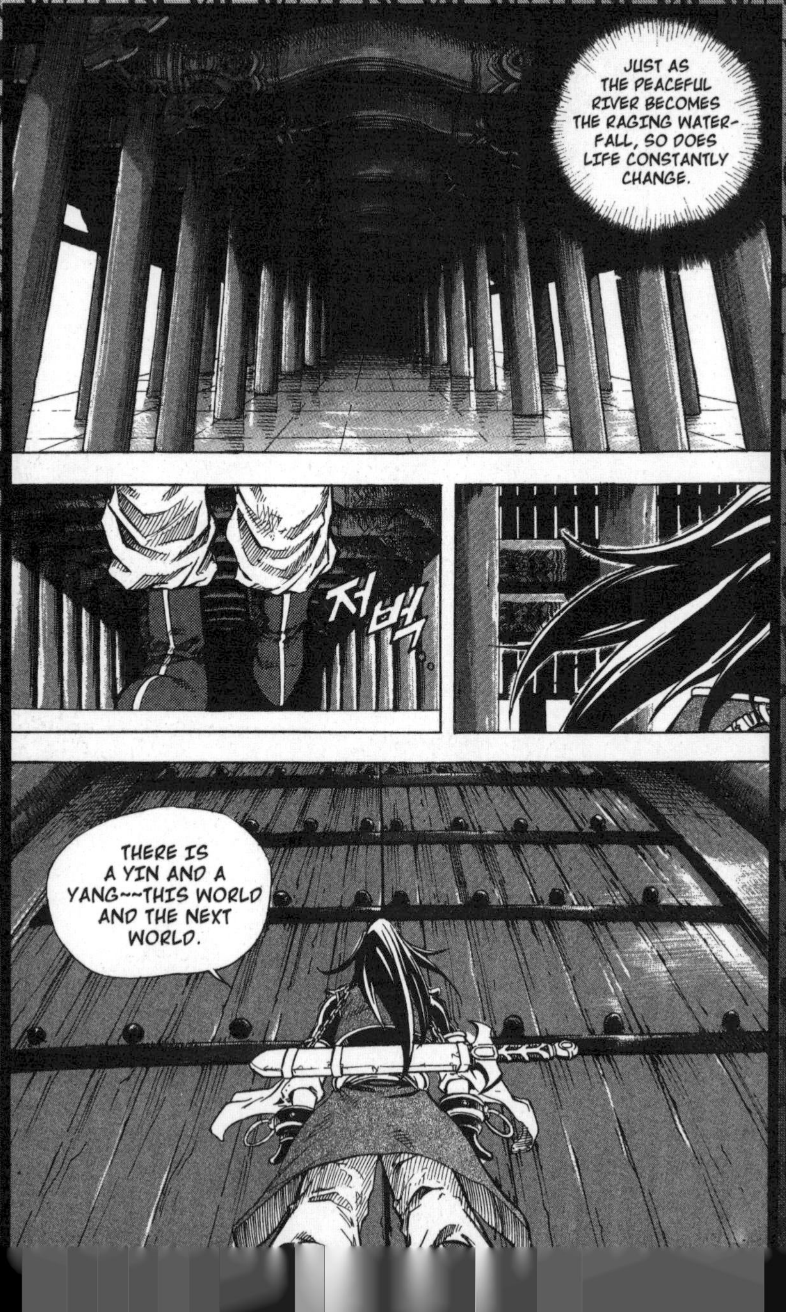
JUST AS THE PEACEFUL RIVER BECOMES THE RAGING WATER-FALL, SO DOES LIFE CONSTANTLY CHANGE.
저벅
THERE IS A YIN AND A YANG--THIS WORLD AND THE NEXT WORLD.

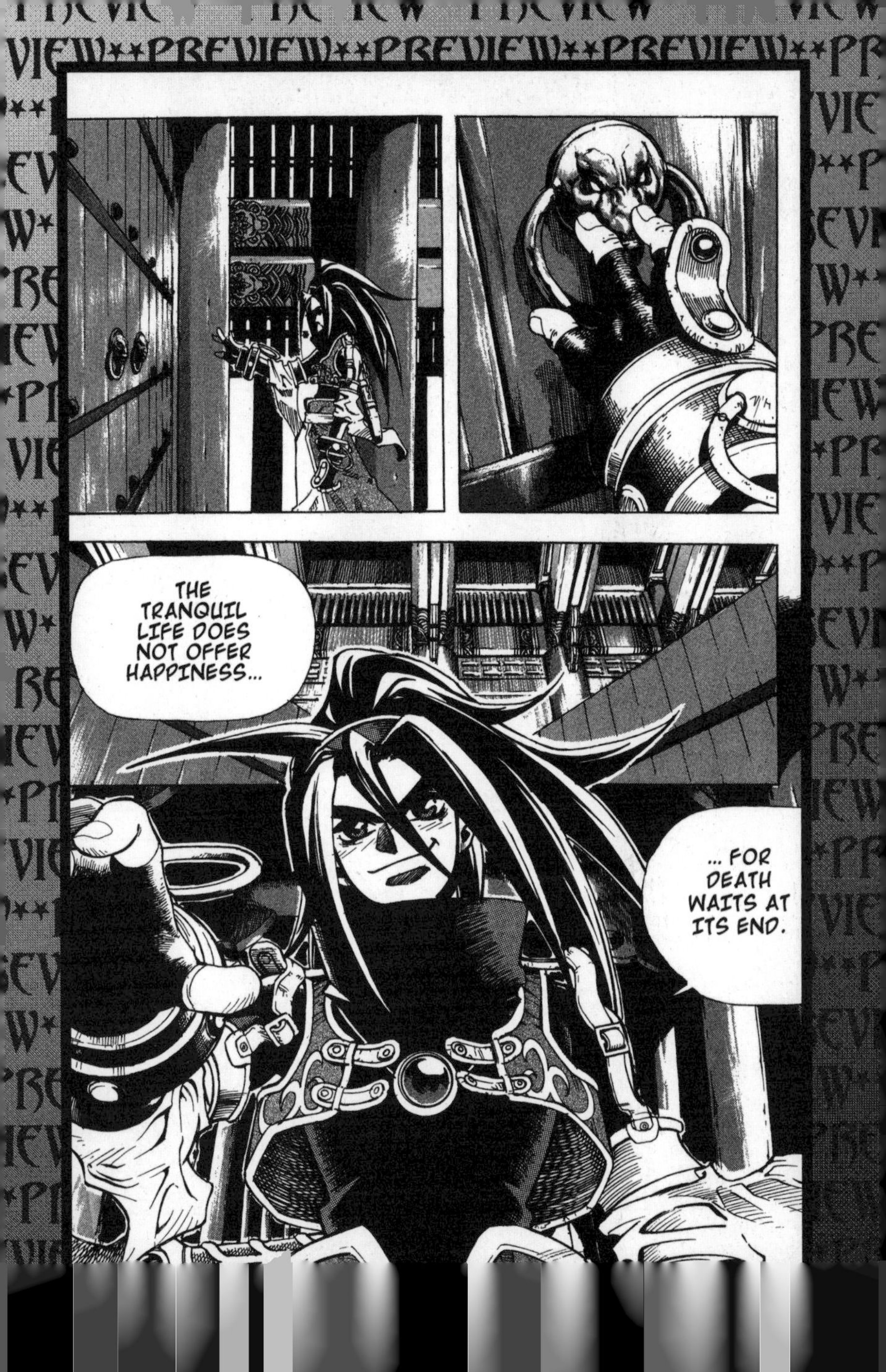
THE TRANQUIL LIFE DOES NOT OFFER HAPPINESS...
... FOR DEATH WAITS AT ITS END.

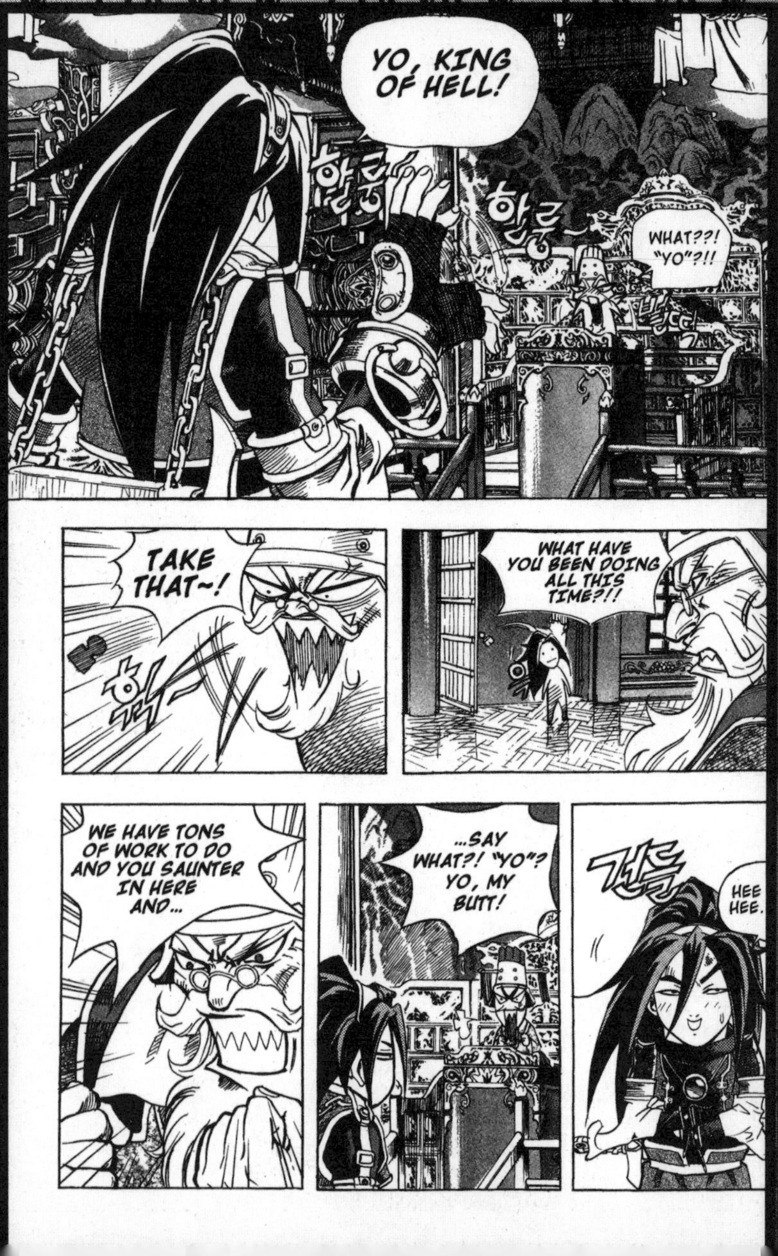
YO, KING OF HELL!
WHAT??! "YO"?!!
TAKE THAT~!
WHAT HAVE YOU BEEN DOING ALL THIS TIME?!!
WE HAVE TONS OF WORK TO DO AND YOU SAUNTER IN HERE AND...
...SAY WHAT?! "YO"? YO, MY BUTT!
HEE HEE.

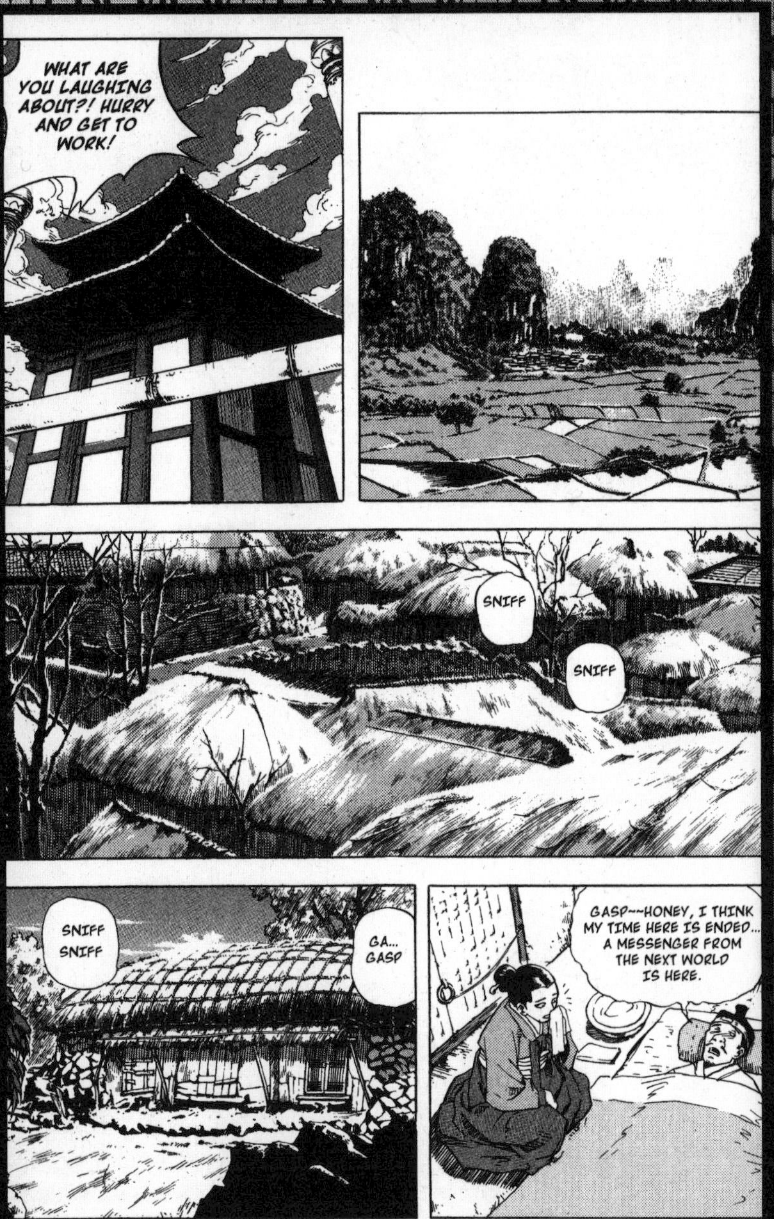
WHAT ARE YOU LAUGHING ABOUT?! HURRY AND GET TO WORK!
SNIFF
SNIFF
SNIFF SNIFF
GA... GASP
GASP--HONEY, I THINK MY TIME HERE IS ENDED... A MESSENGER FROM THE NEXT WORLD IS HERE.

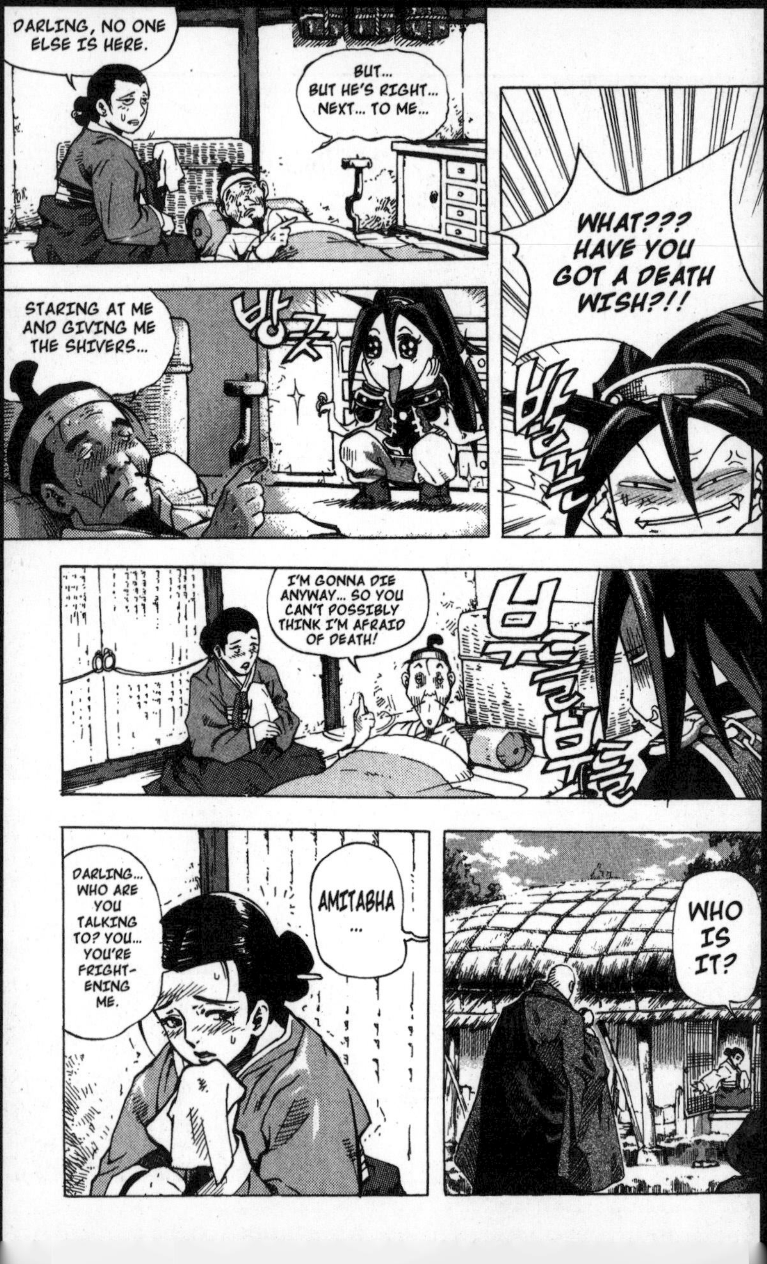
DARLING, NO ONE ELSE IS HERE.
BUT... BUT HE'S RIGHT... NEXT... TO ME...
STARING AT ME AND GIVING ME THE SHIVERS...
방긋
WHAT??? HAVE YOU GOT A DEATH WISH?!!
I'M GONNA DIE ANYWAY... SO YOU CAN'T POSSIBLY THINK I'M AFRAID OF DEATH!
DARLING... WHO ARE YOU TALKING TO? YOU... YOU'RE FRIGHT-ENING ME.
AMITABHA ...
WHO IS IT?

WOULD YOU PLEASE GIVE AN OFFERING?

AMITABHA ~

WHY DON'T YOU ASK THE MONK TO PRAY TO BUDDHA FOR YOU? YOU NEVER KNOW! YOU MIGHT BE ABLE TO GET INTO PARADISE.

ALTHOUGH, JUDGING BY YOUR ATTI-TUDE---YOU'RE BOUND FOR HELL... HEH HEH...!

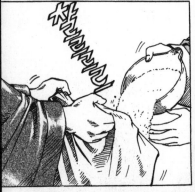

THANK YOU VERY MUCH.